Effective Supervision

A Guidebook for Supervisors, Team Leaders, and Work Coaches

David L. Goetsch

Upper Saddle River, New Jersey
Columbus, Ohio

Library of Congress Cataloging-in-Publication Data

Goetsch, David L.
    Effective supervision : a guidebook for supervisors, team leaders, and work coaches ⁄ David L. Goetsch.
        p. cm.
    Includes bibliographical references and index.
    ISBN 0-13-031583-4
        1. Supervision of employees.   I. Title.

HF5549.12 .G638   2002
658.3'02—dc21   00-066891

Vice President and Editor in Chief: Stephen Helba
Executive Editor: Debbie Yarnell
Associate Editor: Michelle Churma
Production Editor: Louise N. Sette
Copy Editor: Cindy Peck
Design Coordinator: Robin G. Chukes
Cover Designer: Debra Rosario
Cover art: © SuperStock
Electronic Text Management: Marilyn Wilson Phelps, Karen L. Bretz, Melanie Ortega
Production Manager: Brian Fox
Marketing Manager: Jimmy Stephens

This book was set in Clearface by Prentice Hall. It was printed and bound by Banta Book Group. The cover was printed by Phoenix Color Corp.

Prentice-Hall International (UK) Limited, *London*
Prentice-Hall of Australia Pty. Limited, *Sydney*
Prentice-Hall Canada, Inc., *Toronto*
Prentice-Hall Hispanoamericana, S.A., *Mexico*
Prentice-Hall of India Private Limited, *New Delhi*
Prentice-Hall of Japan, Inc., *Tokyo*
Prentice-Hall Singapore Pte. Ltd.
Editora Prentice-Hall do Brasil, Ltda., *Rio de Janeiro*

1 0 9

ISBN: 0-13-0315834

Preface

BACKGROUND

One of the most valuable assets an organization can have in today's hypercompetitive global marketplace is talented supervisors who know how to achieve consistent peak performance from their direct reports and who know how to help their direct reports improve continually. A good supervisor makes the same kinds of contributions to an organization's success that a good coach makes to a professional sports team's success.

Supervisors go by many names in today's workplace—team leader, work coach, foreman, and many other titles. Regardless of what they are called, supervisors are people who are responsible for the performance of a given unit and the people, processes, and procedures that, together, generate that performance. Carrying out this responsibility has become an increasingly complex undertaking. There are many reasons for this. Prominent among them are rapid and continual technological advances; the unrelenting pressure of global competition; a steadily growing body of law relating to employee rights, safety, and health; a national trend toward more conflict and violence in the workplace; the persistent problems associated with substance abuse; the worldwide "quality revolution"; and demands from the public for ethical business practices.

WHY THIS BOOK WAS WRITTEN AND FOR WHOM

This book was written to satisfy the need for (1) an up-to-date teaching text that allows students in colleges, universities, and technical schools to learn "hands-on, real-world" supervision skills in addition to the foundational theories, principles, and concepts on which those skills are built; (2) a practical "how-to" teaching tool for use in business, industry, and government training settings such as seminars, workshops, and short courses; and (3) a "hands-on" oriented text that can be used for teaching supervision in a distance learning format (on-line, simulcast, or self-paced/text-based).

Effective Supervision was developed in a "worktext" format so that it could meet all three of these needs. All of the text material one would expect to find in a traditional textbook on supervision is contained in this book. In addition, each section of text in each chapter is followed by real-world "Application and Discussion" activities that require learners to discuss and apply the material just presented. These activities help learners transform theoretical and conceptual material into practical, hands-on skills. At the end of every chapter, comprehensive "On-the-Job Scenarios" require learners to apply all of the material from the chapter in solving the types of actual problems supervisors confront on the job. The goal of *Effective Supervision* is to develop individuals who don't just know about supervision, but who know how to supervise.

HOW TO USE THIS BOOK

This book was designed to be used in any one or all of the following approaches: (1) as the principal teaching tool in a traditional classroom setting; (2) as a "hands-on" supplement to another text in a traditional classroom setting; (3) as the principal teaching tool for seminars, workshops, or short courses provided for business, industry, and government organizations; and (4) as the principal teaching tool in a distance learning course on supervision. Strategies for using this book most effectively in each of these settings follow.

Traditional Classroom Setting

In this setting, learners should read the text material in the usual manner. The "Application and Discussion" activities can be used in two ways. They can be used to guide and generate discussion during class, and they can be used as written assignments to be completed outside of class. The "On-the-Job Scenarios" at the end of each chapter can be used as group projects, written assignments, or tests, or as the basis for individual or group classroom presentations and research papers. Having students "act out" the scenarios in small groups in class is also an effective learning strategy. Having done so, the rest of the class can then discuss and critique their solutions. Tests are provided as a supplement.

Supplement in a Traditional Classroom Setting

Effective Supervision can be used to supplement other texts, particularly in providing realistic hands-on, skill-building activities. The "Application and Discussion" activities and the "On-the-Job Scenarios" from each chapter are flexible enough to be used in conjunction with any supervision text. Tests are provided in the supplement.

Seminars, Workshops, and Short Courses

Effective Supervision was designed in such a way as to be a complete "seminar in a book." Everything that is needed to provide a comprehensive seminar, workshop, or short course on supervision can be found within its covers. In addition, each chapter can be used as a one-topic seminar that focuses on a particular area of need or concern. The "Application and Discussion" activities and the "On-the-Job Scenarios" are especially effective for helping people who are already working to develop the knowledge and skills needed to be successful supervisors.

Distance Learning Courses

Effective Supervision, along with the supplemental Instructor's Manual that accompanies it, makes an excellent tool for use in a distance learning course. All of the theories, concepts, and principles needed are contained in each chapter. The "Application and Discussion" activities can be used to guide and generate on-line discussion in chat rooms. They can also be used as written assignments that can be submitted electronically. The "On-the-Job Scenarios" can be used for assigning larger projects. Tests are provided in the supplement. Various web page linkages are listed in Appendix A.

HOW THIS BOOK DIFFERS FROM OTHERS

There are many excellent books available on supervision. *Effective Supervision* contains all of the material one would expect to find in these and any other current book on the topic, and it has the following strengths not associated with most supervision texts: (1) All of the discussion, application, and on-the-job activities come from actual work cases and are designed to place learners in the shoes of practicing supervisors and require them to answer the question, "Based on what you just learned, what would you do in this situation?" Learners read about no more than one subtopic at a time in a chapter before being required to apply that reading in dealing with an actual on-the-job problem; (2) All material in this book has been field-tested and revised based on instructor, student, and trainer input. Activities that worked well in a live setting were kept; others were replaced. The material contained herein has been tested in traditional classrooms, seminars, workshops, short courses, and distance learning settings. In all of these settings it has been well received, the practical hands-on approach being its most popular feature; and (3) *Effective Supervision* is up-to-date in terms of both the text material and the hands-on activities. All activities contained in this book are of the kind that supervisors can expect to confront in today's workplace.

ACKNOWLEDGMENTS

I would like to acknowledge the reviewers of this text: Constantine Ciesielski, East Carolina University (NC); Brian Hoyt, Ohio University; and Allen B. Young, Bessemer State Technical College (AL).

ABOUT THE AUTHOR

David L. Goetsch is Provost of the Fort Walton Beach Campus of the University of West Florida and Okaloosa-Walton Community College where he is also Professor of Quality, Safety, and Management. He teaches *Effective Supervision* in all of the formats described earlier and is also President and CEO of the Center for Effective Supervision, a private consulting and training company that specializes in developing supervisors for business, industry, and government organizations.

Contents

CHAPTER THREE
Communication   23

CHAPTER ONE

Leadership

After studying this chapter, you should be able to do the following:

- Define the concept of leadership.
- Explain whether leaders are born or made.
- Explain how leaders motivate others.
- Explain the pros and cons of the various leadership styles.
- Describe how to establish and maintain followership.
- Describe the process of building trust in those you supervise.
- Describe how leaders promote teamwork.

Leadership is an intangible concept that, when applied properly, can bring tangible results. Leadership is sometimes referred to as an art and other times as a science. In reality, it is both.

The effects of good leadership can be seen in any organization. Well-led organizations, whether they are large companies, departments within a company, or small work teams, have several easily identifiable characteristics. These characteristics include high levels of productivity; a positive, can-do attitude; a commitment to accomplishing organizational goals; effective, efficient use of resources; high levels of quality; and a mutually supportive, teamwork approach to getting work done. Supervisors can provide the leadership that will help develop these characteristics in their departments or teams. This chapter is provided to help prospective and practicing supervisors learn to be effective leaders.

WHAT IS LEADERSHIP?

There are many different definitions of leadership. This is because leadership is needed in so many different fields. Leadership has been defined as it applies to the military, athletics, education, business, industry, and many other fields. Leadership as it relates specifically to the supervisor can be defined as follows:

> **Leadership** is the ability to inspire people to make a total and willing commitment to accomplishing organizational goals.

1

WHAT IS A GOOD LEADER?

Good leaders come in all shapes, sizes, genders, ages, races, political persuasions, and national origins. They do not look alike, talk alike, or even work alike. However, good leaders do share several common characteristics:

- Show a balanced commitment to people and work.
- Set a positive example.
- Use good communication skills.
- Have influence.
- Are persuasive.
- Exhibit coaching skills.

Good leaders are *committed* to both the job to be done and the people who do the job, and they are able to strike an appropriate balance between the two. Good leaders set a positive example. Supervisors who adopt a "Do as I say, not as I do" attitude will not be effective leaders. To inspire workers to follow them, supervisors must be willing to do what they expect of workers, and do it better. For example, if dependability is important, the supervisor must set an example of dependability. If punctuality is important, the supervisor must set an example of punctuality. To be a good leader, the supervisor must set an example of all the characteristics that are important on the job.

Good leaders are strong communicators. They are willing, patient, skilled listeners, and they are also able to communicate their ideas clearly, succinctly, and in a nonthreatening manner. They use their communication skills to establish and nurture rapport with workers.

Good leaders have influence with the employees they supervise. Influence is the art of getting people to do what you want them to do. Supervisors' influence derives from the authority that goes with their jobs and the credibility that comes from having the advanced knowledge and skills necessary to be a supervisor.

Good leaders are persuasive. Supervisors who expect people to simply do what they are ordered to do will be ineffective. Those who are able to use their communications and interpersonal skills to persuade workers to accept their point of view and to help workers develop ownership in that point of view will be much more effective.

Finally, good leaders have coaching skills. This means they are able to convert a group of individuals into a team, build the team so its performance is optimized, and motivate individual team members to continually improve the team's overall performance.

⎯⎯⎯ APPLICATION AND DISCUSSION ⎯⎯⎯

Margaret Lee has been a supervisor for two years, but things are not working well in her team. Those who report directly to her complain that Lee is dedicated to getting the job done "even if it kills them." They also complain about being in the dark, not knowing what is going on, and a lack of teamwork.

- Based on these complaints, how would you rate Lee's leadership skills? What specific leadership characteristics is Lee lacking?
- What can Lee do to turn things around in her team?

ARE LEADERS BORN OR MADE?

Perhaps the oldest debate relating to leadership revolves around the question, "Are leaders born or made?" This debate has never been settled and probably never will be. The point of view set forth in this book is that leaders are much like athletes. Some are born with a great deal of potential whereas others develop their ability through determination and hard work. Inborn ability, or the lack of it, represents only the starting point. Success from that point forward depends on the individual's willingness and determination to develop and improve.

Some athletes are born with tremendous natural ability but never live up to their potential. On the other hand, some athletes with limited natural ability, through hard work and determination, perform beyond their apparent potential. This is also true of supervisors who want to be good leaders. Some supervisors have more natural leadership ability than others.

Regardless of their individual starting points, however, all supervisors can become good leaders through education, training, practice, determination, and effort.

APPLICATION AND DISCUSSION

Some believe that leadership ability is like height; you either have it or you don't. Others believe that with the proper training, mentoring, and experience any person can become a good leader. Yet others believe that the best leaders have natural potential that they develop continually over a lifetime.

- ■ What is your point of view in this debate? Why?
- ■ Develop a list of people you think are good leaders (famous or unknown). Were these individuals born leaders or did they learn leadership?

LEADERSHIP AND MOTIVATION

Motivation is the act of influencing people in a positive direction. One characteristic good leaders share is the ability to inspire and motivate others to make a commitment. The key to motivating people lies in the ability to relate their personal needs to the organization's goals. The key to inspiring people lies in the ability to relate what they *believe* to the organizational goals. Implicit in both cases is the leader's need to know and understand people.

Understanding Individual Human Needs

Perhaps the best model for understanding individual human needs is the one developed by psychologist Abraham H. Maslow. Maslow's **hierarchy of needs** summarizes the five successive levels of human needs as follows (Figure 1-1):

1. *Basic Survival:* Air, food, water, clothing, and shelter
2. *Safety/Security:* Money, laws, law enforcement
3. *Social:* Family, friends, colleagues, organizations
4. *Esteem:* Respect of others, dignity, worth
5. *Self-Actualization:* Fulfillment

The lowest level in the hierarchy encompasses basic survival needs, such as air to breathe, food to eat, water to drink, clothing to wear, and shelter in which to live. The next level encompasses safety/security needs. People need to feel safe and secure in their personal world. To this end, people enact laws, pay taxes to employ police and military personnel, buy insurance, try to save and invest money, and perhaps install security systems in their homes.

The next level encompasses social needs. People are social by nature. People place great importance on ties to family, friends, social organizations, civic groups, special clubs, and even work-based groups such as work teams.

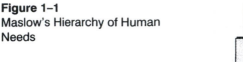

Figure 1–1
Maslow's Hierarchy of Human Needs

The next level on the hierarchy encompasses esteem needs. Self-esteem is a key ingredient in the personal happiness of individuals. People all need to feel self-worth, dignity, and respect. This can be seen in the clothes people wear, the cars they drive, and the behavior they exhibit in public. It can also be seen in job titles. When garbage collectors refer to themselves as sanitation engineers, they are exhibiting the human need for the respect and worth associated with status.

The highest level of the hierarchy encompasses self-actualization needs. The need for complete self-fulfillment is rarely satisfied in people. The need for self-actualization manifests itself in a variety of ways. Some people seek to achieve it through their work, others through their hobbies and associations.

It is important for supervisors to understand how to apply Maslow's model if they hope to use it to motivate workers. Rules for applying this model are as follows:

1. Needs must be satisfied in order from the bottom up (basic survival first).
2. Once a need is satisfied, it no longer works as a motivating factor.
3. For example, people who have satisfied their need for **financial security** (sufficient funds to maintain a certain standard of living) will not be motivated by a pay raise.

    People will focus most intently on their lowest unmet need. For example, employees who have not met their security needs will not be motivated by factors relating to their social needs.

=========== **APPLICATION AND DISCUSSION** ===========

Supervisors who understand where their direct reports (those who report to them) are on Maslow's hierarchy of needs can use this information when attempting to lead, inspire, and motivate them.

■ Examine each of the five categories of human needs. How can a person's job help meet these needs?

■ How might a supervisor use an employee's esteem needs to motivate that employee to higher levels of performance?

■ How might a supervisor use the social needs of employees to promote teamwork?

THEORIES OF LEADERSHIP

Douglas McGregor, late professor of industrial management at Massachusetts Institute of Technology (MIT), became famous for classifying management and leadership styles as being examples of either Theory X or Theory Y. Theory X is a prescriptive, even dictatorial approach. Theory Y is based on a belief in the inherent positive potential of human beings. Modern supervisors should be familiar with Theory X, Theory Y, and Theory XY. Theory XY is a leadership theory that draws on the other two theories as appropriate. (Figure 1–2).

Theory X and Leadership

Traditional management/leadership styles are based on a set of assumptions that lead to a directive approach, an approach that, in the long run, can be counterproductive and have a negative effect on productivity. **Theory X** is based on the following assumptions:

1. Most people have an inherent dislike of work and will avoid it if possible.
2. Because most people dislike work, they must be coerced, threatened, and directed to exert the effort necessary to achieve organizational goals.
3. Most people do not want responsibility, prefer to be directed, have little ambition, and want security more than anything else.

A Theory X supervisor will say, "I'm the boss. Do what I say and don't ask questions."

Theory Y and Leadership

If Theory X represents one end of the leadership spectrum, Theory Y represents the opposite end. It is based on an inherent belief in the almost unlimited potential of people and their capacity for work. The **Theory Y** approach to leadership is based on the following assumptions:

1. The expenditure of energy on work is as natural as the expenditure of energy on play.
2. When committed to objectives, people will work to achieve them without external control or the threat of punishment.
3. People will commit to objectives if appropriate rewards are made, particularly rewards that relate to an individual's self-respect and personal improvement.
4. Under the right conditions, people will not just accept responsibility, they will seek it.
5. People have the capacity to exercise creativity and imagination in solving organizational problems.
6. In most work settings, the intellectual potential of employees is only partially tapped.

A Theory Y supervisor will say to employees, "We have a problem. How do you think we should solve it?"

Figure 1–2
Basic leadership theories

> **Leadership Theories**
>
> ____✓____ **Theory X** Humans must be directed, coerced, controlled and manipulated.
>
> ____✓____ **Theory Y** Under the right conditions, humans will not just accept responsibility; they will seek it.
>
> ____✓____ **Theory XY** Theory Y works most of the time, but not always. Supervisors must be flexible enough to apply appropriate leadership strategies based on existing circumstances.

Theory XY and Leadership

Theory XY is a practical approach to leadership that incorporates some of the Theory X and some of the Theory Y approaches depending on the individuals involved and the needs of the specific situation. The underlying assumptions of Theory XY are as follows:

1. Under the right circumstances, *most* people can be as happy at work as they are at play or even more so.
2. Under the right circumstances, *most* people will commit to organizational goals and exercise self-control in working to accomplish them.
3. Under the right circumstances, *most* people will accept and seek responsibility.
4. Under the right circumstances, *most* people will respond to rewards as long as the rewards are tied to their security, personal satisfaction, and societal contribution needs.

A key term in each of these assumptions is the word *most*. If, under the right circumstances, most people will respond in a certain way, it also follows that some will not. These assumptions also imply that there will be times when the right circumstances cannot be created. In either case, even the most devoted Theory Y leader may, on occasion, need to apply Theory X strategies. Theory XY leaders use what works in a given situation with a given employee. They lean in the direction of Theory Y and use Theory X only when absolutely necessary.

APPLICATION AND DISCUSSION

John Marshall and Beth Benson have both been recently promoted to supervisory positions. It appears from his first month as a supervisor that Marshall is a Theory X person. Benson, on the other hand, appears to favor the Theory Y philosophy. Both are having problems getting an acceptable level of performance from their teams.

- What types of problems do you think John Marshall might be having with his employees?
- What types of problems do you think Beth Benson might be having with her employees?
- How might Theory XY be applied by Marshall and Benson to solve these problems?

LEADERSHIP STYLES

Leadership styles grow out of the theories explained in the previous section. They have to do with how supervisors interact with the people they want to lead. Leadership styles have many different names, but most styles fall into the following categories:

- Autocratic leadership
- Democratic leadership
- Participative leadership
- Goal-oriented leadership
- Situational leadership

Autocratic Leadership

Autocratic leadership is also called directive or dictatorial leadership. Leaders who take this approach make decisions without consulting the employees who will have to implement these decisions. They tell employees what to do and expect them to comply obediently. Autocratic leaders subscribe to the assumptions encompassed in Theory X. Critics of this approach say that although it can work in the short run or in isolated instances, in the long run it can lead to morale problems, half-hearted "malicious" compliance, and labor/management disputes.

Democratic Leadership

Leaders who take the **democratic leadership** approach, also called consultive or consensus leadership, involve the employees who will have to implement the decision in making it. The leader makes the final decision, but only after receiving the input and recommendations of all team members. One drawback to democratic leadership is that it can result in the selection of the most popular decision as opposed to the most appropriate decision, and the most popular decision is not necessarily the best one. It can also lead to ineffective compromises. Democratic leadership is based on Theory Y assumptions.

Participative Leadership

In **participative leadership**, also called open or nondirective leadership, leaders exert less direct control over the decision-making process. Rather, they provide information about the problem and ask team members to recommend solutions. The underlying assumption of this style is that workers will more readily accept responsibility for the solutions, goals, and strategies they help develop. But this approach breaks down fast if team members are not mature, responsible, and committed to the best interests of the organization. Participative leadership is based on the Theory XY philosophy.

Goal-Oriented Leadership

Leaders who take the **goal-oriented leadership** approach, also called results-oriented leadership, ask team members to focus only on the goals at hand. Only strategies that make a definite and measurable contribution to accomplishing organizational goals are discussed. The influence of personalities and other factors unrelated to the specific goals of the organization are minimized. Critics of this approach say it can break down when team members focus so intently on specific goals that they overlook opportunities or potential problems that fall outside their narrow focus. Goal-oriented leadership grows out of Theory X assumptions.

Situational Leadership

In **situational leadership**, also called contingency leadership, leaders select a style appropriate to the circumstances and the individuals involved. In identifying these circumstances, leaders consider the following factors:

- Relationship of the supervisor and team members
- How precisely actions taken must comply with specific guidelines
- Amount of authority the leader actually has with team members

Depending on what is learned when these factors are considered, the supervisor decides whether to take the autocratic, democratic, participative, or goal-oriented approach. Under different circumstances, the same supervisor would apply a different leadership style. Situational leadership is based on the Theory XY philosophy.

=========== APPLICATION AND DISCUSSION ===========

Of the five leadership styles presented in this section, which would you be most likely to use? As an employee, which type of leader would you prefer to have as your supervisor? Why?

SELECTING THE APPROPRIATE LEADERSHIP STYLE

Supervisors are responsible for continually improving the productivity of the people they supervise. One of the keys to accomplishing this goal is selection of the appropriate leadership style. The most appropriate style is the one that allows supervisors to achieve the best results in both the short and long run. Since the people doing the work and the conditions under which they do it can change, situational leadership may have the most potential for modern supervisors.

Leadership styles are like tools. The key is to select the right tool for the task at hand. For example, a hammer is an excellent tool if the problem involves driving a nail. However, it's not a good tool for changing a tire. This rule of thumb also applies to selecting a leadership style.

Depending on the conditions and the people involved, the same supervisor might apply one leadership style today and a different style tomorrow. Some situations allow for **people-oriented styles** (democratic and participative); others require **task-orientated styles** (autocratic and goal-oriented). Still others require combinations of the elements from different styles. Situations faced by modern supervisors are increasingly fluid. Consequently, supervisors should be familiar with all the leadership styles, perceptive enough to determine which style is called for in a given situation, and flexible enough to move from style to style as dictated by the situation.

=========== **APPLICATION AND DISCUSSION** ===========

All of the various leadership styles have their good points and bad. The key is to select the style that is needed in the given situation and with the individuals involved. A commonly made mistake is when supervisors select the style that is *comfortable for them* rather than selecting the style that is likely to work best when all things are considered.

- ■   What is an example of a situation that calls for goal-oriented leadership?
- ■   What is an example of a situation that calls for participative leadership?
- ■   Are you aware of a supervisor who applies the same style regardless of the situation? What problems have you seen with this approach?

WINNING AND MAINTAINING FOLLOWERSHIP

Supervisors can be good leaders only if the people they supervise follow them willingly and steadfastly. Followership must be won and, having been won, must be maintained. This section explains how supervisors can win and maintain the followership of the people they supervise.

Popularity and the Leader

Many new supervisors confuse popularity with followership. An important point to understand in supervising people is the difference between popularity and respect. Long-term followership grows out of respect, not popularity. Good leaders may be popular with those they supervise, but they must be respected. Not all good leaders are popular, but they are all respected.

All supervisors must occasionally make unpopular decisions. This is why leadership positions are sometimes described as lonely positions. Making an unpopular decision does not necessarily cause leaders to lose followership, provided the leader is seen as being fair, objective, and impartial. Correspondingly, leaders who make inappropriate decisions that are popular in the short run may actually lose followership in the long run. If the long-term consequences of a decision turn out to be detrimental to the team, team members will hold the supervisor responsible no matter how strongly they originally supported the decision.

Leadership Characteristics that Win and Maintain Followership

Leaders win and maintain followership by engendering the respect of their followers. Some characteristics of leaders that build respect are as follows:

- A sense of purpose
- Self-discipline
- Honesty
- Credibility
- Common sense
- Stamina
- Commitment
- Steadfastness
- Fairness
- Impartiality

Pitfalls that will Undermine Followership

The preceding list contains the positive characteristics that help supervisors win and maintain the respect and loyal followership of team members. In addition, supervisors should be aware of several common pitfalls to avoid. The following pitfalls can quickly undermine the respect supervisors must work so hard to build (Figure 1–3).

- *Trying to be a buddy instead of a supervisor*. Positive relations and good rapport are important, but supervisors cannot be a buddy to those they hope to lead. The nature of the relationship will not allow it.
- *Having an intimate personal relationship with an employee*. This practice is both unwise and unethical. A positive supervisor-employee relationship cannot exist under such circumstances. Few people can succeed at being both the lover and the boss, and few things can damage the morale of a team as quickly and completely.
- *Trying to keep things the same when supervising former peers*. The supervisor-employee relationship, no matter how positive, is different from the peer-peer relationship. This can be a difficult fact to accept and an even more difficult adjustment to make. But it must be made if the supervisor is going to succeed in the long run.

Figure 1–3
Mistakes that can cause a supervisor to fail

Three Mistakes To Avoid
✓ Trying to be a buddy to those you supervise.
✓ Having an intimate relationship with an employee you supervise.
✓ Failing to recognize that the relationship changes immediately when you supervise former peers.

Juan Gonzalez was a member of the team for three years before he was promoted to team leader. He now supervises the same employees he used to work side by side with. Gonzalez still dates one of the team members he now supervises. He also continues to bowl with and socialize with three or four of his "old buddies" from the team. The other six team members don't bowl or participate in the social activities.

- What kinds of problems might Juan Gonzalez eventually face as a result of dating an employee who reports directly to him?
- What kind of problems might Juan Gonzalez face as a result of his "buddy" relationship with the team members he supervises?

TRUST BUILDING AND LEADERSHIP

Trust is a necessary ingredient for success in the highly competitive modern workplace. Building trust requires leadership on the part of supervisors. Trust-building strategies include the following:

- *Taking the blame, but sharing the credit.* Supervisors who point the finger of blame at their employees, even when the employees are at fault, will not build trust. Leaders must be willing to accept responsibility for the performance of people they hope to lead. Correspondingly, when credit is due, leaders must be prepared to spread it around appropriately. Such unselfishness on the part of supervisors will build trust among employees.
- *Pitching in and helping.* Supervisors can show leadership and build trust by rolling up their sleeves and helping out when a deadline is approaching. A willingness to get their hands dirty when circumstances warrant will help supervisors build trust among employees.
- *Being consistent.* People trust consistency. It lets them know what to expect. Even when employees disagree with supervisors, they appreciate consistent behavior.
- *Being equitable.* Supervisors cannot play favorites and hope to build trust. Employees want to know that they are treated not just well, but as well as all other employees. Fair and equitable treatment of all employees will build trust.

The following scenarios represent the types of situations supervisors can expect to encounter on the job. They are provided to give readers opportunities to learn appropriate responses to such situations.

1. When Mark Crawford went through Marine Corps boot camp at Parris Island, South Carolina, his drill instructors were tough, demanding, and unforgiving. Crawford was impressed with his drill instructors. To him they were outstanding leaders who got their recruits to perform at levels higher than they ever thought they could. In Crawford's eyes the drill instructors knew how to get results. Consequently, when he was promoted to supervisor yesterday, Crawford knew just how he planned to lead. This morning he called a team meeting and did his best impersonation of a Marine Corps drill instructor. Among other things, Crawford said: "This team is going to be the best producing unit in the history of this company. We are going to outwork and outthink every other team on the payroll. As of now you work for me

and I expect results. No whining, no excuses, and no complaining. I want results. I will be here early and I will stay late. You follow my example and we will get along just fine. Anyone who doesn't want to follow my example can request a transfer. You are dismissed. Let's get to work!"

- How do you think Crawford's introductory speech was received by his team members?
- Do you think Crawford's approach will be effective in the long run? Why or why not?

2. Du Van Tram prides himself on being a "people" person. His fellow employees know that Van Tram will always give them a shoulder to cry on and an empathic ear. Consequently, they are looking forward to his replacing their current supervisor who has given his two-week notice. Van Tram has asked all members of the team to write down the three worst complaints they have about current working conditions. Knowing that morale in the team is low, Van Tram intends to begin his planned improvements by focusing on morale. In his opinion just improving the morale of team members will also solve the team's quality, productivity, and absenteeism problems. Van Tram knows that some of his team members are loafing on the job, overlooking quality problems, and taking sick days when they are perfectly well. These things don't bother Van Tram. He thinks if he is nice to team members, listens to their complaints, and is a friend to them, things will turn around.

- How well do you think Van Tram's approach is going to work?
- Can you foresee any problems that Van Tram might have? If so, what are these problems likely to be?

KEY TERMS AND PHRASES

Autocratic leadership	Participative leadership
Democratic leadership	People-oriented styles
Financial security	Situational leadership
Goal-oriented leadership	Task-oriented styles
Hierarchy of needs	Theory X
Leadership	Theory Y
Motivation	Theory XY

REVIEW QUESTIONS

1. Define the term *leadership*.
2. List five characteristics of good leaders.
3. Briefly state your opinion concerning the following statement: "Leaders are born, not made."
4. What are the key factors in becoming a good leader?
5. What is the key to motivating people?
6. What are the five levels of Maslow's hierarchy of needs?
7. Briefly explain three procedures for applying the hierarchy of needs model in motivating people.
8. Briefly explain the following theories of leadership: Theory X, Theory Y, and Theory XY.
9. List and briefly explain five leadership styles.
10. List eight leadership characteristics that win and maintain followership.

CHAPTER TWO

Facilitating Change

LEARNING OBJECTIVES

After studying this chapter, you should be able to do the following:

- Explain how a supervisor can play a leadership role in facilitating change.
- Describe a change-management system and the role supervisors play in it.
- Explain the supervisor's role in each step of the change-implementation model.
- Explain the supervisor's role when an organization undergoes restructuring.

The one thing that can be depended on not to change in today's competitive marketplace is the ever-present reality of change. Processes, products, people, services, and technology in the workplace have always changed. However, there were times when the rate and magnitude of change were less than they are now. In today's marketplace, an organization that is not changing is falling behind. Consequently, supervisors in the contemporary workplace must be effective change agents. This chapter explains the role supervisors play in helping organizations respond proactively and systematically to change and how they can play their role more effectively.

FACILITATING CHANGE AS A LEADERSHIP FUNCTION

A facilitator is someone who helps make things happen. Facilitators are not usually in a position to simply order, command, or direct that something happen. Rather, they must use persuasion, influence, and communication to "grease the organization's wheels." In addition, facilitators use their experience, judgment, and common sense to identify barriers and help eliminate them. The following general strategies will help supervisors be effective facilitators of change in their organizations:

- Ask higher management to paint a "word picture" of the change in question and how things will be after the change is implemented. One reason employees sometimes resist change is that it represents the unknown, and people are uncomfortable with the unknown.
- Communicate the "word picture" to all employees who will be affected by the change. Those who will be affected by change are more likely to go along if they are "in the know."
- Take responsibility for the change. Ask, "What can I do to make this change succeed?" Supervisors and employees who are opposed to change do not have to

actively fight against it to ensure it fails; they can simply sit back and do nothing. Therefore, taking responsibility is critical.

- Write down what you can do to help successfully implement the change. Convert your "To Do" list into objectives and establish a schedule for accomplishing the objectives. Writing things down and setting a schedule will keep you focused.
- Identify hidden barriers to successful implementation of the change. Make those barriers known to higher management and assist in removing them.
- When dealing with employees affected by the change, explain the need to change in terms of how they will benefit. People tend to personalize the issues they deal with. Put the need to change in personal terms.
- Ask employees for input concerning what the change will mean to them and barriers they see to successful implementation. People tend to support change more readily when they are participants rather than spectators.
- Involve every employee affected by a change in developing the plan for successfully implementing the change. This will promote buy in and cause employees to see the change as "theirs" rather than "yours."
- Stay positive, never react defensively, and listen, listen, listen. Supervisors who become defensive when questioned might appear to be hiding something.

APPLICATION AND DISCUSSION

For years, the Hecto Company has processed change orders manually. Deviations from the contract cannot be made without an approved change order. Field personnel complete a "Change Order Form," route it to the office by courier, and then wait until the form is processed and approved by a manager with an appropriate level of authority before actually making the change in question. If the manager whose signature is needed is not available, if the change order is misplaced, or if the courier's van breaks down, a whole crew might find itself sitting idle waiting for approval. This happens frequently enough that Hecto's CEO has decided to convert to an electronic system. He plans to give each field crew and all managers a laptop computer with an e-mail connection. Change orders will be submitted electronically and approvals will be sent electronically.

You supervise three field crews. The CEO has called a meeting of all supervisors to discuss the change. He wants to know what problems to expect and what can be done to facilitate a smooth conversion.

- What problems do you foresee in this conversion?
- As the most senior supervisor, you feel an obligation to develop a facilitation plan for supervisors. Develop a plan that shows supervisors how they can be effective facilitators in making the conversion go smoothly.

CHANGE-MANAGEMENT SYSTEM

Change is an ever-present reality for organizations operating in a competitive marketplace. Change is not a one-time inconvenience to be disposed of so things can get back to normal. Unfortunately, though, this is how many organizations handle change. What such organizations fail to realize is that change is constant; it is the normal state of things. Consequently, organizations need to respond proactively and systematically to change as a normal part of their everyday operations.

This requires the adoption of a **change-management system**. Such a system should have at least the following components (Figure 2–1):

- Scanners
- Receiving points
- Deliberative groups
- Executive committee

Scanners

This component of the change-management system consists of employees at all levels who constantly scan the environment in which the organization operates. Every employee from the CEO to the lowest-paid wage earner should be a scanner for the organization. **Scanners** constantly look outside and inside the organization to identify developments and trends that could signal the need for change. In other words, scanners help anticipate change so the organization can respond proactively and get out in front of it.

Managers monitor economic trends, feedback from customers, and demographic trends. Supervisors read professional literature, attend seminars and workshops, and talk to colleagues in the business. Employees read work-related literature and observe technological developments in their fields. All of these activities are scanning opportunities.

Supervisors play a critical role in operationalizing this component of an organization's change-management system. The extent to which employees will identify potential changes that might help the organization will be determined by how supervisors receive their recommendations. Supervisors who "shoot the messenger" will soon find they receive no messages. On the other hand, supervisors who let employees know that they not only welcome, but expect scanning input will benefit from a steady flow of information.

Receiving Points

If all employees are supposed to continually scan the environment and make recommendations for dealing with change they see on the horizon, there must be a mechanism for facilitating the process. This mechanism is the receiving point. A **receiving point** is a place (or a person) where employees can make a recommendation for change.

Since all employees in an organization, other than the CEO, have a supervisor, the obvious choice when establishing receiving points is the supervisor. With this approach, every supervisor in the organization becomes the receiving point for his or her direct reports. Using supervisors as receiving points has several advantages:

Figure 2–1
Purposes of each component in a change-management system

Components of a Change-Management System
• **Scanners.** All employees at all levels should "scan" the organization's environment continually in an attempt to anticipate the need for change.
• **Receiving Points.** Supervisors who receive recommendations for change and act on them in one of the following ways: 1) approve, 2) disapprove, 3) return for additional information, or 4) forward for deliberation by an appropriate group.
• **Deliberative Groups.** Discuss the ramifications of recommendations and give advice concerning appropriate action.
• **Executive Committee.** Final approval, planning, and budgeting.

- It "plugs this function in" without creating another level or another unit in the organization.

- It builds in a measure of informed judgment at the front end of the process. Supervisors are in the best position to distinguish between promising and frivolous recommendations relating to their teams, units, or departments.

- It gives supervisors opportunities to work with team members to focus on strengthening their recommendations before sending the recommendations up the chain.

Receiving, acknowledging, processing, and monitoring recommendations can be simplified by purchasing one of the many tracking software packages available. With such packages, each supervisor has tracking software on a personal computer or a laptop. Once a recommendation is entered into the supervisor's computer, a printed acknowledgement is produced and forwarded to the employee. From that point forward the recommendation can be processed, monitored, and modified electronically.

Deliberative Groups

Sometimes supervisors have the authority to act directly on recommendations from their direct reports. However, supervisors often need a second opinion before approving or denying a recommendation. For example, an employee might make a recommendation having to do with employee safety. The supervisor likes the recommendation, but is concerned that it might conflict with a state or federal safety regulation. She consequently forwards the recommendation to the organization's "Safety Committee" for review. A customer-service-related recommendation might be forwarded to the "Customer Service Committee."

In-house groups such as these are deliberative groups. **Deliberative groups** provide a review process and advice when recommendations might have cross-departmental or organization-wide impact. Most of the commercially available electronic tracking packages allow supervisors to interact electronically with deliberative groups.

Executive Committee

The **executive committee** consists of the organization's top managers. These individuals have final authority for approving and budgeting recommendations for changes. No significant change will happen in an organization without the commitment and support of the executive managers. Supervisors who make recommendations for change or endorse those made by subordinates should prepare their justification with executive management in mind.

=========== APPLICATION AND DISCUSSION ===========

Some think that change should come from the bottom up. Others think that it should be initiated only from the top down. The most effective organizations welcome and promote both approaches.

- What do you see as the supervisor's role in facilitating change that is initiated from the bottom up? Top down?

- How does the change-management system described in this section accommodate both the bottom up and the top down approaches to initiating change?

CHANGE IMPLEMENTATION MODEL

The change-management system explained in the previous section serves the following purposes: (1) empowers all employees at all levels to help the organization respond proactively and systematically to change; (2) establishes the supervisor as a key player in managing organizational change; and (3) establishes a system for making, tracking, revising, approving, and disapproving recommendations for change.

Once a change recommendation is approved and necessary funds have been budgeted, the change must be implemented. Implementation is rarely automatic. An organization's managers cannot simply decree that a given change take place. Too many factors work against organizational change. These factors include employee resistance, structural inhibitors, and organizational inertia (the tendency of an organization to continue doing things the way it "always has").

Consequently, implementing change requires a concerted, systematic effort. The following **change-implementation** model is an effective way to systematically implement specific changes in an organization:

- *Develop a "picture" of how things will be after the change.*
- *Communicate with all stakeholders about the change.*
- *Provide any training that will be necessary.*
- *Implement the change.*
- *Monitor and adjust.*

The model should be applied in the order presented with no steps skipped. Supervisors have a role to play in each step, a role that can vary depending on the origin and scope of the change in question.

Develop the Change "Picture"

People take comfort in the familiar and fear the unknown, even when they do not particularly like the familiar. This trait of human nature is what gave rise to the adage "the devil you know is better than the devil you don't know." Because of this trait, the first step in successfully implementing change is to eliminate uncertainty by developing a **change "picture"** of how things will be after the change.

This means that supervisors must analyze changes carefully and be able to answer the following questions: "How will this change affect my team? What will be different and how? How will the new way be better?" The answers to these questions form the change "picture" that is then communicated to team members. It is important for supervisors to remember that employees personalize change. Therefore, the change "picture" should be personalized. It should show clearly what will be different after the change and how things will be better.

Supervisors should be prepared to meet with opposition, grumbling, and questions. These things are all part of the transition process people go through when confronted with change. The key for supervisors is to be patient and apply the following guidelines:

- Give employees opportunities to express their misgivings. Let them vent and listen. They might see something that has been overlooked. If so, it can be dealt with or factored into the implementation process.

- Stay positive. No matter what is said, do not become defensive. Employees will sense the defensiveness and wonder what you are hiding.

- Let employees know that "we are in this together." It is important that employees know they are not being singled out or picked on.

- Help employees see that change is driven by market forces that must be responded to if the organization is going to stay competitive. Change is not being driven by top managers who become bored with the same way of doing things and order change for the sake of change. The issue is competitiveness and survival, and all employees have a personal interest in the survival of their employer.

- Listen, listen, listen, and listen some more.

Communicate With All Stakeholders about the Change

When the issue is change, a stakeholder is any person who will be affected by the change. People do not resist change so much because they want things to stay as they are, but because change is often "inflicted" on them. Consequently, employees often see change as something done *to* them rather than something done *with* them or *for* them. The implementation process will be more effective if employees go along with the change and do their part to make it work rather working overtly or covertly against it.

The best way to make this happen is to communicate with all stakeholders about the change. Let them know what is going to happen, when it will happen, and why. Show them both the big picture and the little picture (their role in the big picture). Let them know what is expected of them, what they will need to do and *not* do for the change to succeed. Communicate continually throughout the implementation until the new way becomes the accepted way. Ask how they are doing, listen to their feedback, deal with any unforeseen difficulties, and recognize their efforts.

Provide Any Necessary Training

One of the main reasons employees like to do things the way they have always done them is familiarity. They know how to do them this way. Too often changes are implemented in organizations without proper consideration of how they will affect the minute-by-minute, day-to-day lives of employees. Any person would rather do something in a familiar way. This is just human nature.

Consequently, it is important to provide training when a change requires employees to do things differently. The classic example of this phenomenon is a software change or upgrade. People who work with computers become accustomed to specific software packages. When these packages are changed or just upgraded, employees are often left on their own to figure out how to use them. Naturally, they would rather use the former package. However, if part of changing to a new software package included employee training, in short order the familiar way would be the new way. This is true about any change that affects work procedures and processes. Give employees the training they need to do things the new way, and their grumbling about having to change will last no longer than the training.

Implement the Change

Once employees can see the change "picture," understand what is going to happen and when, embrace the role they need to play, and have been trained in the new way, it is time to implement the change. On the official "change-over" day, the organization stops doing things the old way and begins using only the new way. At this point, the new way becomes the only and official way. Up to now the organization might have continued to use old procedures while the new were being tested and while employees were being trained. But not any longer. There comes a point when the new way cannot succeed unless the organization lets go of the old way.

Monitor and Adjust

Any implementation must be followed by a period of adjustment. The new procedures must be monitored to determine their effectiveness, and sometimes adjustments must be made. One of the most difficult things to deal with when implementing change is that productivity sometimes declines for a brief period following implementation of new procedures. This is because employees have used the old procedures long enough to hone their skills, gain experience, and work out the bugs. In other words, with the old procedures employees were on the positive side of the learning curve. This will not be the case with new procedures, at least not at first. When supervisors first realize this, it can be tempting to put aside the new procedures and go back to the old way, especially when the team begins to fall behind in its work. This is a mistake. The only way employees will become proficient in using the new procedures is to use them. Therefore, it is important for supervisors to patiently help employees work through the frustrations of the learning curve when implementing new procedures.

=============== APPLICATION AND DISCUSSION ===============

Identify an organizational change that has occurred or that is happening now. It can be from an organization you work in, have worked in, or are familiar with. It can also be from a case in a professional journal.

■ Put yourself in the place of a supervisor in the organization in question. What types of resistance to the change are being offered by employees or would you expect to be offered?

■ Apply each step of the change-implementation model to this situation. Explain your role as a supervisor in each step and what you would say and do.

RESTRUCTURING AND CHANGE

Few words can strike fear into the hearts of employees as quickly as the term *restructuring*. This word has become synonymous with layoffs, terminations, plant closings, and workforce cuts. As a result, the typical employee response to the term is uncertainty and panic.

Because of the ever-changing conditions of the global marketplace, few organizations will escape the necessity of restructuring, and few people will complete a career without experiencing one or more restructurings. Acquisitions, mergers, buyouts, and downsizing—common occurrences in today's marketplace—all typically involve organizational restructuring. This fact is market driven and can be controlled by neither individuals nor organizations. However, organizations and individuals can control how they respond to the changes brought by restructuring, and this response determines the effectiveness of the restructuring effort (Figure 2–2).

Figure 2–2
Four steps for handling the changes brought by restructuring an organization

Steps for Making Restructuring Effective
Step 1: Be smart and empathetic.
Step 2: Communicate the "change picture."
Step 3: Establish incentives that promote change.
Step 4: Continue to train.

Be Smart and Empathetic

Supervisors should remember that restructuring can be traumatic for employees when implementing the changes that go with restructuring. The challenge is to be both **smart and empathetic**. The following strategies can help maintain employee loyalty and calm employee fears during restructuring:

- Take time to show employees that management cares and is concerned about them on a personal level.
- Communicate with employees about why the changes are necessary. Focus on market factors.
- Encourage management to offer outplacement assistance for all employees who might lose their jobs.
- Be fair, equitable, and honest with employees. Select employees to be laid off according to a definite set of criteria rather than as the result of a witch-hunt or friendship.

Communicate the Change "Picture"

One of the best ways to minimize the disruptive nature of change is to have a clear "picture" of what the organization is going to look like after the change. A good question to ask is "What are we trying to become?" Supervisors should have a clear "picture" and be able to articulate it. This will eliminate the problem of uncertainty.

Establish Incentives That Promote the Change

People respond to incentives, especially when those incentives are important to them personally. Supervisors can promote the changes that accompany restructuring by establishing incentives for those who contribute to making changes. Incentives can be monetary or nonmonetary, but they should motivate employees on a personal level.

An effective way to identify incentives that will work is to form ad hoc committees of employees that are chaired by supervisors. Each committee lists as many monetary and nonmonetary incentives as the group can identify. Then the members discuss the list with their fellow employees. Once a broad base of employee input has been collected, the committees meet again and rank the incentives that are most likely to promote change. A final list or "menu" of incentives is the result of this collaboration. The menu concept allows employees to select from among a list of options each time they earn an incentive.

Continue to Train

During times of intense change, the tendency of organizations is to put training on hold. The idea is "we'll get back to training again when things settle down." In reality, putting off training during restructuring is the last thing an organization should do. One of the primary reasons employees oppose change is that it requires skills they do not have. Training should actually be increased during times of intense change to ensure that employees have the skills required during and after the transition period.

=========== **APPLICATION AND DISCUSSION** ===========

The two terms that best describe how people feel when they learn that their employer is going to restructure are *uncertainty* and *fear*. They will want to know what is going to happen to them. The less they are told, the more they will worry.

- What types of problems would you expect as a supervisor in the following situation: Out of the blue, your employer's CEO announces in a local newspaper interview that he is going to initiate a major restructuring over the next six months. His mandate to executive managers is "Keep a lid on this." He tells the newspaper, but will not let supervisors talk to employees.

■ Now explain how this situation should have been handled.

ON-THE-JOB SCENARIOS

The On-the-Job Scenarios in this book represent the types of situations supervisors can expect to encounter on the job. They are provided to give readers opportunities to learn appropriate responses to such situations.

1. The CEO of Sumcom, Inc. wants the company to get better at responding to change. She thinks that Sumcom just reacts to change and, as a result, is always operating in a "catch-up" mode. She has formed a task force to develop a plan for turning Sumcom into an organization that accurately predicts change and effectively responds to it. You, as the senior supervisor at Sumcom, have been selected to chair the task force. Develop a plan for accomplishing the following:
   - Implementing a change-management system.
   - Ensuring that Sumcom has a model in place for implementing changes that are approved by top managers.

2. The CEO of Sumcom, Inc. has approved the plan your task force developed. Now she wants you to analyze the plan and develop another plan that does the following:
   - Describes the supervisor's role in the change-management system.
   - Describes the supervisor's role in implementing change. She would like the plan to be a "how-to" guide that can be distributed to all supervisors at Sumcom. Develop the plan/guide.

KEY TERMS AND PHRASES

Change implementation model

Change-management system

Change "picture"

Deliberative groups

Executive committee

Receiving points

Scanners

Smart and empathetic

REVIEW QUESTIONS

1. Explain why employees sometimes resist change.
2. Why is it so important for supervisors to take responsibility for change?
3. List and explain the four components of a change-management system.
4. What are the advantages of using supervisors as receiving points?
5. What three purposes does a change-management system serve?
6. What is organizational inertia?
7. List the five steps in the change-implementation model.
8. What is a change "picture"?
9. Explain the guidelines supervisors can use to deal with the opposition and grumbling that sometimes accompany change.
10. Explain the steps for improving the effectiveness of organizational restructuring.

CHAPTER THREE

Communication

════════ LEARNING OBJECTIVES ════════

After studying this chapter, you should be able to do the following:

- Define communication.
- Explain communication as a process.
- Explain the most common inhibitors of communication.
- Explain the concept of communication networks.
- Demonstrate how to communicate better by listening.
- Demonstrate how to communicate better nonverbally.
- Demonstrate how to communicate corrective feedback.
- Explain six steps to improved communication.

Of all the skills needed by supervisors, communication is the most important. All other supervision skills presented in this book depend either directly or indirectly on effective communication. It is fundamental to leadership, motivation, problem solving, training, discipline, ethics, and all other areas of concern to the supervisor. This chapter helps supervisors become more effective communicators. Note that although communication is important enough to warrant its own unit, in practice it must be fully integrated into all the other functions supervisors perform.

COMMUNICATION DEFINED

Inexperienced supervisors often confuse *telling* with *communicating*. When a problem develops, they are likely to explain, "But I told him what to do." Inexperienced supervisors also often confuse *hearing* with *listening*. They are likely to say, "This isn't what I told you to do. I know you heard me. You were standing right next to me!"

In both cases, the supervisor has confused telling and hearing with communicating. This point can be illustrated by a quotation attributed to less-than-forthright politicians: "I know you believe you understand what you think I said, but I am not sure you realize that what you heard is not what I meant."

This is an amusing quote, but it does make a point. What you say is not necessarily what the other person hears, and what the other person hears is not necessarily what you intended to say. The key word is *understand*. This word is the key to communication. Communication may involve telling, but it is not *just* telling. It may involve hearing, but it is not *just* hearing. For the purpose of this book, communication is defined as follows:

> ***Communication*** *is the transfer of information that is received and fully understood from one source to another.*

A message can be sent by one person and received by another, but until the message is fully understood, there is no communication. This applies to spoken, written, and nonverbal messages.

Communication Versus Effective Communication

When information conveyed is received and understood, there is communication. However, understanding by itself does not necessarily make effective communication. **Effective communication** occurs when the information that is received and understood is acted on in the desired manner (Figure 3–1).

For example, a supervisor might ask her team members to arrive at work fifteen minutes early for the next week to ensure that an important order goes out on schedule. All of the team members verify that they understand both the facts and the reasons in the message. However, without informing the supervisor, two team members decide they are not going to comply. This is an example of ineffective communication. The two nonconforming employees understood the message, but decided against complying with it. The supervisor in this case failed to achieve acceptance of the message. Consequently, the communication was ineffective.

Effective communication is a higher level of communication. It implies not just understanding, but understanding and acceptance. This means that effective communication will require persuasion, motivation, monitoring, and leadership.

Communication Levels

Communication can take place on several levels in an organization. These levels are as follows:

- One-on-one level
- Team or unit level
- Organization level
- Community level

Although supervisors are actively engaged primarily in the first two levels, they may be involved at all levels, at least indirectly. Consequently, supervisors should be familiar with all four levels of communication.

- **One-on-one-level communication** is just what the name implies—one person communicating with one other person. This might involve face-to-face conversation, a telephone call, or even a simple gesture or facial expression.
- **Team- or unit-level communication** is communication within a peer group. The primary difference between one-on-one and team communication is that, with the

| Understanding | Acceptance | = | Effective communication |

Figure 3–1
Elements of effective communication

latter, all team members are involved in the process at once. A team meeting to solve a problem or set goals would be an opportunity for team-level communication.

- **Company-level communication** is communication among groups. A meeting involving the sales department, design department, and a production team would represent an opportunity for company-level communication.
- **Community-level communication** occurs among groups inside an organization and groups outside the organization. Perhaps the most common examples of community-level communication are a company's sales force with potential clients and a company's purchasing department with vendors.

=== APPLICATION AND DISCUSSION ===

Eugene Washington is fond of quoting a favorite line from an old movie: "What we have here is failure to communicate." He does this any time there seems to be a breakdown in communication in the team he supervises. Lately, he has been using this quote a lot. He still gets the performance he wants out of his experienced team members, but the three new members act as if they have hearing problems. Washington tells them what he wants, and he knows they hear him. However, more times than not they fail to do what he asks.

- What problem is Eugene Washington facing in this situation?
- Put yourself in Washington's place. How would you improve communication with the three new employees?

COMMUNICATION AS A PROCESS

Communication is a process that involves several components. These components are the sender, the receiver, the medium, and the message itself. The **sender** is the originator or source of the message. The **receiver** is the person or group for whom the message is intended. The **message** is the information to be conveyed, understood, accepted, and acted on. The **medium** is the vehicle used to convey the message (Figure 3-2).

There are three basic categories of mediums: verbal, nonverbal, and written. **Verbal communication** includes face-to-face conversation, telephone conversation, speeches, public address announcements, press conferences, and other approaches for conveying the spoken word. **Nonverbal communication** includes gestures, facial expressions, voice tone, and body poses. **Written communication** includes letters, e-mail, memorandums, billboards, bulletin boards, manuals, books, and any other method of conveying the written word.

Technological developments are having a major impact on our ability to convey information. These developments include word processing, satellite communication, computer modems, cordless telephones, car telephones, telephone answering machines, facsimile machines, pocket-size dictation machines, electronic mail, and the Internet.

Figure 3–2
Communication process

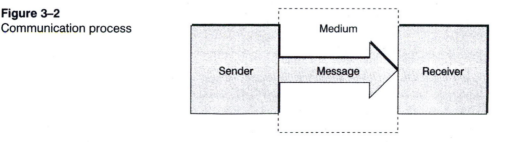

===================== APPLICATION AND DISCUSSION =====================

With cellular telephones, beepers, overnight express mail, FAX machines, e-mail, and other technological innovations, communication has become more immediate. We can now transmit a message to almost anybody, almost anywhere, and almost any time. Consequently, the quality of communication has improved markedly, or has it?

■ List of the different modes of communication you might use in a typical week.

■ Have the various technological aids available to you made your communication more *effective* or just more *immediate*? Why or why not?

INHIBITORS OF COMMUNICATION

As advanced as communication-enhancing devices have become, there are still as many inhibitors of effective communication as ever. Supervisors should be familiar with these inhibitors to be able to avoid or overcome them. The most common inhibitors of effective communication are as follows:

■ Differences in meaning
■ Insufficient trust
■ Information overload
■ Interference
■ Condescending tones
■ Listening problems
■ Premature judgments
■ Inaccurate assumptions
■ Technological glitches

Differences in Meaning

Differences in meaning are a common problem in communication. We all have different backgrounds and levels of education. We might even come from different cultures and have different national origins. As a result, words, gestures, and facial expressions can have altogether different meanings to different people. This is why supervisors must invest the time to know their team members.

Insufficient Trust

Insufficient trust can inhibit effective communication. If receivers do not trust senders, they may be overly sensitive and guarded. They might concentrate so hard on reading between the lines for the "hidden agenda" that they miss the real message. This is why trust building between supervisors and employees is so important. It is well worth all the time and effort required.

Information Overload

Information overload is more of an inhibitor than it has ever been. Computers, modems, satellite communication, facsimile machines, electronic mail, the Internet, and the many other technological innovations developed to promote and enhance communication can actually cause a breakdown in communication. Because of advances in communication technology and the rapid and continual proliferation of information, we often find ourselves with more information than we can process effectively. This is **information overload**. Supervisors can guard against information overload by screening, organizing, summarizing, and simplifying the information they convey to employees.

Interference

Interference is any external distraction that inhibits effective communication. It might be something as simple as background noise or as complex as atmospheric interference with satellite communications. Regardless of its source, interference either distorts or completely blocks the message. This is why supervisors must be attentive to the environment when they plan to communicate with employees.

Condescending Tones

A condescending tone when conveying information can inhibit effective communication. People do not like to be talked down to. Problems in this regard typically result from the tone rather than the content of the message. Supervisors should never talk down to employees.

Listening Problems

Listening problems are one of the most serious inhibitors of effective communication. Problems can result when the sender does not listen to the receiver and vice versa. An entire section is devoted to listening later in this unit.

Premature Judgments

Premature judgments by either the sender or the receiver can inhibit effective communication. This is primarily because they interfere with listening. As soon as we make a quick judgment, we are prone to stop listening. You cannot make premature judgments and maintain an open mind. Therefore, it is important for supervisors to listen nonjudgmentally when talking with employees.

Inaccurate Assumptions

Our perceptions are influenced by our assumptions. Consequently, **inaccurate assumptions** can lead to inaccurate perceptions, as in the following example. John Andrews, a technician, has been taking an inordinate amount of time off from work lately. His supervisor, Joe Little, assumes John is goldbricking. As a result, whenever John makes a suggestion in a team meeting, Joe assumes he is just lazy and suggesting the easy way out.

It turns out this is an inaccurate assumption. John is actually a highly motivated, highly skilled worker. His excessive time off is the result of a problem he is having at home, a problem he is too embarrassed to discuss. In this case, because of an inaccurate assumption, the supervisor is missing opportunities to take advantage of the suggestions of a highly motivated, highly skilled employee. In addition, he is overlooking a need for building trust. Perhaps if John Andrews trusted his supervisor more, he would be less embarrassed to discuss his personal problem with him.

Technological Glitches

Software "bugs," computer viruses, dead batteries, power outages, and conversion problems between software packages are only a few examples of technological glitches that can interfere with communication. The more dependent we become on technology in conveying messages, the more often these glitches will interfere and inhibit.

Communication is an imperfect process at best. Numerous inhibitors are at work every time one attempts to communicate. Most people have experienced all of the various inhibitors set forth in this section.

- List the inhibitors explained in this section. Now, identify an instance in which you have experienced each of the inhibitors. What problems were caused in each case?
- Have you experienced other inhibitors? What are they and what problems did they cause?

COMMUNICATION NETWORKS

In most organizations, much of the communication that takes place goes through networks, either formal or informal. A **network** is a group of senders linked by some means with a group of receivers. A formal network might consist of all supervisors in a company linked electronically to each other and higher management. Any person in the system can be a sender or receiver. The networking mechanism is the electronic system.

An informal network would be what is alternately referred to as *the gossip circle, water cooler crowd*, or **grapevine**. In this case, all participants in the network can be senders and receivers. The network itself is one-on-one conversation passed along from person to person. Formal networks are used for communicating official company messages. Informal networks are used to convey unofficial and often inaccurate messages (Figure 3–3).

We often think of a network as an electronic system onto which organizations load the software they use. All employees who have access to the network are able to use the various software packages contained therein, the e-mail system, and so on. In reality, the

Figure 3–3
Supervisors should be aware of both formal and informal networks.

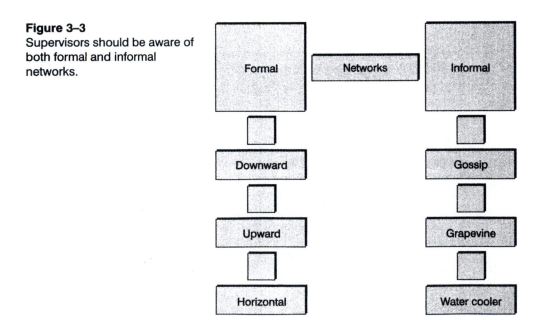

people who use this electronic system make up the network. This is why people who attend professional conferences and similar meetings say that part of their motivation for doing so is the opportunity to "network" with colleagues.

- How many different forms of networks—formal and informal—do you use (or have you used)? What are they?
- What problems/advantages have you experienced with each form of network you have used?

COMMUNICATION BY LISTENING

Perhaps the most important communication skill of supervisors is listening. It is also the one people are least likely to have. Are you a good listener? Consider the following questions:

1. When in a group of people, are you more likely to talk or listen?
2. When talking with someone, do you often interrupt before the speaker completes the statement?
3. When talking with someone, do you find yourself tuning out and thinking ahead to your response?
4. When talking with someone, could you paraphrase what the speaker said and repeat it?
5. In a conversation, do you tend to state your opinion before other speakers have made their case?
6. When talking with someone, do you give your full attention or continue with other tasks simultaneously?
7. When you do not understand, do you ask for clarification?
8. In meetings, do you tend to daydream or stray from the subject?
9. When talking with someone, do you fidget and sneak glances at your watch?
10. Do you ever finish statements for people who do not move the conversation along fast enough?

A skilled listener will respond to these questions as follows:

1. Listen	6. Full attention
2. No	7. Yes
3. No	8. No
4. Yes	9. No
5. No	10. No

A better way to find out if you are a good listener is to ask. Ask a friend, your spouse, a fellow supervisor, and an employee you can trust to give an objective answer. Do not be overly concerned if you find you are a poor listener. Listening is a skill and, like all skills, it can be developed. To become a good listener you need to know (1) what listening is, (2) barriers that inhibit listening, and (3) strategies that promote effective listening.

What Is Listening?

Hearing is a natural process, but listening is not. A person with highly sensitive hearing abilities can be a poor listener. Conversely, a person with impaired hearing can be an excellent listener. Hearing is simply the physiological process of decoding sound waves, but listening requires *perception*. Listening can be defined in numerous ways. In this book, we define listening as follows:

> **Listening** is receiving the message, correctly decoding it, and accurately perceiving what is meant.

Inhibitors of Effective Listening

Listening breaks down when the receiver does not accurately perceive the message. Several inhibitors can cause this to happen:

- Lack of concentration
- Preconceived ideas
- Thinking ahead
- Interruptions
- Tuning out

To perceive the message accurately, listeners must *concentrate on what is being said, how it is being said, and in what tone*. Part of effective listening is properly reading nonverbal cues (covered in the next section).

Concentration requires the listener to eliminate as many extraneous distractions as possible and to mentally shut out the rest. Supervisors who cling to preconceived notions cannot listen effectively. **Preconceived ideas** can cause supervisors to make premature judgments that turn out to be wrong. Be patient, wait, and listen.

Supervisors who jump ahead to where they think the conversation is going may get there and find they are all alone. *Thinking ahead* is typically a response to being hurried, but supervisors will find it takes less time to hear an employee out than it does to start over after jumping ahead to the wrong conclusion.

Interruptions not only inhibit effective listening, they frustrate and often confuse the speaker. If clarification is needed during a conversation, make a mental note and wait for the speaker to reach an interim stopping point. Mental notes are preferable to written notes. Writing notes can distract the speaker or cause the listener to miss a critical point. If you find it necessary to make written notes, keep them short.

Tuning out inhibits effective listening. Some people become skilled at using body language to make it appear they are listening while their mind is focusing on other areas of concern. Supervisors should avoid the temptation to engage in such ploys. A skilled speaker may ask you to repeat what he or she just said (Figure 3–4).

Supervisors can become effective listeners by applying several simple strategies:

- Remove all distractions.
- Put the speaker at ease.
- Look directly at the speaker.
- Concentrate on what is being said.
- Watch for nonverbal cues.
- Make note of the speaker's tone.
- Be patient and wait.
- Ask clarifying questions.
- Paraphrase and repeat.
- No matter what is said, control your emotions.

Figure 3–4
These factors can form
impenetrable barriers to effective
listening.

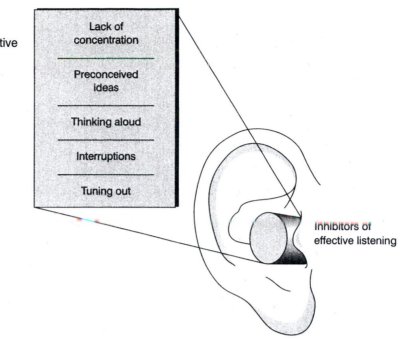

| Lack of concentration |
| Preconceived ideas |
| Thinking aloud |
| Interruptions |
| Tuning out |

Inhibitors of
effective listening

APPLICATION AND DISCUSSION

Listening is a skill to be learned for most people. Few people are natural listeners. As a supervisor, you will have to be a good listener. Your effectiveness will depend on it.

- Take the ten-question quiz on page 29. List the areas in which you need to improve.
- Select a partner and a topic of mutual interest. Discuss this topic with your partner using the strategies presented at the end of this section. What nonverbal cues did you pick up from your partner? Were you able to paraphrase and repeat your partner's main points?

COMMUNICATING NONVERBALLY

Nonverbal messages represent one of the least understood, but most powerful, modes of communication. Often nonverbal messages are more honest and telling then verbal messages provided the receiver is attentive and able to read nonverbal cues.

It has become popular to call nonverbal communication "body language." However, body language is only part of nonverbal communication. There are actually three components:

- Body factors
- Voice factors
- Proximity factors

Body Factors

A person's posture, body poses, facial expressions, gestures, and dress—**body factors**—can convey a message. Even such extras as makeup or lack of it, well-groomed or unkempt hair, and shined or scruffy shoes can convey a message. Supervisors should be attentive to these body factors and how they add to or detract from the verbal message.

One of the keys to understanding nonverbal cues lies in the concept of ***congruence***. Are the spoken message and the nonverbal message congruent? They should be. To illustrate this point, consider the hypothetical example of Chem-Tech Company. An important element of the company's corporate culture is attractive, conservative dress. This is especially important for Chem-Tech's sales force. For the men, white shirts, dark suits, and shined shoes are the norm.

John McNamara is an effective sales representative, but lately he has taken to flashy dressing. He wears loud sports coats, open-neck print shirts, and casual shoes. When questioned by his supervisor, John said he understands the dress code and agrees with it. This is ***incongruence***. His verbal message says one thing, but his nonverbal message says another. This is an exaggerated example. Incongruence is not always so obvious. A simple facial expression or a subtle gesture can be an indicator of incongruence.

When verbal and nonverbal messages are not congruent, supervisors should take the time to dig a little deeper. An effective way to deal with incongruence is to gently but frankly confront it. A simple statement such as, "Cindy, your words agree with me, but your eyes disagree" can help draw an employee out so the supervisor gets the real message.

Voice Factors

Voice factors are also an important part of nonverbal communication. In addition to listening to the words, supervisors should listen for **voice factors** like volume, tone, pitch, and rate of speech. These factors can reveal feelings of anger, fear, impatience, uncertainty, interest, acceptance, confidence, and a variety of other messages.

As with body factors, it is important to look for congruence. It is also advisable to look for groups of nonverbal cues. Supervisors can be misled by attaching too much meaning to isolated nonverbal cues. A single cue taken out of context has little meaning. But as one of a group of cues, it can take on significance.

For example, if you look through the office window and see a man leaning over a desk pounding his fist on it, it would be tempting to interpret this as a gesture of anger. But what kind of look does he have on his face? Is his facial expression congruent with desk-pounding anger, or could he simply be trying to knock loose a desk drawer that has become stuck? On the other hand, if you saw him pounding the desk with a frown on his face and heard him yelling in an agitated tone, your assumption of anger would be well based. He might just be angry because his desk drawer is stuck. But, nonetheless, he would still be angry.

Proximity Factors

Proximity factors range from where you position yourself when talking with an employee to how your office is arranged, to the color of the walls, to the types of fixtures and decorations. A supervisor who sits next to an employee conveys a different message than one who sits across a desk from the employee. A supervisor who makes his or her office a comfortable place to visit is sending a message that invites communication. A supervisor who maintains a stark, impersonal office sends the opposite message (Figure 3–5). Supervisors who want to send the nonverbal message that employees are welcome to stop and talk should consider the following guidelines:

■ Have comfortable chairs available for visitors.

■ Arrange chairs so you can sit beside visitors rather than behind the desk.

■ Choose soft, soothing colors rather than harsh, stark, or overly bright or busy colors.

■ If possible, have refreshments such as coffee, soda, and snacks available for visitors.

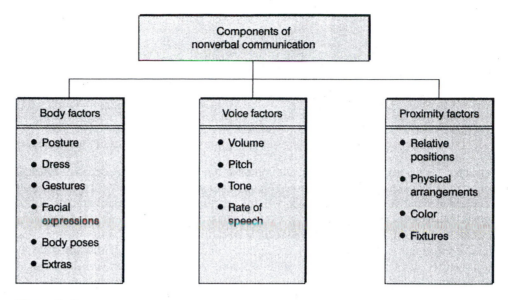

Figure 3–5
Nonverbal communication encompasses more than just body language.

=========== APPLICATION AND DISCUSSION ===========

The ability to understand nonverbal communication begins when we are just children. We learn at an early age to sense another person's mood, attitude, or frame of mind by observing nonverbal cues. Supervisors need to apply this ability on the job.

■   Over the next three days, observe people in conversation from a distance so that you cannot clearly hear the words being spoken. Make written notes of what cues you can observe (anger, happiness, sadness, reluctance, agreement, boredom, and impatience).

■   Be an observer in all of the conversations you have for the next week. Keep a log in which you describe examples of instances in which there was incongruence between the words spoken and non-verbal cues.

COMMUNICATING VERBALLY

Verbal communication ranks close to listening in its importance to the modern supervisor. Supervisors can improve their verbal communication skills by being attentive to the following factors:

Interest

When speaking with employees, show an interest in your topic. Show that you are sincerely interested in communicating your message to them. Also, show interest in the receivers of the message. Look them in the eye and, when in a group, spread your eye contact evenly among all receivers. If you sound bored, reluctant, or indifferent, employees will follow your example.

Attitude

A *positive, friendly attitude* enhances verbal communication. A caustic, superior, condescending, or disinterested attitude will shut off communication. So will an argumentative attitude. Be patient, be friendly, and smile.

Flexibility

Be flexible. *Flexibility* can enhance verbal communication. For example, if a supervisor calls his team together to explain a new company policy, but finds they are uniformly focused on a problem that is disrupting their work schedule, he or she must be flexible enough to put the message aside for the time being and deal with the problem. Until the employees work through what is on their minds, they will not be good listeners.

Tact

Tact is an important ingredient in verbal communication, particularly when delivering a sensitive or potentially controversial message. Tact has been called the ability to hammer in the nail without breaking the board. The key to tactful verbal communication lies in thinking before talking.

Courtesy

Courtesy promotes effective verbal communication. Being courteous means showing appropriate concern for the needs of the receiver. For example, calling a team meeting ten minutes before quitting time is discourteous and will inhibit communication. Most employees have after-work obligations. A meeting called ten minutes before the end of the workday is likely to threaten these obligations. Courtesy also means not monopolizing. When communicating verbally, give the receiver ample opportunities to ask questions to seek clarification and to state his or her point of view.

IMPROVING VERBAL COMMUNICATION BY QUESTIONING

In addition to applying the preceding factors, supervisors should learn to be skilled questioners. Knowing how and when to question is an important verbal communication skill. It is how supervisors can find out what employees really think. What follows are some general rules of questioning that professional counselors use to draw out the feelings and thoughts of their clients. Supervisors can apply these rules to enhance their verbal communication with employees:

Drop Your Defenses

Human interaction is emotional interaction. There is no such thing as fully objective discourse between people. We all have our public and private faces, and it is rare when what we say matches completely what we feel. People learn early in life to build walls and put up defenses. To communicate effectively, it is necessary to get behind the walls and break through the defenses. A strategy counselors use is to drop their defenses first. When employees see you open up, they will be more likely to follow suit and respond more honestly to your questions.

State Your Purpose

The silent question people often ask themselves when a supervisor asks them a question is, "Why is he asking that? What does he really want?" By stating your purpose before asking a question, you can remove the employees' concerns about hidden agendas and, by doing so, get a more honest response.

Acknowledge Emotions

Avoid what counselors call the "elephant-in-the-living-room" syndrome when questioning employees. Human emotions can be difficult to deal with. As a result, some people respond by simply ignoring them. This is like walking around an elephant in the living room and pretending you don't see it. Ignoring the emotions of people you question may cause them to close up. If a person shows anger, you might respond by saying, "I see that you are angry," or "You seem to feel strongly about this." Such nonjudgmental acknowledgments will usually help draw a person out.

Use Open-Ended Questions and Phrase Questions Carefully

To learn the most from your questions, make them open-ended. This allows the person being questioned to do most of the talking and lets you do most of the listening. Supervisors learn more when listening than when talking. Closed-ended questions force restricted or limited responses. For example, the question, "Can we meet our deadline?" will probably elicit only a "Yes" or a "No" response. However, the question, "What do you think about this deadline?" gives the responder room to offer opinions and other potentially useful information.

=========== APPLICATION AND DISCUSSION ===========

Supervisors must be good at communicating verbally. It is the most frequently used approach. The best communicators never just "wing it." Rather they practice and develop their communication skills continually.

- Try this experiment. Ask a friend to do something with you (go to a movie or play a game, e.g.), but show no interest. Sound bored and disinterested. How does your friend respond? Now, repeat the experiment with another friend, but this time show interest and excitement. How does this friend respond?

- Try this experiment. Ask a friend the following question: "Do you like _____?" (You fill in the blank). Note the length and depth of your friend's response. Now ask another friend the same question in an open-ended format: "What do you think about _____?" Compare the responses you get from the open-ended question with the response you got to the "Yes-No" question. Which approach elicited the most information?

COMMUNICATING CORRECTIVE FEEDBACK

In dealing with employees, it is important for supervisors to give **corrective feedback**. This is information that will help them improve their performance. However, to be effective, corrective feedback must be communicated properly. The following guidelines can be used to enhance the effectiveness of corrective feedback:

- *Be positive*. To be corrective, feedback must be accepted and acted on by the employee. This is more likely to happen if it is delivered in a positive manner.
- *Be prepared*. Focus on facts. Do not discuss personality traits. Give specific examples of the behavior you would like to see corrected.
- *Be realistic*. Make sure the behaviors you want to change are controlled by the employee. Don't expect an employee to correct a behavior he or she does not control. Find something positive to say. Give the employee the necessary corrective feedback, but don't focus only on the negative. Tell the employee about the behavior, ask for his or her input, and listen to that input.

===== APPLICATION AND DISCUSSION =====

Marcia Maddox does not like to give corrective feedback to her employees. She gets nervous, and she hates hurting an employee's feelings. Consequently, she has gotten into the habit of giving corrective feedback by e-mail. This approach relieves her feelings of anxiety, but it does not seem to be working very well. Her e-mail messages seem to be doing more harm than good.

- What problems do you think might be caused by Maddox's use of e-mail for giving corrective feedback? Analyze this practice in terms of the four strategies presented in this section (be positive, be prepared, be realistic, and say something good).

- Think back to the last time you received corrective feedback. Analyze the interaction in terms of the same four principles set forth in this section. How could the person giving the feedback have improved its effect?

STEPS TO IMPROVED COMMUNICATION

Effective communication is a must for supervisors. The following strategies can be used to improve your communication skills:

- *Keep up to date.* Stay up to date with new information relating to your workplace. You cannot communicate what you don't know.

- *Prioritize and determine time constraints.* Communicating does not mean simply passing on to employees everything you learn. Such an approach will only overload them and inhibit communication. Analyze information and decide what your employee needs to know. Then prioritize it from *urgent* to *when time permits* and share the information accordingly.

- *Decide whom to inform.* Once you prioritize your information, decide who needs to have it. Employees have enough to keep up with without receiving information they don't need. Correspondingly, don't withhold information that employees do need. Achieving the right balance will improve communication.

- *Determine how to communicate.* There are a variety of ways to communicate (i.e., verbal, electronically, one-on-one, in groups, etc.). A combination of methods will probably be the most effective. The next section in this unit deals with this issue in more depth.

- *Communicate the information.* Don't just tell your employees what you want them to know. Tell, ask, listen, paraphrase, and follow up. Ask questions to determine if they have really gotten the message. Encourage them to ask you questions for clarification. Agree on the next steps (i.e., what they should do with the information).

- *Check accuracy and get feedback.* Check to see that your communication was accurate. Can the employee paraphrase and repeat your message? Is the employee undertaking the next steps as agreed? Get feedback from employees to ensure that their understanding has not changed and that progress is being made.

Selecting the Appropriate Communication Method

One of the steps to improved communication recommended in the previous section was "determine how to communicate." Since most workplace communication is either verbal or written, supervisors need to know when each method is the most and least effective. What follows are summaries of when written and verbal communication should and should not be used. Written communication is *least* effective in the following instances:

- *To communicate a message requiring immediate action on the part of employees.* The more appropriate approach in such a case is to communicate the message verbally and follow it up in writing.

- *To commend an employee for doing a good job.* This should be done verbally and publicly and then followed up in writing.

- *To reprimand an employee for poor performance.* This message can be communicated more effectively if given verbally in private. This is particularly true for occasional offenses.

- *To resolve conflict among employees about work-related problems.* The necessary communication in such instances is more effectively given verbally and in private.

Verbal communication is *least* effective in the following instances:

- To communicate a message requiring future action on the part of employees. Such messages are more effectively communicated when given verbally and followed up in writing.

- To communicate general information such as company policies, personnel information, directives, or orders.

- To communicate work progress to an immediate supervisor or a higher manager.

- To promote a safety campaign.

By following the guidelines set forth in this section, supervisors can choose a method of communication appropriate to the situation at hand, thereby enhancing the effectiveness of their communication.

APPLICATION AND DISCUSSION

Juan Arballo wants to improve the quality of his communication with members of the team he supervises, but is unsure how to go about it. He never seems to get it right. Three weeks ago Arballo's team members complained about his not keeping them informed. Now they complain that they have to spend so much time reading his e-mail messages they have no time to do their work. Just this morning an employee asked, "Why are you telling us this? That's Cynthia's issue." Because of the complaints about too much e-mail to read, Arballo has been communicating new company policies verbally. Lately, team members have seemed confused about several policies as if they had never heard about them.

- Analyze this situation. What is Arballo doing wrong?
- Assume that Arballo presents this situation to you and asks for help. What advice will you give him?

ELECTRONIC COMMUNICATION

Electronic communication is an important means of sending written messages. Electronic mail, or e-mail, consists of written messages transferred electronically from computer to computer. Electronic communication is doing for written communication what the telephone did for verbal communication.

- *Messages can be transmitted rapidly.* For example, consider the time it might take to send a message to a supplier in another city. Even if overnight express services are used, it will take as much as twenty-four hours. The same message sent electronically would be received in a matter of seconds.

■ *Messages can be transmitted simultaneously to more than one person.* This is particularly helpful when the same notification must be sent to a large number of people. The sender inputs the message and enters the group name of all who are to receive it. The message is sent instantly.

■ *Messages can be printed if a hard copy is needed.* A hard copy is a paper printout of the information shown on the screen of a computer. Electronic messages can be printed if a hard copy is needed.

■ *Messages can be stored for future reference.* The computer can serve as an electronic filing cabinet for storing messages that have been sent in case they must be referred to later.

■ *Messages can be acknowledged electronically and recipients can be prompted.* Recipients of electronic messages can acknowledge their receipt with just a few key strokes. This allows the sender to know not just that the message was received, but when. Recipients can also be prompted. This means a message, light, or some other type of visual prompt can inform the receiver that a message is waiting.

Just as there are advantages with electronic communication, there are also potential disadvantages (Figure 3–6). The first disadvantage is one inherent in any form of written communication: inability to transmit body language, voice tone, facial expressions, and eye contact. All of these factors enhance verbal communication but are missing with electronic communication.

Another disadvantage is the potential for overuse of electronic communication. Because of the ease of sending a written message by simply pressing a few keys, users may send more messages than they really need to, send frivolous messages, or send messages that could be more appropriately delivered verbally. Electronic communication is an appropriate mode when written communication is called for.

═══════ APPLICATION AND DISCUSSION ═══════════════════

E-mail has become one of the most widely and frequently used forms of communication. It has advantages such as immediacy and convenience, but it also has disadvantages.

■ Do you use e-mail as a mode of communication? How frequently and in what ways? What problems do you experience using this mode of communication?

■ Use your own workplace or identify an individual in another workplace for completing this activity. What advantages have been gained by supervisors who have access to e-mail? What problems have been caused? Answer these questions from the perspective of a supervisor.

Figure 3–6
Weaknesses of on-line communication

Disadvantages of Electronic On-Line Communication
• Inability to transmit body language
• Inability to transmit voice tone
• Inability to transmit facial expressions
• Inability to make eye contact

ON-THE-JOB SCENARIOS

1. Taxton, Inc. is experiencing serious communication problems. If you ask the employees, they will say, "There is no communication in this company." If you ask managers and supervisors, they will say, "We tell employees what they need to know." If you ask employees, they will say, "Nobody listens to us." If you ask managers, they will say, "Our employees don't listen." The rumor mill seems to be the most active communication network in the company. Whatever the problem is, regardless of who you believe, Taxton's bottom line is suffering.

   - Assume that you have been hired by Taxton, Inc.'s new CEO to analyze this situation. Summarize in a brief report the problems as you see them.
   - Assume that Taxton, Inc.'s new CEO liked the report you submitted. He asks you to prepare a plan for establishing effective communication at Taxton, Inc. Develop the plan.

2. You are a new supervisor at Hershfeld Services Company (HSC). Just before being hired by HSC, you completed a comprehensive course called "Effective Communication." Your new boss was in the seminar too and was impressed by your performance. She has asked you to do the following:

   - Develop a seminar for all of HSC's supervisors on effective listening. Develop the seminar.
   - Develop a seminar for all of HSC's other supervisors on how to give corrective feedback. Develop the seminar.
   - Develop guidelines for supervisors for when and where to *not* use e-mail as an aid to communication.

KEY TERMS AND PHRASES

Body factors	Listening
Brevity	Medium
Classes of communication	Message
Communication	Network
Community-level communication	Nonverbal communication
Company-level communication	One-on-one level communication
Congruence	Preconceived ideas
Corrective feedback	Proximity factors
Effective communication	Receiver
Electronic communication	Sender
Grapevine	Tact
Inaccurate assumptions	Team- or unit-level communication
Incongruence	Voice factors
Information overload	Verbal communication
Interference	Written communication

REVIEW QUESTIONS

1. Define the term *communication*.
2. Distinguish between communication and effective communication.

3. Explain the communication process.

4. List five communication inhibitors.

5. What is a network? Give two examples.

6. Define the term *listening*.

7. List five inhibitors of effective *listening*.

8. What are the three components of nonverbal communication?

9. Explain the concept of congruence.

10. Explain how to be more effective in communicating corrective feedback.

11. What are the advantages and disadvantages of electronic communication?

CHAPTER FOUR

Ethics

LEARNING OBJECTIVES

After studying this chapter, you should be able to do the following:

- Define the term *ethics*.
- Explain the importance of ethical behavior in organizations.
- Demonstrate the supervisor's role in promoting ethical behavior.
- Explain the organization's role in promoting ethical behavior.
- Demonstrate how to handle ethical dilemmas.

There is almost universal agreement that the business practices of organizations should be above reproach with regard to ethical standards. Few people are willing to defend unethical behavior, and for the most part businesses in the United States operate within the scope of accepted legal and ethical standards. However, unethical behavior occurs frequently enough that supervisors should be aware of the types of ethical dilemmas they will occasionally face and know how to deal with these dilemmas. This chapter is designed to help prepare supervisors to deal effectively with ethics on the job.

AN ETHICAL DILEMMA

According to Edward Stead, Dan Worrell, and Jean Stead,

> Managing ethical behavior is one of the most pervasive and complex problems facing business organizations today. Employees' decisions to behave ethically or unethically are influenced by a myriad of individual and situational factors. Background, personality, decision history, managerial philosophy, and reinforcement are but a few of the factors which have been identified by researchers as determinants of employees' behavior when faced with ethical dilemmas.

Tom Richards is a supervisor for Alloy Tech Corporation. He is an effective supervisor, and his team is efficient and productive. But Tom has a problem. Alloy Tech is losing market share to Morton Metal, Inc., its chief competitor. His manager has made it clear to Tom that his team is partially to blame and he expects the situation to be corrected quickly.

Tom knows the source of his problem, and well he should; he trained him. Jake Bronkowski is the secret to Morton Metal's recent success in the marketplace. He is the most talented Computer Numerical Control (CNC) machinist Tom Richards has ever known. He represents the quintessential example of the student who surpasses the teacher. Not only does he know process planning, resource planning, setup, tooling, and

41

programming, but he can retrofit manual machines for CNC operation, troubleshoot inoperable machines, and repair both the electronic and mechanical components of machines that are down. In short, Jake Bronkowski is a one-person operation.

Since he was lured away by Morton Metals just six months ago, Alloy Tech has seen its market share decline steadily and that of Morton Metals increase correspondingly. In desperation, Tom has talked with Jake in an attempt to get him back. This is where Tom's problem became an ethical dilemma. Jake Bronkowski is willing to return to Alloy Tech. In fact, he would like to. However, he knows his value on the open market. He knows that several companies would like to hire him. As a result, Jake has made some demands that Tom feels are not just exorbitant, but unethical.

Jake wants a wage and benefits package that far exceeds the salary schedule approved by Alloy Tech's management. He wants his own office and a four-day work week. These demands are tough, but Tom can meet them. In fact, Tom had already received his manager's approval to meet all of Jake's demands and put him to work, but Jake made one more demand that is causing Tom's crisis of conscience.

Jake's final demand is that Tom move Alice McCormick, a machine operator at Alloy Tech, out of the metal cutting shop. Alice was a secretary who became a machine operator through the company's upward mobility program. She went to night school, completed the requisite training, and started work as a trainee in the metal cutting shop. Alice loves her job and has realized a significant pay increase with it. At this point in her development, Alice is just an average machine operator, but she works hard and has the potential to develop into a good technician.

Jake and Alice had a personal relationship when Jake worked at Alloy Tech. But the relationship did not last and Jake is still bitter. As a result, Tom Richards faces an ethical dilemma not unlike those faced by supervisors every day. He is caught between the demands of his company to protect the bottom line and the demands of morality to behave ethically.

What should Tom Richards do? Is there an acceptable compromise here? Does the end justify the means in these cases? These are the types of questions supervisors face on the job as they deal with concerns such as privacy, hiring, firing, promotions, performance appraisal, working conditions, product quality, production quotas, and other people-oriented problems.

APPLICATION AND DISCUSSION

Ethical dilemmas often occur in the workplace as a result of "bottom line" pressures. If we do "X" we will improve the bottom line, but "X" is ethically questionable. What should we do? One problem supervisors face in such situations is that doing the right thing often "pays off" only in the long run. In the short run it might appear to have a negative financial effect.

- Have you ever faced an ethical dilemma on the job or elsewhere? What kinds of pressures did you face when trying to decide what to do? Did you have the support of people important to you to do the "right thing"?

- Put yourself in the place of Tom Richards in the preceeding example. What do you think he should do? What problems will he face if he meets Jake's demands?

ETHICS DEFINED

There are many definitions of the term *ethics*. However, no one definition has emerged as universally accepted. Ethical dilemmas in the workplace are more complex than ethical situations in general. They involve societal expectations, competition, and social responsibility as well as the potential consequences of an employee's behavior to customers, fellow workers, competitors, and the public. The result of the often conflicting and contradictory interests of workers, customers, competitors, and the general public is a propensity for ethical dilemmas to occur frequently in the workplace.

Any time ethics is the topic of discussion, terms such as *conscience*, *morality*, and *legality* will be frequently heard. Although these terms are closely associated with ethics, they do not by themselves define it. For the purposes of this book, ethics is defined as follows:

> *Ethics* is the study of morality. *Ethical behavior* means doing the "right thing" within a moral framework.

Morality refers to the values that are widely subscribed to and fostered by society in general and by individuals within society. Ethics attempts to apply reason in determining rules of human conduct that translate morality into everyday behavior. Ethical behavior is that which falls within the limits prescribed by morality. Doing what is ethical is often called doing the "right thing."

How, then, does the supervisor know if someone's behavior is ethical? Ethical questions are rarely black and white. They typically fall into a gray area between the two extremes of clearly right and clearly wrong, and this gray area is often clouded further by personal experience, self-interest, point of view, and external pressure.

Guidelines for Determining Ethical Behavior

Before presenting the guidelines supervisors can use to sort out matters that fall into the gray area between clearly right and clearly wrong, it is necessary to distinguish between what is legal and what is ethical. They are not necessarily the same thing.

In fact, it is not uncommon for people caught in the practice of questionable behavior to use the "I didn't do anything illegal" defense. A person's behavior can be well within the scope of the law and still be unethical. The following guidelines for determining ethical behavior assume that the behavior in question is legal:

- Apply the *morning-after test*. If you make this choice, how will you feel about it and yourself tomorrow morning?
- Apply the *front-page test*. Make a decision that would not embarrass you if printed as a story on the front page of your local newspaper.
- Apply the *mirror test*. If you make this decision, how will you feel about yourself when you look in the mirror?
- Apply the *role-reversal test*. Trade places with the people affected by your decision and view the decision through their eyes.
- Apply the *common sense test*. Listen to what your instincts and common sense are telling you. If it feels wrong, it probably is (Figure 4–1).

Figure 4–1
Tests supervisors can use when making ethical decisions

Tests for Making Ethical Choices
• Morning-after test
• Front page test
• Mirror test
• Role-reversal test
• Common sense test

Kenneth Blanchard and Norman Vincent Peale suggest their own test for determining the ethical choice in a given situation. Their test consists of the following three questions:

1. Is it legal?
2. Is it balanced?
3. How will it make me feel about myself?

If a potential course of action is not legal, no further consideration of it is in order. If an action is illegal, it is also unethical. As to the second question, a course of action that is balanced will be fair to all involved. This means supervisors and their team members have responsibilities that extend beyond the walls of their unit, organization, and company. As to the final question, a course of action that leaves you feeling good about it and yourself is one that is in keeping with your own moral structure.

Blanchard and Peale also discuss what they call "The Five P's of Ethical Power."

■ *Purpose*. Individuals see themselves as ethical people who let their conscience be their guide and in all cases want to feel good about themselves.

■ *Pride*. Individuals apply internal guidelines and have sufficient self-esteem to make decisions that may not be popular with others.

■ *Patience*. Individuals believe right will prevail in the long run and they are willing to wait when necessary.

■ *Persistence*. Individuals are willing to stay with an ethical course of action once it has been chosen and see it through to a positive conclusion.

■ *Perspective*. Individuals take the time to reflect and are guided by their own internal barometer when making ethical decisions.

These tests and guidelines can help supervisors and their team members make ethical choices in the workplace. In addition to internalizing the guidelines themselves, supervisors should share them with the employees they supervise.

APPLICATION AND DISCUSSION

Mary Todd faces an ethical dilemma. James Crawford, a top-producing member of her team, is "moonlighting" for a competitor across town, a practice that is strictly forbidden by their employer. She has counseled Crawford several times, but he refuses to give up his part-time job. "I need the money. My wife is seriously ill, and the medical bills are eating me alive," is his response whenever Todd raises the issue. What really troubles Todd is that this loyal, productive employee is telling the truth. She has checked. On the other hand, Crawford's other employer—always a tough competitor—has gained significant market share since he started moonlighting. Clearly he is helping the competitor and hurting his "real" employer.

■ Put yourself in Todd's place. Decide how you would handle this dilemma by applying the morning-after, front-page, mirror, role-reversal, and common sense tests.

■ Put yourself in Crawford's place. Apply the "Five P's of Ethical Power." Can you justify working for a competitor or should you find another answer to your financial problem?

■ Explain the rationale for your decision.

ETHICAL BEHAVIOR IN ORGANIZATIONS

Research by L. K. Trevino suggests that ethical behavior in organizations is influenced by both individual and social factors. Trevino identified three personality measures that can influence an employee's ethical behavior: (1) ego strength, (2) Machiavellianism, and (3) locus of control.

An employee's **ego strength** is the ability to undertake self-directed tasks and to cope with tense situations. **Machiavellianism** is the extent to which workers attempt to deceive and confuse others. **Locus of control** refers to the perspective of people concerning who or what controls their behavior. Employees with an internal locus of control feel they control their own behavior. Employees with an external locus of control feel their behavior is controlled by external factors (i.e., rules, regulations, their supervisor, peer pressure, etc.).

Social factors also influence ethical behavior in organizations. These factors include gender, role differences, religion, age, work experience, nationality, and the influence of other people who are significant in an individual's life. People learn appropriate behavior by observing the behavior of significant role models (i.e., parents, teachers, public officials, etc.). Since supervisors represent perhaps the most significant role model for their team members, it is critical that they exhibit ethical behavior that is beyond reproach in all situations.

APPLICATION AND DISCUSSION

Doing the right thing often comes down to a battle between external pressures, such as the bottom line, job security fears, and peer pressure, versus an individual's internal commitment to a set of values. Consider the follow situation:

Mark Payette supervises a team of machinists responsible for making 100 parts per day. Recently Payette's manager increased the quota to 150 parts, but refused to authorize overtime or hire another machinist. Consequently, the only way to produce 150 parts per day is to remove the safety guards from all machines, which speeds their operation but makes the process dangerous to the machinists. Before the safety guards were installed, Payette's team produced 145 parts per day, but injuries were common. Several had been serious. When Payette brought this fact to his manager's attention, he was told to "Stop whining and get the job done."

- List all the conflicting pressures acting on Mark Payette that you can identify.
- How will Payette's ego strength affect what he does in this situation? How about his locus of control?
- If Payette removes the safety guards from his team's machines and an employee is injured, do you think his manager will support him or blame him? Who will his team members blame? Payette or his manager?

THE SUPERVISOR'S ROLE IN ETHICS

Using the guidelines set forth in the previous section, supervisors should be able to make responsible decisions concerning ethical choices. Unfortunately, deciding what is ethical is often easier than actually *doing* what is ethical. In this regard, trying to practice ethics is like trying to diet. It is not so much a matter of knowing you should cut down on eating; it is a matter of following through and actually doing it.

It is this fact that defines the role of supervisors with regard to ethics. Supervisors have a three-part role. First, they are responsible for setting an example of ethical behavior. Second, they are responsible for helping employees make the right decision when facing ethical questions. Finally, supervisors are responsible for helping employees follow through and actually undertake the ethical option once the appropriate choice has been identified. In carrying out their roles, supervisors can adopt one of the following approaches:

- Best ratio approach
- Black and white approach
- Full potential approach (Figure 4–2)

Best Ratio Approach

The **best ratio approach** is the pragmatic option. Its philosophy is that people are basically good and under the right circumstance will behave ethically. However, under certain conditions they can be driven to unethical behavior. Therefore, the supervisor should do everything possible to create conditions that promote ethical behavior and try to maintain the best possible ratio of good choices to bad. When hard decisions must be made, supervisors should make the choice that will do the most good for the most people. This is sometimes referred to as *situational ethics*.

Black and White Approach

In the **black and white approach**, right is right and wrong is wrong. Circumstances and conditions are irrelevant. The supervisor's job is to make ethical decisions, carry them out, and help employees choose the ethical route regardless of circumstances. When difficult decisions must be made, supervisors should make fair and impartial choices and let the chips fall where they may.

Full Potential Approach

Supervisors make decisions under the **full potential approach** based on how they will affect the ability of those involved to achieve their full potential. The underlying philosophy is that people are responsible for realizing their full potential within the confines of morality. Choices that can achieve this goal without infringing on the rights of others are considered ethical.

Decisions might differ, depending on the approach selected. For example, consider the ethical dilemma presented at the beginning of this unit. If the supervisor, Tom Richards, applied the best ratio approach, he might opt to go along with Jake Bronkowski's demand to move Alice McCormick out of the metal cutting shop. He might justify this choice based on what he perceives as the best decision for the most people. On the other hand, if he took the black and white approach, he could not justify giving in to Jake's demand.

Figure 4–2
Three approaches supervisors can take to handle ethical problems

Approaches to Ethical Behavior

- **Best ratio approach** Pragmatic option sometimes called situational ethics.
- **Black-and-white approach** Right is right and wrong is wrong. Circumstances are irrelevant.
- **Full-potential approach** Make decisions based on how they will help those involved achieve their full potential.

================ APPLICATION AND DISCUSSION ================

Alma DeJesus faces an ethical dilemma. A corporate buyout and restructuring strategy is going to eliminate five of the fifteen positions in the unit she supervises. DeJesus is very close to three of the employees who will lose their jobs. She has worked with them for years and knows their spouses and children. DeJesus was even in the wedding of one of these employees. On a personal level she would like to warn her employees about the upcoming restructuring, but the CEO of her company has forbidden "early announcements" under any circumstances. According to the CEO, a leak to the press could undermine the buyout that is causing the restructuring. If this happens, the company's survival might be in question. Should she forewarn her employees or not? This is DeJesus's ethical dilemma.

■ Apply the best ratio, black and white, and full potential approaches to this case. What is your decision in each case?

■ Does the concept of the "greater good" come into play in this situation? If so, how? If not, why not?

THE ORGANIZATION'S ROLE IN ETHICS

Organizations have a critical role to play in promoting ethical behavior among their employees. Supervisors cannot expect employees to behave ethically in a vacuum. An organization's role in ethics can be summarized as (1) creating an internal environment that promotes, expects, and rewards ethical behavior; and (2) setting an example of ethical behavior in all internal and external dealings.

Creating an Ethical Environment

An organization creates an ethical environment by establishing policies and practices that ensure all employees are treated ethically and then enforcing these policies. Do employees have the right of due process? Do employees have access to an objective grievance procedure? Are there appropriate health and safety measures to protect employees? Are hiring practices fair and impartial? Are promotion practices fair and objective? Are employees protected from harassment based on age, race, sex, or other reasons? An organization that establishes an environment which promotes, expects, and rewards ethical behavior can answer "yes" to all these questions.

One effective way to create an **ethical environment** is to develop an ethics philosophy and specific guidelines that operationalize the philosophy. These should be put in writing and shared with all employees. What follows is an example of a Code of Ethics for a business:

> The Jones Company will conduct its business in accordance with all applicable laws, rules, regulations; with corporate policies, procedures and guidelines; with honesty and integrity; and with a strong commitment to the highest standards of ethics. We will do business in accordance with both the letter and the spirit of the law.

Such a statement sets the tone for all employees at the Jones Company by letting them know that higher management not only supports ethical behavior, but expects it. This approach makes it less difficult for supervisors when they find themselves caught in the middle between the pressures of business and the maintenance of ethical behavior at work.

Setting an Ethical Example

Organizations that take the "Do as I say, not as I do" approach to ethics will not succeed. Employees must be able to trust their organization to conduct all external and internal dealings in an ethical manner. Organizations that do not pay their bills on time, that pollute, that do not live up to advertised quality standards, that do not stand behind their guarantees, and that are not good neighbors in their communities are setting a poor ethical example. Such organizations can expect employees to mimic their unethical behavior.

In addition to creating an ethical internal environment and handling external dealings in an ethical manner, organizations must support supervisors who make ethically correct decisions—not just when they are profitable, but in all cases. For example, in the ethical dilemma presented at the beginning of this unit, assume that the supervisor decided the ethical choice was to deny Jake Bronkowski's demand to move Alice McCormick. Management gave the supervisor permission to meet Jake's demand, and the sooner the better. This is obviously the profitable choice. But is the ethical choice? If Tom Richards does not think so, will Alloy Tech stand behind him? If not, everything else the company does to promote ethics will break down.

═══════════ **APPLICATION AND DISCUSSION** ═══════════

The Kenton-Combs Company (KCC) has the following code of ethics:

"KCC is committed to maintaining the highest standards of ethics in its dealings with customers, suppliers, employees, and the community. In all cases we will choose what is right over what is expedient."

The executive management team at KCC is under pressure from its largest stockholders to increase profits. As a result supervisors are under pressure to cut anything that can be cut and do more with less. Jason Powers has been a supervisor at KCC for 10 years. He knows that some of the proposed cuts and adjustments raise serious questions about equipment maintenance, employee safety, and product quality. Powers is convinced that KCC will be harmed in the long run if some of the proposed changes are made.

- How do the proposed cuts that concern Jason Powers measure up in terms of KCC's code of ethics?
- How can Jason Powers use KCC's code of ethics to prevent counterproductive changes from being made?
- What do you think will be the effect on employee morale and behavior if KCC's executive management team makes changes that run counter to the company's code of ethics?

HANDLING ETHICAL DILEMMAS

No person will serve long in a supervisory capacity without confronting an ethical dilemma. How then should supervisors proceed when they confront such a problem? (See Figure 4–3.) There are three steps:

- Apply the various guidelines for determining what is ethical that were presented earlier in this unit.
- Select one of the three basic approaches to handling ethical questions.
- Proceed in accordance with the approach selected and do so with consistency.

Apply the Guidelines

In this step, supervisors apply as many of the tests set forth earlier as necessary to determine what the ethically correct decision is. In applying these guidelines, supervisors

Figure 4–3
Three steps for handling ethical dilemmas

Handling Ethical Dilemmas
• Apply the "Tests for Making Ethical Choices."
• Select one of the "Approaches to Ethical Behavior."
• Proceed with the decision (be consistent over time).

should try to block out all mitigating circumstances and other factors that tend to cloud the issue. At this point the goal is only to identify the ethical choice. Deciding whether or not to implement it comes in the next step.

Select the Approach

Supervisors have three basic approaches to use when deciding how to proceed once the ethical choice is identified: the best ratio, black and white, and full potential approaches (Figure 4–3). These approaches and their ramifications can be debated ad infinitum; no one can tell a supervisor which approach to take. It is a matter of personal choice unless higher management specifies the approach. Factors that affect the ultimate decision include the supervisor's own personal makeup, the organization's expectations, and the degree of organizational support.

Proceed with the Decision

The approach selected dictates how the supervisor should proceed. Two things are important in this final step. The first is to proceed in strict accordance with the approach selected. The second is to proceed consistently. **Consistency** is critical when handling ethical dilemmas. Fairness is a large part of ethics, and consistency is a large part of fairness. The grapevine will ensure that all employees know how a supervisor handles a given ethical dilemma. Some will agree, and some will disagree regardless of the decision. Such is the nature of human interaction. However, regardless of the differing perceptions of the problem, employees will respect the supervisor for being consistent. Conversely, even if the decision is universally popular, supervisors may lose respect if the decision is not consistent with past decisions.

=========== **APPLICATION AND DISCUSSION** ===========

Myra Brennan is an ethical supervisor, and her company is usually an ethical employer. But, on occasion, Brennan has seen short-term profits win out over ethics when decisions are made. She is a single parent who needs her job. A job that pays well and that she worked hard for years to get. Brennan is torn between economic necessity and her dissatisfaction with the inconsistent ethical behavior of her employer.

■ Assume Brennan cannot afford to quit her job. Which of the three ethical models (black and white, best ratio, or full potential) is most appropriate for her use?

■ How can Brennan use this model to have the greatest positive effect on the ethical behavior of her employer?

===== ON-THE-JOB SCENARIOS =====

1. Solid Waste Disposal Company (SWDC) has three teams of drivers who transport compacted solid waste to the company's landfill. SWDC is a responsible company that has, at great expense, developed an environmentally sound landfill that can safely handle all of the various types of solid waste the company accepts. Its one disadvantage is its distance from the compacting plant. Drivers complain that the 100-mile round trip required for each load limits their ability to earn the financial incentives available to drivers who exceed their weekly tonnage quotas. These financial incentives are at the heart of Don Morgan's ethical dilemma. Don supervises the three teams of drivers for SWDC. One of his best, most loyal, most experienced drivers needs the financial incentives badly. The driver, Tim McGhee, has a child in the hospital. The child's treatment is stretching Tim's finances to the breaking point. Don has learned that, to maximize the incentive money received, Tim McGhee is dumping every third load in the company's old landfill. This landfill, which has been closed for three years, is not rated to handle some of the potentially hazardous material SWDC accepts. How should Don Morgan handle this dilemma?

2. Leisure Wear Corporation and Modern Apparel, Inc. are major textile producers and competitors. Recently Modern Apparel has been winning almost every time it competes against Leisure Wear. The grapevine has it that this is due to a revolutionary breakthrough in the formula Modern Apparel uses to produce a particular synthetic material. The formula is patented. The new formula is allowing Modern Apparel to produce its fabric at half the cost of Leisure Wear's competing fabric.

   Nancy Davies, supervisor of the research and development unit for Leisure Wear, has been pulling her hair out trying to duplicate Modern Apparel's breakthrough, but to no avail. The pressure on her is tremendous. Top management is pushing her hard to come up with the formula. Friends in other sections of the plant have intimated they may be laid off if things do not turn around soon. If this happens, the first employee to be let go will be Nancy's niece, a new employee in Leisure Wear's mailroom. What makes this even more difficult for Nancy is that Leisure Wear is located in a one-company town. Job prospects will not be good for laid off employees.

   Nancy may have found a solution to her problem. A disgruntled employee in the research and development unit at Modern Apparel has called asking for a job. He has promised that, if hired, he will bring the new formula with him. It happens that Nancy has an opening in her unit. How should she handle this problem?

===== KEY TERMS AND PHRASES =====

Best ratio approach

Black and white approach

Common sense test

Consistency

Ego strength

Ethical environment

Ethical behavior

Ethics

Ethics philosophy

Front-page test

Full potential approach

Locus of control

Machiavellianism

Mirror test

Morality

Morning-after test

Role-reversal test

===== REVIEW QUESTIONS =====

1. Define the term *morality*.
2. Define the term *ethics*.

3. Briefly explain each of the following ethics tests: morning-after test, front-page test, mirror test, role-reversal test, common sense test.

4. What is the supervisor's role with regard to ethics?

5. Briefly explain the following approaches to handling ethical behavior: best ratio approach, black and white approach, full potential approach.

6. Briefly explain a company's role with regard to ethics.

7. Explain how a supervisor should proceed when facing an ethical dilemma.

8. Write a brief ethics philosophy for a plastics recycling company.

9. List the individual and situational factors that might influence an employee's ethical behavior.

10. List and briefly describe the "Five P's of Ethical Power" as described by Blanchard and Peale.

========== **ENDNOTES** ==========

1. E. W. Stead, D. L. Worrell, and J.G. Stead, "An Integrative Model for Understanding and Managing Ethical Behavior in Business Organizations," **Journal of Business Ethics** 9 (1990): 233.

2. K. Blanchard and N. V. Peale, *The Power of Ethical Management* (New York: Ballantine Books, 1988), p 10–17.

3. Ibid., p. 79.

4. L. K. Trevino, "Ethical Decision Making in Organizations: A Person-Situation Interactionist Model," *Academy of Management Review* 11 (1986): 601–17.

CHAPTER FIVE

Motivation

After studying this chapter you should be able to do the following:

- Define the term *motivation*.
- Explain the rationale for motivation.
- Explain the effect of the work ethic on motivation.
- Explain the effect of job satisfaction on motivation.
- Explain the effect of expectancy on motivation.
- Explain the effect of achievement on motivation.
- Explain the effect of job design on motivation.
- Explain the effect of competition on motivation.
- Explain the effect of communication on motivation.
- Explain the effect of promotions on motivation.
- Describe how to motivate new employees.
- Describe how to motivate problem employees.
- Describe how to motivate part-time employees.
- Explain the effect of incentives on motivation.
- Demonstrate how to develop Personal Motivation Plans (PMPs) for individual employees.

People can be extraordinarily creative, innovative, and effective at accomplishing goals they really want to obtain. America's history is replete with stories of individuals who overcame enormous adversity and countless obstacles to accomplish their personal goals. Invariably, one of the keys to their success was their motivation. By coupling motivation with determination, people can accomplish almost anything. Because of this, motivating people and helping them learn to be self-motivating are important responsibilities of the modern supervisor.

DEFINITION AND RATIONALE FOR MOTIVATION

Motivation is a person's drive to do something. This drive can be internal, external, or a combination of the two. Motivation as it relates to the workplace is the drive to do a good job. A motivated employee is one who constantly tries to exceed performance expectations and accomplish team goals. When supervisors talk about motivating employees, they mean getting them to work harder, work smarter, and work better.

The ultimate goal of supervisors with regard to motivation is to develop their direct reports into "self-motivated" employees. **Self-motivated employees** are internally driven to achieve at peak levels. All external motivation strategies applied by supervisors are temporary to jump-start the employees' potential for internal motivation. The rationale for attempting to instill internal motivation is continual improvement.

The coaching aspect of supervision is aimed at achieving this goal: employees who perform at peak levels and continually improve. External factors can motivate employees to perform at peak levels in the short term, but to improve continually, employees must become internally motivated.

WHAT MOTIVATES PEOPLE

All people share two sets of needs that relate to their work. The first set consists of the following needs described in chapter 1 of this book (Figure 5–1):

- Basic survival needs
- Safety/security needs
- Social needs
- Esteem needs
- Self-actualization needs

These human needs relate either directly or indirectly to a person's job. Basic **survival needs** include air, water, food, clothing, and shelter. Most of us generate the income necessary to meet these needs through our work.

Safety/security needs include safety from harm or pain and security from criminal or financial difficulties. Although safety/security needs are never pushed completely from our minds, most working people feel relatively safe and secure. These needs relate directly to our jobs. By working we are able to provide a home in a safe neighborhood, install security systems, make financial investments, and purchase insurance.

Social needs include our needs for family, friends, and a sense of belonging. Our jobs have a great deal to do with meeting these needs. They give us the financial resources to marry and start a family. They determine where we are able to live and, in turn, who our neighbors will be. Many of our friendships are with people we meet either directly or indirectly through our jobs. In addition, our jobs can provide a sense of belonging by making us part of a team.

Esteem needs relate to our need to feel self-respect, worth, and dignity. One of the principle sources of those feelings is our work. One of the primary determinants of status in society is one's job. Many people unfortunately tend to let others define their worth

Figure 5–1
Maslow's Hierarchy of Human Needs

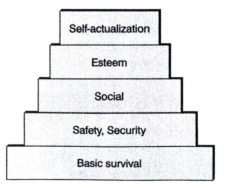

and provide the basis for their feelings of self-respect. This results in people seeing themselves through the eyes of society. Counselors work hard to help people overcome this tendency and to call upon internal stimuli in developing feelings of self-worth. The counselors are right, but it is the rare individual who fully succeeds in this regard. Most of us need positive external stimuli and positive reinforcement to meet our esteem needs. Supervisors who understand this can use it when trying to motivate team members.

Self-actualization needs encompasses our desire to be a whole person completely at ease with all aspects of our life. With work so large a part of our lives, we cannot achieve self-actualization unless we are happy in our jobs. Because of this, supervisors should be familiar with what people need to be happy in their jobs.

Specific Human Needs Related to Work

The needs explained in the previous section relate to work, but they also apply to life in general. Those explained in this section relate specifically to an individual's job. Specific job-related needs are as follows:

- Financial reward
- Personal satisfaction
- Societal contribution

People who work for a living place a high priority on **financial reward** (a paycheck). Until they earn enough money to be comfortable financially, employees will be motivated by the opportunity to earn more. On the other hand, employees who earn enough to be comfortable will be less motivated by money. What complicates this phenomenon for supervisors is the fact that different employees will feel comfortable with different levels of income. Some can never earn enough, whereas others reach their comfort zone at relatively low income levels. For this reason supervisors need to get to know their direct reports well enough to understand their financial needs and to know what level of income will put each individual in his or her financial comfort zone.

Personal satisfaction, how much an employee likes his or her work, is also a high priority for people who work. Some people will do any kind of work as long as the pay is sufficient, but most will not. Most employees want to like what they do in addition to earning sufficient money. People who work spend a large percentage of their lives on the job. Working eight or more hours a day, five or more days a week is a lot of time to spend doing something that gives you no personal satisfaction. Consequently, employees can be motivated by the potential to improve their job satisfaction.

Societal contribution typically becomes a higher priority once employees satisfy their financial and personal satisfaction needs. **Societal contribution** means that the job is important, that it matters. People who like their jobs and have reached their financial comfort zones begin to concern themselves with their "legacy." They ask themselves such questions as, "Am I spending my career in a meaningless, trivial job, or does what I do really matter?" Nobody wants to feel insignificant. Consequently, employees can be motivated by the potential to make a difference or to be viewed as being important.

=========== APPLICATION AND DISCUSSION ===========

Consider your personal needs (survival, security, social, esteem, and self-actualization). Now consider your work-related needs (financial reward, personal satisfaction, and societal contribution).

- How can a job help you meet each of the personal needs all people have? How could your supervisor use each of these needs to motivate you?

■   How do you rank the three work-related needs in terms of their relative importance to you? If your supervisor knew this, how might it affect her attempts to motivate you?

THE WORK ETHIC AND MOTIVATION

It has been said that one of the things that traditionally distinguished Americans from people in other countries was their work ethic. But what is the work ethic? The **work ethic** is a philosophy that can be summarized as follows:

> *Work is intrinsically good and intrinsically rewarding. As such it should be a source of accomplishment and pride.*

An employee with a strong work ethic is internally motivated and will try to do the best job possible in every situation. Such employees take pride in their work and meet their esteem needs by doing a good job.

Improving the Work Ethic

When the work ethic is not what it should be, the natural reaction is to blame the employee, but this is not always appropriate. The fault could be the organization. Supervisors cannot give workers a positive work ethic. However, they can help develop the work ethic in people and also recharge one that has run down.

Supervisors can help employees see a direct connection between the quality/quantity of their work and the amount of their pay. If salary/wage programs are not linked directly to work quality and quantity, supervisors should work with management to restructure the program so that financial incentives are available and tied to job performance.

Do not confuse happy, satisfied, or comfortable employees with productive employees. Whereas productive employees may be happy in their jobs, it does not automatically follow that happy employees are productive employees. Employees might be happy with their jobs because the pay is good, working conditions are good, and nobody pushes them to work too hard.

Job satisfaction, the extent to which an employee likes his or her job, is not necessarily a motivator for better performance. But it cannot be overlooked because a low level of job dissatisfaction is a *demotivator*. Consequently, supervisors must concern themselves with job satisfaction, not as an end unto itself but as one step toward the goal of motivating employees. The relationship between job satisfaction and motivation is presented in the next section.

═══════ **APPLICATION AND DISCUSSION** ═══════

A tale of two employees. Francine comes to work a few minutes early every day, gets started without waiting for prompting from her supervisor, and does the best job she can possibly do. Francine is proud of her work and will not accept second best from herself. Monica is a different sort. She is often late, never starts work without prompting from her supervisor, and does as little as she can get by with. Monica does not seem to care much about the quality of her work.

■   Have you ever met someone like Francine or Monica on the job? Which would you prefer to supervise? Why?

■   If you were the supervisor in this case, what would you do to help improve Monica's work ethic? How could you use Francine to help improve Monica?

JOB SATISFACTION AND MOTIVATION

Job satisfaction is the foundation on which higher levels of productivity can be built. Consequently, it is an important element in the motivation of employees. Supervisors have a key role to play in the job satisfaction of their direct reports. Factors relating to job satisfaction include wages, benefits, working conditions, co-worker relationships, the supervisor/employee relationship, potential for advancement, potential for development, new challenges, and competition (Figure 5–2).

A supervisor trying to motivate employees may find that improving their level of job satisfaction is an effective strategy. In the area of compensation (wages and benefits) supervisors are typically limited in what they can do other than completing periodic performance appraisals, the results of which can affect an employee's wages, but only indirectly. However, supervisors can work with employees and higher management to improve working conditions.

Take the example of Joan Fuller, who supervises a team of customer service representatives. Their interaction with customers is intense and goes on all day long. For six months her "reps" complained to Fuller that they had no place to get a cup of coffee, no temporary refuge from demanding and occasionally angry customers, and nowhere to go to catch their breath. Fuller could see that this situation was undercutting the motivation of even her best employees. Working with management, Fuller got permission to convert a storeroom into what her "reps" now call their "R and R" room (rest and recuperation).

Fuller brought in a coffee maker and an old couch. Her "reps" decorated the room and brought in other accessories. Within a short time Fuller noticed that her "reps" were demonstrating a higher level of motivation, and the quality of their interaction with customers had improved too. Improving working conditions, in this case, helped improve motivation.

Supervisors can do a great deal to promote positive relationships among their direct reports. Team building activities (chapter 15) serve this purpose as does effective conflict management (chapter 9). To promote positive relationships between themselves and their direct reports, supervisors can make a point of being honest, fair, consistent, and productive in communicating effectively.

The potential for advancement can also be an effective motivator, particularly when dealing with ambitious employees. However, dangling the promotion "carrot" in front of ambitious employees when there is no hope of a promotion can backfire and kill an employee's motivation. It is better to be realistic with employees and let them know that you, their supervisor, will be their advocate and will work hard on their behalf when it comes to promotions. Employees who see this happen will be motivated by it.

Development potential is also an effective motivation for ambitious employees. Employees understand that the more job-related skills they develop and the higher the level of those skills, the greater their chances of moving up. Basing access to cross-train-

Figure 5–2
Factors that promote job satisfaction

ing, reimbursement for off-duty education, and other employee development activities on daily job performance can motivate employees to higher levels of performance.

New challenges can be used to motivate employees who feel bogged down or bored with their current positions. Sometimes a change of pace is all that is needed to re-ignite an employee's spark. The opportunity to try something new by taking on a special project, filling in for another team member, or serving on an interesting committee can give employees a new challenge. The new challenge, in turn, can be an effective motivator.

Competition can be an effective motivator if used properly. However, it can also backfire and be a demotivator. The proper and improper uses of competition as a motivator are covered later in this chapter.

The strategies in this section are aimed at motivating by improving the job satisfaction of employees. Better job satisfaction will result in better motivation for some employees. But like all strategies, job satisfaction has its limits. Some employees will respond lethargically even when satisfied with their jobs.

APPLICATION AND DISCUSSION

People are satisfied or dissatisfied with their jobs for a variety of different reasons. Some want only to be comfortable, others want to like what they do, and others want their job to be a stepping-stone or a launching pad.

■ What will it take to satisfy you in a job? What could a supervisor do to improve your job satisfaction in a current, past, or future job?

■ Consider the following strategies for improving job satisfaction. Rank them in the order of how effective they would be in motivating you to higher levels of performance (explain your reasons).

- Compensation (Wages and Benefits)
- Working conditions
- Better co-worker relationships
- Better relationship with the supervisors
- Advancement potential
- Development potential
- New challenge
- Competition

EXPECTANCY AND MOTIVATION

Expectancy is an important factor in motivating employees. It has four components: what management expects, what the supervisor expects of employees, what employees expect in return for performance, and what peers expect of each other. For employees to stay motivated over the long run, there must be consistency between what they expect for performing well and what they actually get. If the incentives established by management and the supervisor come to be viewed as empty promises, their motivational value will be negated. Correspondingly, if the performance expected is so high as to be unattainable, employees will expect to fail and failure will become a self-fulfilling prophecy.

Another side of expectancy that can be a motivator is the expectations of fellow employees. If team members internalize the organization's goals, expectations of performance will manifest themselves through peer pressure. The expectancy of peers can be a powerful motivator (Figure 5–3).

Figure 5–3
Expectancy can play an
important role in motivating
employees.

Expectancy on the Job

- What management expects
- What the supervisor expects of employees
- What employees expect of the employer
- What fellow employees (peers) expect of
  each other

========= APPLICATION AND DISCUSSION ==========

Peer pressure is one of the most powerful motivators known. In an attempt to fit in with their peers and meet their expectations, people will change the way they dress, talk, and even behave. Whether in school or in the workplace, when people interact in groups, there is peer pressure.

- Have you ever been influenced by peer pressure? In what way? Have you ever experienced the negative consequences of failing to meet the expectations of a peer group? If so, what effect did it have on you?
- How can a supervisor use peer pressure as a positive tool in motivating employees?

ACHIEVEMENT AND MOTIVATION

Achievement, a feeling of accomplishment in the job, motivates some people and not others. The key for supervisors lies in being able to (1) identify achievement-oriented people and (2) take advantage of this characteristic for motivating them.

Recognizing Achievement-Oriented Employees

People who are motivated by achievement are not difficult to pick out of a crowd. They tend to be task-oriented, independent, need continual reinforcement, and focus intently on evaluations of their performance. They usually accumulate physical evidence of their achievements such as trophies, plaques, certificates of accomplishment, and other memorabilia.

Using Achievement to Motivate Employees

Perhaps the easiest way to motivate achievement-oriented employees is by sharing the organization's goals with them so that each goal accomplished becomes a personal achievement for them. Another effective strategy is to make achievement-oriented employees responsible for specific goals that they can call their own. In addition, it is also necessary to provide appropriate recognition when they achieve goals. Part of what motivates achievement-oriented people is the recognition achievement brings them (Figure 5–4).

One of the drawbacks of challenging achievement-oriented employees is that it can lead to problems with other workers who are motivated more by affiliation than achievement. Employees with an affiliation orientation are team players who are motivated by the social interaction among peers. They view their achievements in terms of those of the team, and they do not try to stand out in a crowd. Affiliation-oriented employees sometimes resent achievement-oriented employees and criticize them for not being team players. Supervisors can minimize the potential for friction by taking the precautions described in the following paragraphs.

Figure 5–4
How to recognize achievement-
oriented employees

Characteristics of Achievement-Oriented Employees
• Task-oriented
• Independent
• Need recognition
• Need continual positive reinforcement

Talking with both types of employees one-on-one and explaining the strengths and contributions of each will help. Supervisors can explain how achievement- and affiliation-oriented people can complement each other in ways that result in higher productivity for all. Where possible, supervisors should group affiliation types with affiliation types and achievement types with achievements types. Let the achievement types compete with each other under properly controlled circumstances.

Where work is done in teams, supervisors should make sure that there is an appropriate balance between affiliation- and achievement-oriented workers on the teams. An achievement-oriented worker can be a "spark plug" for the team if handled properly.

=========== APPLICATION AND DISCUSSION ===========

Consider the following scenario from Marine Corps boot camp. Drill instructors must teach their platoons to run long distances in the shortest amount of time possible, while arriving at the destination all together and ready to fight. Only by arriving together as a whole platoon can the Marines bring to bear simultaneously all of their combat strengths. It does no good to have a few faster runners arrive ahead of the rest. On the other hand, the sooner the platoon arrives the better. In other words, speed is important, but it is the speed of the whole platoon, not individual Marines, that counts. Drill instructors motivate the faster runners in the platoon by using them to set a challenging pace for the rest of their colleagues while being careful to avoid setting an impossibly fast pace. In this way, the overall platoon gets faster while the faster individuals are rewarded for their talent.

■ Transfer this example to the workplace. How does it relate to motivating achievement-oriented employees without turning off affiliation-oriented members of the team?

■ Give an example of how a supervisor might use this strategy in the workplace.

JOB DESIGN AND MOTIVATION

Job design, how a job's various tasks are determined and structured, can be an important factor in motivating employees and keeping them motivated over time. There are three basic approaches to job design: task-oriented, people-oriented, and balanced.

Task-Oriented Job Design

In the past, job design was typically task-oriented. **Task-oriented job design** means that job processes were set up to get the most out of the floor space available, equipment used, and humans involved. Time and motion studies were used to continually improve processes by identifying and eliminating wasted motion.

Task-oriented job designs resulted in early innovations such as the assembly line. On paper, task-oriented job designs look good. However, in reality they rarely live up to expectations over extended periods of time because they fail to sufficiently consider the psychological and physiological needs of the people doing the work. This leads to boring, unchallenging, monotonous work. As a result, the long-term productivity gains from task-oriented job designs are limited (Figure 5–5).

People-Oriented Job Design

In **people-oriented job design**, the psychological and physiological needs of human workers are the foremost consideration. The philosophy of this approach is that, in the long run, workers who are simultaneously comfortable and challenged will be more productive even if the tasks they perform are not perfectly laid out.

The science of **ergonomics,** which grew out of the people-oriented school of thought, is the study of how human workers interact with technology and how they react in their environment. The buzzword "user-friendly" is part of the language of ergonomics.

Taken to an extreme, even the people-oriented approach can have a detrimental effect on productivity. People can actually become so comfortable that they lose the positive edge that is necessary for high productivity.

Balanced Orientation in Job Design

The **balanced job design** seeks to strike the optimum balance between the other two orientations. The key element of the balanced approach is the maximum participation of people who do a job in the design of the job. They are encouraged to weigh both task and people considerations in trying to arrive at an optimum job design that incorporates the best of both concepts.

There are several advantages of the balanced approach. The most important of these include the following: (1) it brings the firsthand knowledge of the people who actually do a job to bear on designing the job; (2) it focuses attention on the work instead of the people who are doing the work, which is less threatening for employees; and (3) it promotes ownership of the job design by workers.

How to Use Job Design to Motivate

The first step in using job design as a motivator is to adopt the balanced approach. In applying this approach, supervisors may find the following rules of thumb helpful:

- Design the job so that employees see the big picture rather than isolated, seemingly, independent pieces of the job. One of the many problems with the traditional job design is that workers cannot see where their part of the job fits into the overall process or how their task contributes to the organization's mission.
- Design the job so that employees must apply a variety of skills rather than performing one monotonous task that never changes.
- Design the job so that employees can be as autonomous as possible. The more decisions about the work that can be made by the people doing it, the better.
- Design the job so that employees are allowed to come into contact with customers as frequently as possible. Feedback straight from a customer can be a powerful motivator.

Figure 5–5
Superiors should have a
balanced orientation.

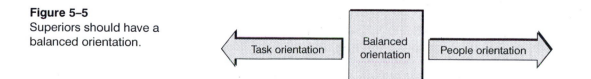

Task orientation | Balanced orientation | People orientation

═══════ **APPLICATION AND DISCUSSION** ═══════

Halim Po supervises twelve people, most of whom complain constantly about the monotonous nature of their job. The company they work for is seventy-five years old, and its work processes have changed little during this time. Po would like to redesign his team's work processes to motivate team members.

■ Put yourself is Po's place. What would you do first? Next?

■ Explain how and why your plan will motivate employees.

COMPETITION AND MOTIVATION

To a degree, most people enjoy **competition**. They like to outperform others when challenged. A child's competitive instinct is nurtured through play and reinforced by sports and school activities. Supervisors can use adults' competitive instinct when trying to motivate employees, but competition on the job should be carefully organized, closely monitored, and strictly controlled. Competition that is allowed to get out of hand can do more harm than good. Uncontrolled competition can lead to cheating and hard feelings among fellow workers.

Competition can be organized between teams, shifts, divisions, or even plants. It can focus on a number of different performance-related factors or combinations of factors such as production, absentee rates, safety records, quality, waste rates, customer satisfaction, and a variety of other factors.

What follows are some tips that will help supervisors use competition in a positive way while ensuring that it is properly controlled (Figure 5–6).

■ Involve the employees who will compete in planning programs of competition.

■ Where possible, encourage competition among groups rather than individuals, while simultaneously promoting individual initiative within groups.

■ Make sure the competition is fair by dividing work equally, making sure that resources available to competing teams are equitably distributed, and that human talent is as appropriately spread among the teams as possible.

═══════ **APPLICATION AND DISCUSSION** ═══════

Competition between A and B shifts produced immediate results at Planco, Inc. when it was initiated six months ago. The absentee rate declined to almost zero, and the produc-

Figure 5–6
Work factors that can be the basis for competition

Potential Areas for Positive Competition

- **Quality.** Based on clearly defined measures.

- **Waste rates.** Measured against clearly defined benchmarks.

- **Production rates.** Measured against an established production goal.

- **Absentee rates.** In conjunction with production rates (it is important to do more than just show up).

- **Safety records.** Close observation is necessary so that injuries or near misses do not go unreported.

tivity and quality measure for both shifts improved markedly. Planco's executive management team was so encouraged by the results that the CEO decided to raise the stakes. He established a new set of performance benchmarks and started a new round of competition between shifts A and B. The new competition was a winner-takes-all program with significant financial incentives for the employees of the winning shift, but nothing for the losing shift, even if it surpassed all of the new performance benchmarks set by the CEO. Before long the two teams began to undercut each other's performance. Shift A began working right up to the last minute of its shift rather than using the last thirty minutes to clean and maintain machines and equipment. This forced shift A to use the first thirty minutes of its shift cleaning and maintaining machines rather than turning out products. Shift B retaliated in the same way. Before long, one shift was actually sabotaging the work of the other. Within 90 days, things had gotten so out of control that Planco's productivity and quality had plummeted. Shift A and shift B employees had stopped being friendly rivals and become bitter enemies.

- What happened here and why? How could this unfortunate situation have been prevented?
- How could this competition program have been designed to prevent what happened and to improve motivation?

COMMUNICATION AND MOTIVATION

Just as people have a natural instinct for competition, they also have a natural desire to be informed. They want to know how they are doing as individuals, how the team is doing, how their division is doing, and how the company is doing. People like to know what is going on. Providing up-to-date, accurate information on a continual basis is an excellent way to motivate employees. In fact, without effective communication, all the other motivation strategies break down.

Communication involves more then just conveying information. It also involves giving instructions, listening, persuading, inspiring, and understanding. For the supervisor, communication can be viewed as preventive maintenance. To use communication to prevent problems and to keep small problems from becoming big ones, supervisors must be tuned into what is being said by employees, verbally and nonverbally, as well as what is going unsaid. This requires supervisors to have the ability to:

- Understand nonverbal communication.
- Empathize with employees and see things through their eyes.
- Read between the lines and determine what the real problem is.
- Keep an open mind and truly listen to what employees are saying.

=========== APPLICATION AND DISCUSSION =============

To Mark Granger, supervisor of Team B at Lotwark, Inc., knowledge is power. What he knows gives him power over others; at least this is what he thinks. Consequently, Granger tells his direct reports only what he thinks they need to know. To know what to do in a given situation, members of Team B must first go to Granger and ask for information.

- Would you want to be a member of Team B? Why or why not?
- What types of problems might be experienced by Team B as a result of Mark Granger's attitude about communication?

PROMOTIONS AND MOTIVATION

Like so many factors relating to motivation, promotions can have positive or negative effects depending on how they are handled. The two basic approaches to promotions are promoting from within and promoting from outside. Of the two, promotion from within is the approach most likely to be a motivator if used properly. What follows are some demotivators that should be avoided when promoting from within:

- *Don't* promote solely on the basis of seniority. A person with ten years' experience might, in reality, have one year of experience that has been repeated ten times. Seniority is a legitimate factor to consider in promotions, but should not be the only factor. If a senior employee is promoted over a less senior but more skilled employee, morale will suffer.

- *Don't* promote on the basis of popularity. Personal popularity is no guarantee of success in a new position. It is not uncommon for an employee who is well liked as a person to struggle and perform poorly when placed in a supervisory role over former coworkers.

- *Don't* promote on the basis of friendship. Of all the *don'ts*, this is the most critical. Promotions viewed by other workers as being influenced by friendship are doomed to failure from the outset.

A good rule of thumb is to promote from within whenever possible, but to base promotions on qualifications rather than seniority, popularity, or friendship. This will ensure that promotions motivate, rather than demoralize.

APPLICATION AND DISCUSSION

The debate between Linda Washington and her direct reports is about a promotion that took place in another team. The supervisor of the other team recommended one of her team members for a promotion to the position of lead technician. This person is a popular team member, a friend of the supervisor, and the most senior member of the team. However, she is not the best technician on the team. In fact, two less experienced technicians on the team are noticeably better. The younger members of Linda Washington's team have heard about the promotion and are upset. They claim that the best technician should have gotten the promotion irrespective of seniority. They are also upset that the promotion appears to be based on a friendship and popularity. The more senior members of Washington's team disagree. They claim that the experience of the more senior employee will more than compensate for any technical shortcomings.

- Join this debate. Which side do you think is right? Why?
- Put yourself in Linda Washington's place. What would you say to your team?

NEW EMPLOYEES AND MOTIVATION

New employees represent a special challenge for supervisors. It is important to help new workers make a positive start. To get new employees motivated, supervisors should take personal responsibility for their introduction to the new job, which should begin with an orientation that is handled personally by the supervisor rather than a subordinate. This serves two purposes. First, it shows new employees that they are important enough to rate the supervisor's personal attention. Second, it shows existing employees that new employees are important enough to rate the supervisor's personal attention.

The next step involves letting new employees know what is expected of them. This will establish the company's corporate culture in the minds of new employees. **Corpo-**

rate culture is the name given to the overall collection of the company's expectations of employees. If the corporate culture encompasses such philosophies as an emphasis on quality and customer service, new employees should know it from the start.

Supervisors should carefully assign the new employee's first task. Success is a powerful motivator that breeds further success. Failure is an equally powerful demotivater. The key is to make a new employee's first assignment a confidence builder. In this way, initial success will breed additional success.

Supervisors should spend more than the usual amount of time with the new employee. A one-on-one, face-to-face conference at the end of each day can be an effective motivating strategy. During the conference, supervisors can identify problems the employee is having and deal with them right away, give the employee feedback on performance, and provide encouragement. The following strategies will help supervisors motivate new employees:

- *Focus on efforts* rather than the person. Compliment the effort, not the person. This will keep employees from tying their personal worth to their performance. Remember, even the best employees can have a bad day. This doesn't make them bad people.

- *Build on strengths and assets* to help new employees build self-esteem. Most new employees will perform well on some aspects of the job. Build on this strength to help overcome and correct weaknesses in other aspects of the job.

- *Recognize improvement* to reinforce the new employee's self-esteem. Success breeds success. By acknowledging improvement, supervisors will encourage additional improvement.

- *Break down complex tasks into simpler ones*. It is discouraging to new employees to face difficult, complex tasks. When possible, supervisors should break tasks down into a series of tasks that successively increase in difficulty. This will encourage employees by allowing them to experience success.

- *Focus on specific contributions*. Giving specific examples when offering encouragement lets new employees know exactly what they did right. Relating the behavior to the accomplishment of one or more of the organization's goals lets employees know the specific contribution that they have made.

- *Turn mistakes into learning activities*. New employees will make mistakes, particularly those who are willing to risk attempting to improve performance. When a new employee makes a mistake, say, "All right, this didn't work. What can we learn from the experience?" This communicates the message that mistakes can be opportunities for improvement rather than failure. This will encourage them to take the calculated risks necessary for improved performance (Figure 5–7).

- *Promote problem solving* by encouraging self-sufficiency. For example, when a new employee comes to you with a problem, try saying, "Think about it for a while and bring me a suggested solution. If you get stuck, we'll put our heads together." This will show employees you have confidence in them, but that you are willing to collaborate if necessary. This approach will promote problem solving.

Encouragement can be an invaluable strategy for supervisors trying to help new employees motivate themselves. A public pat on the back or a compliment can be a powerful motivator for both new and experienced employees.

APPLICATION AND DISCUSSION

Mack Fairlane's biggest fear is getting a new employee on his team. It happens two or three times a year, but for some reason things never seem to work out. The last two times new employees joined his team, they asked for a transfer within three months.

Figure 5–7
Strategies for giving new
employees a good start

Strategies for Motivating New Employees

- **Provide a personal orientation.**
  Supervisors should never turn orientation
  over to a subordinate.

- **Use one-on-one conferences.** Give new
  employees more than the usual amount of
  one-on-one attention.

- **Establish the organization's culture.** Let
  new employees know from the start what
  is expected of them and how things are
  done.

- **Make the first assignment a confidence
  builder.** Never push new employees in
  over their heads before they have learned
  to swim.

Fairlane is developing a reputation for being unable to supervise new employees. If things don't change, his days as a supervisor are probably numbered. Fairlane is sufficiently worried that he has decided to ask for advice.

- What advice would you give Fairlane concerning building the self-esteem and sense of belonging of new employees?

- What advice would you give Fairlane concerning helping new employees experience success as soon as possible and concerning helping employees deal positively with making "rookie mistakes"?

PROBLEM EMPLOYEES AND MOTIVATION

Problem employees—the drug user, slow achiever, sick-leave abuser, grouch, know-it-all, goldbrick, constant complainer, and gossip—have always posed a challenge for supervisors and can strain a supervisor's patience to the breaking point. However, firing a problem employee is not always an option. Employees, no matter how many problems they cause, have rights. In today's workplace, it is difficult to fire an employee in a way that does not leave the company vulnerable to charges of wrongful discharge.

As a result, the modern supervisor is well advised to make a concerted effort to help problem employees become contributing members of the team. The first and most critical step in motivating problem employees is determining what is causing the unacceptable behavior.

Getting to the root cause of unacceptable behavior will not be possible in all cases. In addition, supervisors should resist the temptation to engage in "armchair psychology." However, if supervisors apply the following strategies, they may occasionally succeed in turning a problem employee into an asset:

- *Avoid jumping to conclusions.* Keep an open mind until the causes of the behavior have been identified.

- *Be patient.* It may take time to learn what is causing the negative behavior.

- *Spend as much one-on-one time with problem employees as possible.* Let them do the talking. Listen, make mental notes, and look for clues. To draw the employee out, avoid judgmental comments, gestures, or facial expressions, and ask open-ended questions.

■ If the cause of the negative behavior can be identified, *tailor your motivational techniques as dictated by the cause*.

=============== **APPLICATION AND DISCUSSION** ===============

The diminishing abilities of high school graduates as evidenced by a decade of lower and lower test scores is presenting employers with a difficult challenge. In the old days, an employer could simply fire a problem employee and hire someone better. There were usually more good applicants than jobs. This is no longer the case. Now applicants who replace problem employees may turn out to be even bigger problems than their predecessors. Because of this, employers are finding it necessary to put more effort into turning problem employees around, and supervisors are the key players in implementing these efforts.

■ Have you ever worked with or known someone who was a problem employee because of problems he or she had off the job? Could this person have been turned around and become a contributing employee?

■ Play the role of a supervisor. How would you try to motivate the following types of problem employees: Gossip? Constant complainer? Sick-leave abuser?

MOTIVATING PART-TIME WORKERS

Part-time employees represent approximately 25 percent of the total workforce in this country. The reasons part-time employees work and their needs with regard to work often differ from those of their full-time counterparts. Consequently, what it takes to motivate part-time employees often differs too.

Daniel Kopp and Lois Shufeldt developed a six-phase program called P-TIMER that can be used by supervisors to motivate part-time employees. The P-TIMER program consists of six strategies:

■ *Positive reinforcement* to show part-time employees that they are full members of the team and that their contributions are appreciated.

■ *Team-building* efforts that include part-time employees and let them know they are members of the team.

■ *Information sharing* that allows part-time employees to know what is going on. Better informed employees, part-time or full-time, are better prepared to do their jobs.

■ *Money* paid at a rate that says "You are important" to part-time employees.

■ *Expectations* explained fully so that part-time employees understand what is expected of them.

■ *Feedback* that lets part-time employees know how they are doing. Praise and recognition can be as effective in helping part-time employees motivate themselves as they are with full-time employees.

With part-time employees representing approximately one-fourth of the workforce now and that number likely to increase over time, modern supervisors will need to be able to motivate part-timers. The six strategies set forth in the P-TIMER program can help.

=============== **APPLICATION AND DISCUSSION** ===============

More than 70 percent of the employees in many organizations are part-time employees. They represent the largest part of the workforce in many companies. This can present supervisors with a difficult challenge.

■ Have you ever worked part-time? If so, what was your attitude toward your employer and its customers? Did you feel as much a part of the team as the full-time employees? If not, why not?

■ If you worked in a setting in which 70 percent of the employees you supervise are part-timers, how would you motivate them?

INCENTIVE PROGRAMS AND MOTIVATION

Increasingly, companies faced with intense competition in the marketplace are developing incentive programs to motivate employees to higher levels of productivity, quality, and customer services. For this reason, it is important for supervisors to know how to help higher management establish effective incentive programs. To do this, supervisors need to know which incentives will work best (Figure 5–8).

Pay raises and promotions are still part of the picture, but only part. It is important for supervisors to understand that today's employees are more concerned with personal recognition than with corporate recognition (i.e., the gold watch or jewelry bearing the company logo). They also want to be involved in decision making. The following strategies can help ensure the effectiveness of incentive programs:

■ *Define objectives.* Begin by deciding what is supposed to be accomplished by the incentive program. Higher quality? Higher productivity? Improved safety? Examples of incentive program objectives might be:

 • To increase productivity by 22 percent.

 • To decrease customer complaints by 25 percent.

 • To decrease the accident rate by 50 percent.

■ *Lead by example.* For incentive programs to work, supervisors and higher managers must set a positive example of modeling the type of behavior they want the incentives to reinforce. For example, if an objective is to decrease absenteeism and tardiness, supervisors must set an example of attendance and punctuality.

■ *Develop specific criteria.* On what basis will the incentives be awarded? This question should be answered during the development of the program. Specific criteria define the type of behavior and level of performance that is to be rewarded as well as outline the guidelines for measuring success.

■ *Make rewards meaningful.* For an incentive program to be effective, the rewards must be meaningful to the recipients. Giving employees rewards that they do not

Figure 5–8
Making incentive programs effective takes work.

> **Summary of Strategies for Making Incentive Programs Effective**
>
> • Define objectives.
> • Lead by example.
> • Develop specific criteria.
> • Make rewards meaningful.
> • Ask employees which incentives will motivate them.
> • Solicit feedback from employees.
> • Reward teams.

value will not produce the desired results. To determine if rewards will be meaningful, it is necessary to involve employees in developing the list of potential rewards.

■ *Only the employees who will participate in an incentive program know what incentives will motivate them*. In addition, employees must feel it is their program. This means that employees should be involved in the planning, implementation, and evaluation of establishing an incentive program.

■ *Keep communications clear*. It is important for employees to fully understand all aspects of the incentive program. Communicate with employees about the program, ask for continual feedback, listen to the feedback, and act on it.

■ *Rewards teams*. Rewarding teams can be more effective than rewarding individuals. This is because work in most organizations is more likely to be accomplished by a team than an individual. When this is the case, other team members might resent the recognition given to an individual member. Such a situation can cause the incentive program to backfire.

══════ APPLICATION AND DISCUSSION ══════

The Morgan Jones Company (MJC) has used monetary incentives to motivate its sales force for years, and the incentives seem to work well enough. But when the CEO decided to establish an incentive program for nonsales personnel, problems began immediately. Using a sales-oriented incentive program with nonsales personnel is not working. In fact, it's done nothing but cause problems.

■ What types of problems do you think MJC is experiencing in trying to use a sales-oriented incentive program with nonsales personnel?

■ If you were a supervisor of nonsales personnel at MJC, what advice would you give the CEO about establishing an effective incentive program for nonsales personnel?

DEVELOPING PERSONAL MOTIVATION PLANS (PMPS)

The best motivation plan is the one that is personalized for the individual employee. Employees are so different in their individual strengths, weaknesses, attitudes, and needs that a *one-size-fits-all* motivation plan will always be limited in its effectiveness. For this reason, supervisors need to become proficient in developing **Personal Motivation Plans** (PMPs) that are designed to bring about specific improvements in the performance of individual employees.

With PMPs, supervisors note specific improvements they want individual employees to make. Then they choose some form of reward they think will motivate each respective employee to make the improvements. For example, say a supervisor has a team member, Tim Smith, who is frequently late to work. The supervisor, Dawn Burke, wants Smith to show up on time every day unless there is a justifiable reason for being late. Burke knows that Smith wants to take college classes at night as part of the company's tuition-reimbursement program. Acceptance into the program requires the supervisor's approval.

The PMP Dawn Burke developed for Tim Smith, like all PMPs, has five components: employee name, desired improvement, motivator, action steps, and follow-up statements. Smith's PMP reads as follows:

■ *Employee Name*: Tim Smith.

■ *Desired Improvement*: Show up on time for work every day.

■ *Motivator*: Recommendation for acceptance in the company's tuition-reimbursement program.

- *Action Steps*: Talk to Smith about his tardiness and explain the importance of being on time every day. Explain how to handle valid reasons for being late. Explain that when he has accomplished six straight months of on-time attendance you will recommend him for the tuition-reimbursement program. Also, explain that to stay in the program, he will have to continue his on-time status.

- *Follow-Up Statements*: In this component, Burke will record what she learns and does as a result of attempting to motivate Smith.

This same approach can be used in developing a PMP for any employee. The key is to (1) identify specific improvements the employee needs to make and (2) know the employee well enough to identify what motivator might work.

ON-THE-JOB SCENARIOS

1. Wendell Glover knew he had a tiger by the tail. He had been a supervisor for five years and had faced numerous challenges. But this latest challenge is the biggest yet. He is the new supervisor of a department in turmoil. Two long-time employees have been fired for sabotaging the work of another department during a company competition. Their replacements have just reported for work. Members of his new department seem to be either ill-informed or completely uninformed concerning the companies goals and corresponding departmental goals. The work ethic in the department is nonexistent, and job satisfaction is about as low as it can get. Put yourself in Wendell Glover's place. Develop a plan for turning this department into a highly motivated, peak performing team.

2. Elsa Maxwell supervises five full-time employees and seven part-timers. The full-time employees are motivated and productive. They are happy with their jobs and the company's incentive plan. The part-time employees are a different story. They are unmotivated, unproductive, and complain constantly. Their main complaints are as follows: (1) full-timers get the best tasks, the best hours, and the most support; (2) full-timers get financial incentives that are unavailable to part-timers; and (3) full-timers are included in the decision-making process, but part-timers are not. Maxwell's boss has given her one-week to come up with a plan for transforming these part-time employees into motivated, productive members of the team. Put yourself in Elsa Maxwell's place. Develop the plan.

KEY TERMS AND PHRASES

Achievement	Personal Motivation Plans
Balanced job design	Personal satisfaction
Competition	Problem employees
Corporate culture	Safety/security needs
Ergonomics	Self-actualization needs
Esteem needs	Self-motivated employees
Expectancy	Social needs
Financial reward	Societal contribution
Job design	Survival needs
Job satisfaction	Task-oriented job design
Motivation	Work ethic
People-oriented job design	

REVIEW QUESTIONS

1. What are the five general areas of need all people have?
2. What are the three specific work-related needs all people share?
3. Define the term *work ethic*.
4. Give three reasons you think the work ethic is not as strong as it could be in this country.
5. Briefly explain how supervisors can help enhance the work ethic.
6. What is job satisfaction and how does it affect motivation?
7. List the job satisfaction factors that maintain morale.
8. List the job satisfaction factors that can motivate people to higher levels of performance.
9. Explain the term *expectancy* as it relates to motivation.
10. How can a supervisor recognize an achievement-oriented employee?
11. How can a supervisor use achievement as a motivator?
12. How can a supervisor prevent friction between achievement- and affiliation-oriented employees?
13. Explain the following terms: *people-oriented job design, task-oriented job design, balanced job design.*
14. Explain just one strategy for using job design as a motivator.
15. Explain briefly how supervisors can ensure that competition is a motivator rather than a demotivator.
16. What abilities must a supervisor have to be a good communicator?
17. Explain briefly how to avoid making promotions a demotivator.
18. Explain briefly how to motivate a new employee.
19. Explain briefly how to deal with problem employees.
20. List and briefly explain four strategies supervisors can use for encouraging employees in ways that will help motivate them.
21. List six strategies in the "P-Timer" program.
22. Explain four strategies for ensuring the effectiveness of incentive programs.
23. List the components of a PMP.

ENDNOTES

1. D. G. Kopp and L. M. Shufeldt, "Motivating the Part-Time Worker," *Supervisory Management* (January 1990), 4.

CHAPTER SIX

Decision Making and Problem Solving

After studying this chapter, you should be able to do the following:

- Define *decision making*.
- Explain the problems associated with decision making.
- Describe the decision-making process.
- Demonstrate how to use decision-making models.
- Explain how to involve employees in decision making.
- Describe the role of information in decision making.
- Describe the role of creativity in decision making.

Decision making and problem solving are important responsibilities of supervisors. Supervisors make decisions and solve problems within specified limits defined by their range of authority. These limits should be clearly understood so there is no question as to what decisions supervisors are allowed to make and what problems they have the authority to solve.

DECISION MAKING DEFINED

All people make decisions every day. Some are minor (e.g., What should I wear to work today? What should I have for breakfast?). Some are major (e.g., Should I accept a job offer in another city? Should I buy a new house?). Regardless of the nature of the decision, decision making can be defined as follows:

> *Decision making is the process of choosing one alternative from among two or more alternatives. (Ideally the alternative chosen is the best or at least the optimum alternative available.)*

Decision making is one of the most critical tasks supervisors perform. Decisions can be compared to fuel in an engine. Decision making keeps the engine (organization) running. In a typical case, work cannot progress until a decision is made.

Consider the following example. Because the computer network is down, XYZ Company has fallen behind schedule. The company cannot complete an important contract on time without scheduling at least seventy-five hours of overtime. The functional supervisor faces a dilemma. On the one hand, no overtime was budgeted for the project. On the other hand, there is substantial pressure to complete this contract on time since future contracts with this client could be contingent on an on-time delivery. The supervisor must make a decision.

In this case, as in all such situations, it is important to make the best decision. How do supervisors know when they have made the right decision? In most cases there is no *one* right choice. If there were, decision making would be easy. Typically there are several alternatives, each with its own advantages and disadvantages.

For example, in the case of XYZ Company, the supervisor had two alternatives: authorize seventy-five hours of overtime or miss a deadline and risk losing future contracts. If the supervisor authorizes the overtime, his company's profit margin for this project will suffer, but its relationship with the client will be enhanced. If the supervisor does not authorize the overtime, his company's planned profit will be protected, but its relationship with this client may be damaged.

Since it is not always clear at the outset what the best decision is, supervisors should be prepared to have their decisions criticized after the fact. It may seem unfair to criticize, in the calm aftermath, decisions made during the heat of the battle. However, having one's decisions evaluated is part of accountability, and it can be an effective way to improve a supervisor's decision-making skills.

Evaluating Decisions

There are two ways to evaluate decisions. The first is to examine the results. The result of a decision should advance an organization toward accomplishing its goals. To the extent it does, the decision is usually considered good. Supervisors' decisions typically will be evaluated based on results. However, this is not always the best way. Regardless of results, it is also wise to evaluate the process used in making a decision (Figure 6–1). This is because a positive result can cause you to overlook the fact that you used a faulty process. And in the long run, a faulty process will lead to more negative results than positive.

For example, say a supervisor must choose from among five alternatives. Rather than collect as much information as possible about each, weigh the advantages and disadvantages of each, and solicit informed input, the supervisor simply chooses randomly. There is one chance in five that she might choose the best alternative. Such odds will occasionally produce a positive result, but typically they won't. This is why it is important to examine the process as well as the result, not just when the result is negative, but also when it is positive.

=== APPLICATION AND DISCUSSION ===

We make decisions all day every day. When to get out of bed? What to wear? What to eat? Some of our decisions are almost automatic whereas others require careful deliberation. Some are simple, others complex.

- List every decision you can think of that you made today. Code each as being either simple or complex. What process did you go through in making the complex decisions? How does the process differ when making the simple decisions?

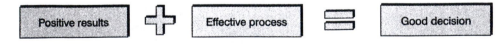

Figure 6–1
Elements of a good decision

■ What is a difficult decision you have made (that you can discuss)? What alternatives did you consider before making your final decision?

PROBLEMS AND DECISION MAKING

Everyone has problems. We have problems at home, at work, in relationships, and in every other human endeavor. But what is a problem? Ask any number of people to describe their biggest problem, and you will get many different responses. Here is a list of responses that might be given to this question:

"I don't make enough money."

"I am overweight."

"I need more education."

"I don't like my job."

What these responses have in common is that they point out a difference between what is desired and what actually exists. Such a condition is a problem. Therefore, a problem can be defined as follows:

> A **problem** is the condition in which there is a discrepancy between what is desired and what actually exists.

Obviously the greater the disparity, the greater the problem, with one exception. A key ingredient in determining the magnitude of a problem is the ability of the person with the problem to solve it. Even a pronounced disparity between what is desired and what exists does not represent a major problem if the person involved can eliminate the disparity. Correspondingly, even seemingly small disparities can represent big problems for people who do not have the ability to eliminate them.

To illustrate this point, consider the following example. A new machine has been installed that can do five times as much work per hour as the one it replaced. But there is a problem. Nobody can remember the correct start-up sequence. Using the wrong sequence can damage the machine. For most operators this is a small problem. They will simply consult the operator's manual, read the proper sequence, and follow it. However, for the operator who cannot read, this is a major problem. The difference is in the ability of the operator to solve the problem.

Characteristics of Problems

Problems can be classified according to the following characteristics: structure, organizational level, and urgency (Figure 6–2). The **structure** of a problem can vary from highly structured to no structure. A highly structured problem exists when the decision maker understands both the problem and how to solve it. An unstructured problem exists when the decision maker is unsure about alternatives and solutions. Highly structured and unstructured problems represent opposite extremes. There are also problems and varying degrees of structure that fall at different points along a continuum connecting these extremes.

Highly structured problems are so predictable that decisions regarding them can be automatic. For example, when the copy machine runs out of paper (a highly structured problem), the solution is obvious: add paper.

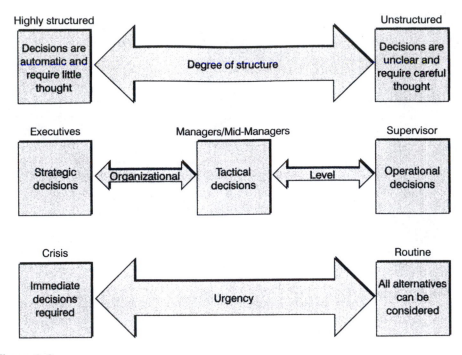

Figure 6–2
Decisions can be classified according to degree of structure, organizational level, and urgency.

Unstructured problems are not as predictable, nor are responses to them automatic. For example, a supervisor in a small business temporarily loses her three best technicians when their Army Reserve unit is suddenly called up to participate in a classified operation. She does not know where they are going or when they will return. Consequently, she does not know whether to defer action and hope they will return soon, put her remaining staff on overtime, advertise for temporary employees, or request an extension on the contract her team is trying to complete. As is always the case with unstructured problems, this supervisor needs to consider all alternatives carefully and seek informed input before making a decision.

Problems also vary according to **organizational level**. Executive-level decision makers or top managers deal with strategic problems. Supervisors deal with operational-level problems, those that affect the day-to-day work of the organization. Supervisors are able to deal with problems within their span of authority without consulting higher management. Problems above the operational level are outside the scope of the supervisor's authority.

Problems can also be classified according to their degree of **urgency**. From this perspective, problems range from routine to those representing a crisis. One of the underlying purposes of such management functions as planning and organization is to minimize the number of crisis problems decision makers face.

Crisis problems require immediate attention and force decision makers to react. **Routine problems**, on the other hand, allow decision makers to study the situation, consider alternatives, brainstorm ideas, and make well-reasoned decisions. In decision making, it is always better to act than to react.

For this reason, supervisors should apply the three-step approach to minimizing crisis problems. The three steps are (1) plan, (2) organize, and (3) learn.

Careful planning and thorough organization will minimize the number of crisis problems supervisors must deal with. However, even the best planning and organization will not completely eliminate crisis problems. This is why the third step—learn—is so important. Supervisors should learn from every crisis.

Could it have been prevented? If so, how? Did I or my organization contribute to causing the crisis? Can changes be made to prevent a similar crisis from occurring in the future? These are questions supervisors should ask themselves after a crisis.

Careful after-the-fact analysis of a crisis can yield two important benefits. First, it can improve the planning and organization processes, thereby minimizing even further the number of future crises. Second, it can make you better prepared to handle a similar crisis should one occur.

APPLICATION AND DISCUSSION

We all deal with problems in our lives. Some are routine; others are crisis problems. Some are structured; others unstructured. Some are strategic, and others are operational. In addition, what represents a crisis to one individual might be nothing more than a routine problem to another. The difference is in the individual's ability to solve the problem in question.

- Identify problems you have faced that were (1) structured and (2) unstructured. How did your handling of the unstructured problems differ from your handling of the structured problems?

- Identify a crisis problem you have dealt with. What made it a crisis? How did you handle it?

THE DECISION-MAKING PROCESS

Decision making is a process.

> The **decision-making process** is a logically sequenced series of activities through which decisions are made.

Numerous decision-making models are available to supervisors. The one described here in Figure 63 approaches every decision as a problem to be solved and divides the decision-making process into three distinct steps:

1. Identify/anticipate the problem.
2. Consider the alternatives.
3. Choose the best alternative, implement, monitor, and adjust.

Identify/Anticipate the Problem

If supervisors can anticipate problems, they may be able to prevent them. Anticipating problems is like driving defensively. You never assume anything. You look, listen, ask, and sense. For example, if you hear through the grapevine that a key employee was injured in this weekend's company softball game, you can anticipate the related problems that may occur. She is likely to be absent or, if she can still work, her pace may be slowed. Knowing this, the supervisor can take the appropriate steps to fill in for this employee. The better supervisors know their employees, systems, products, and processes, the better able they will be to anticipate problems.

Even the most perceptive supervisors will not always be able to anticipate problems. For example, a supervisor notices a "Who cares?" attitude among his team members. This

Figure 6–3
Tasks involved in solving
problems

Decision-Making/Problem-Solving Process

Identify/anticipate the problem

- Don't wait for problems to occur; look for them.
- Identify the root cause of the problem. Don't just treat the symptoms.

Consider the alternatives

- Cost/benefit analysis
- Time considerations
- Permanent solution or temporary fix?
- Ethical considerations
- Morale considerations
- Think creatively

Choose the best alternative, implement, monitor, and adjust

- Implement the apparently best solution
- Evaluate results
- Adjust as necessary

---

supervisor might identify the problem as lagging employee morale and begin trying to make improvements. However, he would do well to identify what is behind the negative attitudes. It could be that employees are upset about an unpopular management policy.

The process at the heart of a problem might include those for which a supervisor is responsible, such as scheduling and work processes, as well as a variety of others he does not control. These include purchasing, inventory, delivery of material from suppliers, in-house delivery, quality control, and work methods. For example, a supervisor's organization is having problems meeting production deadlines. She might suspect sandbagging on the part of employees and take steps to solve that problem. However, the real problem could be the need to redesign production processes.

Resources that might be at the heart of a supervisor's problem include time, money, supplies, material, personnel, and equipment. Is the problem caused by a lack of time? Insufficient funding? Poorly trained personnel? Outdated equipment? New highly technical equipment that employees have not yet learned to operate proficiently? Poor quality materials? All of these are possible causes of the types of problems supervisors commonly deal with.

The purpose of the following checklist is to help supervisors look beneath the surface when attempting to identify the cause of a problem. This approach can save time and energy that might be wasted dealing with symptoms rather than actual causes.

People/Processes

- Higher management (policies)
- Resource personnel
- Suppliers
- Clients
- Employees
- Training
- Processes
- Purchasing
- Inventory
- In-delivery
- Out-shipping
- In-work processes
- Quality control
- Methods
- Scheduling

Resources

- Time
- Money
- Supplies
- Equipment/technology
- Personnel
- Material

Consider Alternatives

This is a two-step process. The first step is to list all the alternatives available. The second step is to evaluate each alternative. The number of alternatives identified in the first step will be limited by several factors, including practical considerations, the supervisor's range of authority, and the cause of the problem. Once the list has been developed, each entry on it is evaluated. The main criterion against which alternatives are evaluated is the desired outcome. If the problem is that a client's order is not going to be completed on time, will the alternative being considered solve the problem? If so, at what cost?

Cost is another criterion used in evaluating alternatives. The costs might be expressed in financial terms, employee morale, the organization's image, or a client's goodwill. In addition to applying objective criteria, supervisors will also need to apply their experience, judgment, and intuition when considering alternatives.

Choose the Best Alternative, Monitor, and Adjust

Once all alternatives have been considered, one must be selected and implemented. Then supervisors monitor progress and adjust appropriately. Is the alternative having the desired effect? If not, what adjustments should be made?

Selecting the best alternative is an inexact process requiring logic, reason, intuition, guesswork, and luck. Occasionally the alternative chosen for implementation will not produce the desired results. When this happens and adjustments are not sufficient, it is important for supervisors to cut their losses and move on to another alternative. This is what is meant by the adage, "If the horse you are riding dies, get off and find another."

Do not fall into the "ownership trap." This happens when supervisors invest so much ownership in a given alternative that they refuse to change even when it becomes clear the idea is not working. This can happen any time, but is more likely to happen when supervisors select an alternative that (1) runs counter to the advice they have received, (2) is unconventional, or (3) is unpopular. Remember, the supervisor's job is to solve the problem. Showing too much ownership in a given alternative can impede one's ability to do so.

═══════ APPLICATION AND DISCUSSION ═══════

The problems you solve will not stay solved unless you go beyond just treating their symptoms and actually remove their root causes. Most workplace problems are the result of root causes that fall into one or more of the following categories: people, processes, and resources. For example, consider the following problem. Juan Herrera, a shift supervisor for ABC Production, Inc., has noticed an increase in minor injuries among his machine operators. After observing for half a day, Herrera thought he had identified the problem. The machine operators were neglecting proper safety procedures, procedures they had learned during safety operation training. To solve the problem, he required all of his direct reports to complete a three-hour updating seminar on safety procedures. Just one week after the seminar the injury rate among machine operators on Herrera's shift was back up to a dangerously high level. A more systematic analysis revealed that the neglect of safety procedures was just a symptom. The root cause turned out to be a resource issue. Three of Herrera's top machine operators had been transferred to another shift and had not been replaced.

Operating with three fewer technicians, Herrera's shift was still expected to meet the previous production quota. Failure to do so would cost the remaining machine operators incentive dollars they were accustomed to receiving. Herrera's machine operators were ignoring the safety rules in an attempt to compensate for the loss of three team members. To eliminate this root cause, Herrera will have to do one of two things: (1) employ three new machine operators whose skills are equal to or better than those of the operators who were transferred or (2) convince higher management to reduce his shift's production quota to compensate for the loss of three operators.

- Select a problem you are currently dealing with that can be discussed. Apply the "People-Processes-Resources" checklist to identify the root cause(s).

- Identify as many symptoms of the problem as you can that might be considered a cause by a less systematic observer.

DECISION-MAKING MODELS

Most of the many decision-making models available to supervisors fall into one of two categories: objective or subjective. In actual practice, the model used by supervisors may have characteristics of both.

Objective Approach to Decision Making

The **objective approach** is logical and orderly. It proceeds in a step-by-step manner and assumes that supervisors have the time to systematically pursue all steps in the decision-making process. It also assumes that complete and accurate information is available and that supervisors are free to select what they feel is the best alternative.

Because these assumptions are rarely accurate, a completely objective approach to decision making is infrequently used. Supervisors seldom, if ever, have the luxury of time and complete information. This does not mean supervisors should rule out objectivity in decision making. Quite the contrary. Supervisors should be as objective as possible. However, it is important to understand that the day-to-day realities of the workplace may limit the amount of time and information available. When this is the case, the degree of objectivity is decreased correspondingly.

Subjective Approach to Decision Making

Whereas the objective approach to decision making is based on logic and complete, accurate information, the **subjective approach** is based on intuition, experience, and incomplete information. This approach assumes decision makers will be under pressure, short on time, and operating with limited information. The goal of subjective decision making is to arrive at the best decision possible under the circumstances.

In using this approach, there is always the danger that supervisors might make quick, knee-jerk decisions based on no information and no input from other sources. The subjective approach does not give supervisors license to make sloppy decisions. If time is short, use the little time available to list and evaluate alternatives. If information is incomplete, use as much information as you have. Then call on your experience and intuition to fill in the rest of the picture. Never allow subjective decision making to become necessary because you were too lazy to collect accurate information or to budget time wisely.

APPLICATION AND DISCUSSION

If you plan to take a vacation six months from now and there are three potential destinations on your list, an objective decision will be possible. You have time to collect and analyze complete, accurate information, and you have the freedom to select the best alternative. However, assume an unexpected new contract at work forces you to change your plans. Now you have to leave for vacation tomorrow if you plan to go at all. An objective decision is no longer possible. Work-related decisions are often like this.

- Think of a decision you have had to make when there was time to be objective. Now think of one for which there was insufficient time.

- Compare the process you went through in making these decisions. What were the differences? Were there any similarities?

INVOLVING EMPLOYEES IN DECISION MAKING

A strategy that can improve decision making is to involve employees who will have to carry out the decision or who are affected by it. Employees are more likely to show ownership in a decision they had a part in making, and they are more likely to support a decision for which they feel ownership. There are advantages and disadvantages associated with involving employees in decision making.

Advantages of Employee Involvement

Involving employees in decision making can have a number of advantages for supervisors. It can result in a more accurate picture of what the problem really is and a more comprehensive list of alternatives. It can help supervisors do a better job of evaluating alternatives and selecting the best one to implement. Perhaps the most important advantages are gained after the decision is made. Employees who participate in the decision-making process are more likely to understand and accept the decision, and they have a personal stake in making sure the alternative selected succeeds.

Disadvantages of Employee Involvement

Involving employees in decision making can also have its disadvantages. The major disadvantage is that it takes time, and supervisors do not always have time. It takes employees away from their jobs and can result in conflict among team members. Next to time, the most significant disadvantage is that employee involvement can lead to democratic compromises that do not necessarily represent the best decision. In addition, disharmony can result if the supervisor rejects the advice of the group. Several techniques can help supervisors increase the effectiveness of group involvement. Prominent among these are brainstorming, the nominal group technique, and quality circles.

Brainstorming

With **brainstorming**, the supervisor serves as a catalyst in drawing out group members to share any idea that comes to mind. All ideas are considered valid. Group members are not allowed to make judgmental comments or evaluate any suggestions that are made. Typically, one member of the group is asked to serve as a recorder. All ideas suggested are recorded, preferably on a marker board, flip chart, or another medium that allows group members to review them continuously.

Once all ideas have been recorded, the evaluation process begins. Participants are asked to go through the list one item at a time weighing the relative merits of each. This process is repeated until the group narrows the choices to a specified number. For example, supervisors may ask the group to narrow the number of alternatives down to three, reserving the selection of the best of the three to themselves.

Nominal Group Technique

The **nominal group technique (NGT)** is a sophisticated form of brainstorming. It has the following five steps:

1. Problem is stated.
2. Group members silently record ideas.
3. Ideas of each member are reported publicly.
4. Ideas are clarified.
5. Ideas are silently voted on.

In the first step, the supervisor states the problem and clarifies if necessary to make sure all group members understand. In the second step, each group member silently records his or her ideas. At this point, there is no discussion among group members. This strategy promotes free and open thinking unimpeded by judgmental comments or peer pressure.

In the third step, each group member shares one idea with the group. The ideas are recorded on a marker board or flip chart. The process is repeated until all ideas have been recorded. Each idea is numbered. There is no discussion among group members during this step. Taking the ideas one at a time from group members ensures a mix of recorded ideas, making it more difficult for participants to remember what ideas belong to which member.

In the fourth step, the ideas are voted on silently. There are a number of ways to accomplish this. One simple technique is to ask all group members to record the numbers of their five favorite ideas on five separate 3×5 cards. Each member then prioritizes his or her five cards by assigning them a number ranging from one to five, with the "five" representing the best idea and so on down to the card that receives a "one."

The cards are collected, and the points assigned to ideas are recorded on the marker board or flip chart. Once this process has been completed for all five cards of all group members, the points are tallied. The idea receiving the most points is selected as the best idea.

Quality Circles

A **quality circle** is a group of employees convened to solve problems relating to their jobs. The underlying principle of the quality circle is that people who do the work know the most about the work. Consequently, they should be involved in solving work-related problems. A key difference between a brainstorming group and a quality circle is that members of the latter are volunteers who convene themselves without being directed to do so by the supervisor. In addition, they don't wait for a problem to occur before they meet. Rather, they confer regularly to discuss their work, anticipate problems, and identify ways to improve productivity. A quality circle does have a team leader who acts as the facilitator. However, this person is not necessarily the supervisor. In fact, it may be a different person each time a quality circle convenes.

Potential Problems with Group Decision Making

Supervisors interested in improving decision making through group techniques should be familiar with the concepts of groupthink and groupshift. These two concepts can undermine the effectiveness of the group techniques set forth in this section.

Groupthink is the phenomenon that exists when people in a group focus more on reaching a decision than on making the right decision. A number of factors can contribute to groupthink, including the following: overly prescriptive group leadership, peer pressure for conformity, group isolation, and unskilled application of group decision-making techniques. The following strategies can be used to overcome groupthink:

- Encourage constructive criticism.
- Encourage the development of several alternatives. Do not allow the group to rush to a hasty decision.
- Assign a member or members to play the role of devil's advocate.
- Include people who are not familiar with the issue.
- Hold "last-chance meeting." Once a decision is reached, arrange a meeting for a few days later. After group members have had time to think things over, call a last-chance meeting in case group members are having second thoughts (Figure 6–4).

Groupshift is the phenomenon that exists when group members exaggerate their initial position hoping that the eventual decision will be what they really wanted in the first place. If group members get together prior to a meeting and decide to take an overly risky or overly conservative initial view, it can be difficult to overcome. Leaders can help minimize the effects of groupshift by discouraging reinforcement of initial points of view and by assigning group members to serve as devil's advocates.

=========== APPLICATION AND DISCUSSION ==========

Learning to use decision-making strategies such as brainstorming and the nominal group technique (NGT) takes practice. Do the following activities in groups of four to six.

- Your team is responsible for maintaining the company's fleet of automobiles. It is time to replace all ten cars. Lead your team in a brainstorming session to identify all of the pros and cons of buying versus leasing. Be aware of such phenomena as groupthink and groupshift. Take the appropriate action to prevent these problems.
- Reconstitute the group and conduct the session again using the NGT. Arrive at a decision.

INFORMATION AND DECISION MAKING

Information is a critical element in decision making. Although having accurate, up-to-date, comprehensive information does not guarantee a good decision, lacking such information can guarantee a bad one. The old saying that "knowledge is power" applies in decision making, particularly in a competitive situation. To make decisions that will keep their organizations competitive, supervisors need timely, accurate information.

Information can be defined as data that have been converted into a usable format that is relevant to the decision-making process. Data that are relevant to decision making have an impact on the decision.

Figure 6–4
Supervisors should overcome the tendency toward groupthink.

Strategies for Preventing Groupthink

- Encourage constructive criticism among participants.
- Do not accept rushed or hasty decisions. Ask for several different alternatives.
- "Plant" devil's advocates among the participants.
- Invite people to participate in the group who are not familiar with the issue in question.
- Wait a few days and call a "last chance" meeting to accommodate second thoughts.

Recall that communication requires a sender, a medium, and a receiver. In this process, information is what is sent by the sender, transmitted by the medium, and received by the receiver. For the purpose of this unit, supervisors are receivers of information who base decisions at least in part on what they receive.

Advances in technology have ensured that modern supervisors can have instant access to information. Computers and telecommunications technology give supervisors information quickly and easily. Of course, the quality of the information depends on people receiving accurate data, entering it into these technological systems, and updating it continually. This condition gave rise to the saying "garbage in—garbage out" that is now associated with computer-based information systems. It means that information provided by a computer-based system can be no better than the data put into it.

Data Versus Information

Data for one person may be information for another. The difference is in the needs of the individual. A supervisor's needs will be dictated by the types of decisions he or she makes. In deciding on the type of information they need, supervisors should ask themselves these questions:

- What are my responsibilities?
- What are my organizational goals?
- What types of decisions do I have to make relative to these responsibilities and goals?

Value of Information

Information is a useful commodity. As such, it has value. Its value is determined by the needs of the people who will use it and the extent to which it will help them meet their needs. Information also has a cost. Because it must be collected, stored, processed, continually updated, and presented in a usable format when needed, information can be expensive. Therefore, supervisors must weigh the value of information against its cost when deciding what information they need when making decisions. It makes no sense to spend $100 on the information needed to make a $10 decision.

Amount of Information

There used to be a saying that went like this: "A manager can't have too much information." This is no longer true. With advances in information technology, not only can managers have too much information, they frequently do. This phenomenon has come to be known as **information overload**, or the condition that exists when people receive more information than they can process in a timely manner. *In a timely manner* means in time to be useful in decision making. Information overload can cause the following problems:

- Confusion
- Frustration
- Too much attention given to unimportant matters
- Too little attention given to important matters
- Unproductive delays in decision making

To avoid information overload, supervisors can apply the following strategies:

- Change daily reports to weekly reports wherever possible.
- Make weekly reports monthly reports wherever possible.

- Examine all reports provided on a regular basis. Eliminate unnecessary reports.
- Apply the "reporting-by-exception" technique.
- Format reports for efficiency.
- Use on-line/on-demand information retrieval.

First, examine all reports received on a regular basis. Are they really necessary? Do you receive daily or weekly reports that would meet your needs just as well if provided on a monthly basis? Do you receive regular reports that would meet your needs better as exception reports? In other words, would you rather receive reports every day that say "Everything is all right" or occasional reports only when there is a problem? The latter is called an **exception report**, provided only when conditions are other than normal. It can cut down significantly on the amount of information supervisors must deal with.

Another strategy for avoiding information overload is *formatting for efficiency*. This involves working with personnel who provide information, such as management information systems (MIS) personnel, to ensure that reports are formatted for *your* convenience, not theirs. Supervisors should not have to wade through reams of computer printouts to locate the information they need. Nor should they have to become bleary-eyed reading rows and columns of tiny figures. Talk with MIS personnel and recommend an efficient report format that meets your needs. Also, ask that information be presented graphically whenever possible.

Finally, make use of *on-line, on-demand information retrieval*. In the modern work setting, most reports are computer-generated. Rather than relying on periodic hard copy reports, learn to retrieve information on-line.

=============== **APPLICATION AND DISCUSSION** ===============

Information is critical when making decisions. Getting the information needed requires at least two preliminary steps: (1) identifying what information is needed and (2) identifying a reliable source for the information. Consider the following situation. You need to purchase a new computer for your office. It must have all of the capabilities you require, but funding is limited. Your manager told you to "get the computer needed, but spend as little as possible."

- What types of information will you need before making a purchase? Make a list.
- Where can you get this information? Make a list of sources.

CREATIVITY IN DECISION MAKING

The increasing pressures of a competitive marketplace are making it more and more important for organizations to be flexible, innovative, and creative in decision making. To survive in an unsure, rapidly changing marketplace, organizations must be able to adjust rapidly and change directions quickly. To do so requires creativity at all levels of the organization.

Creativity Defined

Like leadership, creativity has many definitions, and there are varying viewpoints concerning whether creative people are born or made. For the purpose of modern organizations, a definition that works well is this:

> **Creativity** *is the process of developing new, different, imaginative, and innovative perspectives on situations.*

Developing such perspectives requires that decision makers have knowledge and experience regarding the issue in question.

Creative Process

The creative process proceeds in four stages: investigation, incubation, clarification, and review.

- *Investigation* involves learning, gaining experience, and collecting/storing information in a given area. Creative decision making requires that people involved be thoroughly prepared through investigation and research.

- **Incubation** means giving ideas time to develop, change, grow, and solidify. Ideas incubate while decision makers drive, relax, sleep, and ponder. Incubation requires that decision makers get away from the issue in question and give the mind time to sort things out. Incubation is often accomplished by the subconscious mind.

- *Clarification* follows incubation. It is the point when a potential solution becomes clear. This point is sometimes seen as a moment of inspiration. However, inspiration rarely occurs without having been preceded by the perspiration of investigation and incubation.

- *Review* refers to analyzing the decision to determine if it will actually work. At this point, traditional processes such as feasibility studies and cost-benefit analyses are used.

Factors that Inhibit Creativity

The following factors tend to inhibit the creative process:

- *Looking for the right answer*. There is seldom just one right solution to a problem.
- *Focusing too intently on being logical*. Creative solutions sometimes defy perceived logic and conventional wisdom.
- *Adhering too closely to the rules*. Sometimes the best solutions come from stepping outside the box and looking beyond the limits established by prevailing rules.
- *Focusing too intently on practicality*. Impractical ideas can sometimes trigger practical solutions.
- *Avoiding ambiguity*. Ambiguity is a normal part of the creative process. This is why the incubation step is so important.
- *Avoiding risk*. When organizations can't seem to find a solution to a problem, it often means decision makers are not willing to take a chance on a creative decision.
- *Forgetting how to play*. Adults sometimes become so serious they forget how to play. Playful activity can stimulate creative ideas.
- *Fear of rejection or looking foolish*. This fear can cause people to hold back what might be creative solutions.
- *Saying "I'm not creative."* People who decide they are not creative won't be. Any person can think creatively and can learn to be even more creative.

APPLICATION AND DISCUSSION

As a supervisor with XYZ Corporation, you face an interesting problem. A new contract is going to double your team's workload for a period of one year. You have a number of questions to answer. Should you authorize overtime or hire new employees? What about contract employees? If you hire more employees, where will you put them? What about equipment?

- Form an ad hoc group to brainstorm the problem. Begin by defining the needs in broad terms (i.e., personnel, space, equipment, etc).

- Engage in the creative process and brainstorm solutions. Identify several different creative solutions to the problem.

ON-THE-JOB SCENARIOS

1. Joan Cotton, CEO of Class Rings, Inc., (CRI), is an entrepreneur from the old school. Playing it safe while the competition moves ahead is not her style. CRI makes graduation rings for the high school and college markets. Five years ago, Cotton began to notice increased competition. She faced a tough decision. Should CRI continue its traditional approach to production and risk stagnation, diversify into other related products (caps and gowns, diplomas, etc.), or make the heavy investment needed to modernize its production facilities and risk being overloaded with debt?

   Cotton chose to modernize and stay focused on CRI's core market. It took two years, but CRI is once again the market leader in producing class rings. Its future looks bright.

   - Put yourself in Cotton's place. Explain how you might have used brainstorming to help in making your decision.

   - What types of information would you have wanted before making such a decision?

2. Your company currently collects plastic gallon milk bottles, cleans and disinfects them, and sells them to dairies. The CEO would like to expand the company's business base. He has asked all supervisors to hold team meetings to identify as many potential new uses for recycled plastic milk bottles as possible. Form a group to discuss the problem. Use brainstorming or NGT and encourage creativity. Develop your team's list for the CEO.

KEY TERMS AND PHRASES

Brainstorming	Information overload
Creativity	Nominal group technique
Crisis problems	Objective approach
Decision-making process	Organizational level
Decision making	Problem
Exception report	Quality circle
Groupshift	Routine problems
Groupthink	Structure
Incubation	Subjective approach
Information	Urgency

REVIEW QUESTIONS

1. Define the term *decision making*.

2. Explain the concept of right choice as it relates to decision making.

3. Briefly explain two ways to evaluate decisions.

4. What is a problem?

5. Explain the three characteristics of problems.

6. What is a crisis problem?

7. Explain how supervisors can minimize the number of crisis problems they have to deal with.

8. Define the term *decision-making process*.

9. Briefly explain the three steps in the decision-making process.

10. Compare and contrast the objective and subjective approaches to decision making.

11. What are the advantages of involving employees in decision making?

12. What are the disadvantages of involving employees in decision making?

13. Briefly explain the following strategies for involving employees in decision making: brainstorming, NGT, quality circles.

14. Explain how the concepts of groupthink and groupshift can affect decisions made in groups.

15. Define the term *information*.

16. Explain the difference between data and information. What determines the difference?

17. Explain the concept of value versus cost relative to information.

18. Explain the concept of information overload and how supervisors can avoid it.

19. List and explain the four stages of the creative process.

CHAPTER SEVEN

Performance Appraisal

After studying this chapter, you should be able do the following:

- Explain the rationale for conducting performance appraisals.
- Describe what constitutes an effective performance appraisal.
- Describe the supervisor's role in performance appraisal.
- Explain how to complete a performance appraisal form.
- Explain how to conduct a performance appraisal interview.
- Explain how to give corrective feedback to employees.
- Describe the legal aspects of performance appraisal.

"How are we doing?" "Where can we do better?" "What are our strengths?" "What are our weaknesses?" "Who should be rewarded for performance?" "Who needs additional development?" Supervisors must answer these questions if they are going to achieve the continual improvement their organizations need in order to compete in the modern marketplace.

Why then is the performance appraisal process so often viewed in negative terms by both supervisors and employees? One reason is that performance appraisal systems are often poorly designed, improperly administered, and inappropriately used. This chapter will help the reader be an effective participant in performance appraisal systems that help employees and organizations continually improve their performance.

RATIONALE FOR PERFORMANCE APPRAISALS

The rationale for **performance appraisal** is simple—to improve performance. Consequently, every aspect of an organization's appraisal system should serve this purpose either directly or indirectly. An appraisal system should identify weak areas so that they can be corrected. It should also identify areas of strength so that they can be capitalized on.

If the results are used as the basis for rewards or promotions, this should be done in such a way as to be an incentive for **improved performance**. When designing a new appraisal system, keep this purpose in mind at every step. When working with an existing system, examine all aspects of it critically. In both cases, ask the following question every time you make a decision about some element of an appraisal system: How will this element improve performance? Any element that does not serve this purpose should be eliminated.

APPLICATION AND DISCUSSION

Performance appraisals often resemble tests taken in school in three ways: (1) employees feel the same way about performance appraisals as students feel about tests; (2) supervisors feel the same way about rating employees as teachers feel about assigning grades; and (3) employees can focus more attention on their rating scores than on improving performance, just as students can focus more attention on grades than on learning.

- How do you generally feel about tests taken in school? Are they productive or punitive? Why?
- Have you ever had a teacher who used tests to improve performance? How was this done?

EFFECTIVE PERFORMANCE APPRAISAL

Effective performance appraisals are those that improve the performance of the employees being evaluated. This is easy to say, but can be difficult to accomplish. Before evaluating an employee's performance, it is important to ensure that both the supervisor and the employee clearly understand what the job entails.

The best way to clearly delineate what a job entails is through the development of a well-written job description. Before attempting to evaluate employee performance, supervisors should make sure that employees have a clearly written **job description** and that they understand it. If there isn't one, work with the Human Resources Department to write one. If there is, make sure it meets the following criteria:

- States the work descriptions in an action-oriented format (e.g., writes programs; loads software; operates fax machine, etc.).
- States all information clearly in as few words as possible.
- Gives comprehensive descriptions (list all work required of the employee).
- Gives specific types and models of all machines, tools, or equipment that are to be used.
- Indicates which work tasks are more important than others. Lists them in order of importance or with notation.

Once a job description is complete, validate it by asking other supervisors and senior employees to review it. Then make sure all employees performing the job in question have a copy and that they understand it.

The next step involves using the information in the job description as well as other sources such as company rules and regulations, work standards, and widely accepted practices to develop an appraisal instrument. This step is covered later in this unit. At this point, it is necessary to understand only that there should be no surprises in performance appraisals. Employees should know what is expected of them and how they will be evaluated. This is fundamental to making performance appraisal systems effective.

APPLICATION AND DISCUSSION

There should be a close match between employee job descriptions and the performance criteria contained in performance appraisal forms. When the job descriptions and performance appraisal criteria are not closely aligned, employers are asking workers to do one thing and evaluating them on another.

- Identify an organization that will cooperate with you in completing the following three-part assignment: (1) copy a job description for a given employee or category of employee; (2) copy the performance appraisal form used to evaluate this employee; and (3) compare the job description requirements with the performance appraisal criteria. Note any differences.

■ Revise the performance appraisal criteria as necessary to more closely match the job description.

SUPERVISOR'S ROLE IN PERFORMANCE APPRAISAL

Supervisors play a key role in an organization's performance appraisal system. The system cannot succeed unless supervisors play their role effectively. The supervisor's responsibilities with regard to performance appraisal are shown in the following list. These responsibilities fall into three broad categories: (1) preparing for the appraisal, (2) doing the appraisal, and (3) following up the appraisal. The supervisor's responsibilities in these areas are as follows:

1. Preparing for the Appraisal
   * Writing or updating job descriptions
   * Reviewing and revising appraisal instruments
   * Making sure employees know what is expected of them and how they will be evaluated
2. Doing the Appraisal
   * Completing the appraisal instrument
   * Ensuring objectivity
   * Preparing for the appraisal interview
   * Listening and soliciting employee input
   * Conducting the appraisal interview
   * Ensuring against interruptions
   * Ensuring privacy
3. Following up the Appraisal
   * Encouraging
   * Assisting
   * Monitoring

APPLICATION AND DISCUSSION

Supervisors play a key role in any performance appraisal system. Some organizations give supervisors more responsibility than do others in conducting performance appraisals. In the most effective organizations, supervisors are the key players in the process.

■ Identify two supervisors who will work with you in completing this assignment. Ask each supervisor (separately) to explain the role he or she plays in each of the following areas: (1) preparing for the appraisal, (2) doing the appraisal, and (3) following up the appraisal.

■ Compare the notes from interviewing the two supervisors with the checklist provided in this section. Are the supervisors you interviewed playing a comprehensive or limited role in the process?

DEVELOPING AND COMPLETING THE APPRAISAL FORM

Supervisors should be able to help develop a new appraisal form, sometimes called an appraisal instrument, and complete an existing one. **Appraisal instruments** are written documents that contain the evaluation criteria and on which supervisors record their feedback for employees. It is more likely that supervisors will have opportunities to revise existing forms than to actually develop new forms from scratch. However, if supervisors can develop a form, they can revise one. Therefore, this section describes how to develop a performance appraisal form. All performance appraisal forms should have at least the following components: (1) a list of performance criteria, (2) a way to rate performance according to each criteria, (3) space for written comments, (4) an employee response section, and (5) a supervisor's report section.

Performance Criteria

Performance criteria are statements of expectation relative to the employee's performance on the job. Typical performance criteria include quality of work, quantity of work, consistency, job skills, job knowledge, adaptability, attitude, punctuality, dependability, judgment, ability to innovate, initiative, safety practices, personality, team skills, and growth potential. These are just some of the many performance criteria that might be included on an appraisal form. Others can be added based on the individual situation. Regardless of what criteria are included, they should tie directly to the job description.

In deciding what performance criteria to include on an appraisal form, supervisors should select only those that are truly important relative to the job in question. An appraisal form might be challenged in court or before a grievance board. If this happens, supervisors might be called on to justify their performance criteria. Keep this in mind when developing a new form and when revising existing forms. Include only those criteria that an objective panel of your peers would agree have a definite relationship to the job.

Rating Methodology

An appraisal form must contain a **rating methodology** for recording and quantifying an employee's performance. There are a number of different ways of doing this. Numerical rating scales ranging from 1 to 5 or 1 to 10 are common. Continuums ranging from *poor* to *outstanding* are widely used. Some take the simple approach and use just two ratings for each criterion: *satisfactory* and *needs improvement*. Another approach is to follow each criterion with a set of several descriptive statements. The supervisor circles the statement that comes closest to describing the employee's performance for that category.

For example, if the criterion statement concerns quality of work, it might be accompanied by statements such as the following:

- Always meets or exceeds standards
- Usually meets or exceeds standards
- Occasionally below standards
- Does not meet standards

Regardless of the rating system used, make sure that the approach is simple, easy to understand, and lends itself to factual documentation. Subjectivity should be avoided, even in the comments section.

Comments Section

The **comments section** gives supervisors an opportunity to expound on why a certain performance criterion shows a low rating, make suggestions for improvement, comment on strengths, or clarify ratings when necessary. Caution is encouraged when adding written comments to an appraisal form. As with the performance criteria, supervisors should have factual documentation to back up their comments.

Employee's Response Section

The **employee's response section** is not always included on appraisal forms, but it should be. This section gives employees an opportunity to respond to an appraisal and make their response a matter of record. Supervisors should work with employees to reach agreement on the evaluation. However, there will be times when the supervisor and the employee cannot agree. Having a response section for the employee can keep such situations from developing into a problem. Giving employees the opportunity to state their disagreement in writing tells them their point of view is important and that their exception has been noted.

Supervisor's Report Section

In the **supervisor's report section**, the supervisor has the final word. In this section supervisors can comment on the employee's response to the evaluation and his or her attitude. Does the employee agree or disagree with selected ratings? What was his or her attitude toward the evaluation process? Did the employee take a positive approach? Will the employee make a sincere effort to improve? Supervisors answer questions such as these in this section. Figure 7—1 is an example of a performance appraisal form used in a modern work setting.

=========== APPLICATION AND DISCUSSION ==============

Identify an organization that will cooperate with you in completing this activity. Secure a copy of the organization's various performance appraisal forms.

- ■ Analyze the performance appraisal forms. Are the performance criteria appropriate? What type of rating methodology is used? Is there a comments section? Is there an employee-response section?
- ■ How would you improve these performance appraisal forms?

KEEPING PERFORMANCE APPRAISALS CONSISTENT AND OBJECTIVE

Objectivity is important when conducting performance appraisals. This is easier to say than it is to accomplish, since people are not objective by nature. However, objectivity is the best approach both from a legal perspective and from the perspective of improved performance. Strategies that will help enhance objectivity are summarized in the paragraphs that follow.

Review Performance Standards

Appraisal instruments typically use rating scales to describe **performance standards** (i.e., satisfactory/unsatisfactory, above average, average, below average; 0–5; etc.). Before assigning a rating, establish clearly in your mind what each option on the rating scale means to you. Share your interpretation with every employee you plan to evaluate. Make sure all employees understand how you interpret the rating scale. Then stick to this interpretation.

Performance Evaluation

Employee: _____   Division: _____   Date: _____
Job Title: _____   Dept: _____

Rating Factors (Use any rating number from one to the maximum shown in each category)

Quality of Work

3	6	9	12	15	Rating
Almost always makes errors. Quality is someone else's responsibility.	Quite often makes errors. Quality not important; just show.	Makes errors, but equals job standards. Employee is quality oriented.	Makes few errors, has high accuracy. Makes quality and productivity suggestions.	Almost never makes errors. Actively participates in performance enhancement activities.	_____

Comments:

Quantity of Work

3	6	9	12	15	Rating
Almost never meets standards.	Quite often doesn't meet standards.	Volume of work is satisfactory.	Quite often produces more than required.	Always exceeds standards; exceptionally productive.	_____

Comments:

Job Knowledge

3	6	9	12	15	Rating
Inadequate	Requires considerable assistance/ training.	Adequate grasp of essentials; some assistance required.	Knowledge thorough enough to perform without assistance.	Expert in all phases of work expected	_____

Comments:

Attendance/Punctuality

3	6	9	12	15	Rating
Excessively absent or tardy.	Frequently absent or tardy.	Occasionally absent or tardy. No uncompensated time.	Infrequently absent or tardy. No uncompensated time. Has accumulated sick leave and vacation.	Almost never absent or tardy. Never abuses sick leave or vacation.	_____

Comments:

Initiative

3	6	9	12	15	Rating
Requires constant supervision. No self-improvement.	Too frequently requires supervision. Little self-improvement	Requires average supervision. Some self-education.	Works independently with limited supervision. Takes courses, reads books pertaining to job improvement.	Consistent self-starter. Needs minimal supervision. Participates in college classes.	_____

Comments:

Appearance

3	6	9	12	15	Rating
Unacceptable; offensive.	Poor, careless in appearance.	Adequate for position.	Good; usually neat and clean.	Excellent; Always neat and clean.	_____

Comments:

Total Performance Rating: _____

Figure 7–1
Sample performance evaluation

Base Ratings on Facts

Do not assign a rating for a given criterion unless you have actual evidence on which to base the rating. Documentation is just as important with high ratings as it is with low ratings. One of the surest ways to ensure objectivity in performance evaluations is to base ratings on facts. If the facts are not available, respond with the phrase "insufficient

Overall Evaluation

Total Performance Rating

( ) Does not meet standards. (0-50)	( ) Partially meets standards. (51-70)	( ) Meets standards. (71-84)	( ) Exceeds standards (85-94)	( ) Always exceeds standards. (95-100)

Performance Improvement

What are employee's specific strengths, including training received?

_____

_____

_____

_____

What are specific recommendations that can improve the employee's performance, including training recommendations?

_____

_____

_____

_____

Use This Space for Additional Comments if Needed

Certification of Rater:	I hereby certify that this evaluation constitutes my best judgment of the performance of this employee and is based on personal observations and knowledge of the employee's work.
	Signature: _____ Date: _____
Certification of Employee:	I hereby certify that I have personally reviewed this evaluation.
	Signature: _____ Date: _____

information." But do not do this to avoid assigning a rating. If you do not have the facts for this rating period, make sure you get them before the next one.

Avoid Personality Bias

It is difficult to be impartial when evaluating people who are different. Correspondingly, there is a natural human tendency to rate those who are like us more highly. This tendency is known as **personality bias**. Keep personality bias in mind when conducting performance appraisals. Before assigning a rating, ask yourself, "Is this rating influenced in either direction by personality factors?" It should not be.

Avoid Extremes in Assigning Ratings

Some supervisors develop reputations as tough evaluators; others are known as soft touches. Either extreme should be avoided. If supervisors develop a reputation regarding performance appraisals, it should be one of fairness and objectivity. If you find your natural tendency is toward either extreme, be conscious of the fact and work to overcome the tendency.

Avoid the Halo Effect

The **halo effect** is a phenomenon that can occur when an employee's strong points cause you to overlook weak points. It happens like this. An employee has a couple of strong qualities that are important to you and that you rate highly. By focusing on these strengths you may rate the employee higher than he or she deserves in other areas. When assigning ratings, be cognizant of the halo effect.

Avoid Pecking Order Bias

In any organization there is a pecking order; that is, some jobs are more important to the supervisor than others. Since this is the case, supervisors sometimes rate employees in the more important jobs higher than those in the less important jobs, a problem referred to as a **pecking order bias.** Be conscious of it when assessing ratings. You are not rating jobs as to their relative importance, but employees as to their performance in their respective jobs. There should be no relationship between ratings in a job and the relative importance of the job. More important employees should be rewarded with higher wages, not inflated performance appraisals.

=== APPLICATION AND DISCUSSION ===

Pierce LaMarche does not like to evaluate the performance of his direct reports. In fact, he dreads it. He likes to give high ratings, but hates to give low ratings. He rarely documents performance. He even has trouble remembering when its time to rate employees. His usual response is to rate a couple of employees who are especially important to him high and give everyone else "average" ratings.

- What types of problems do you think LaMarche's team experiences after each performance appraisal period?
- What specific strategies can LaMarche use to improve his performance appraisals?

CONDUCTING THE APPRAISAL INTERVIEW

The **appraisal interview** is an important part of the appraisal process, perhaps the most important. In this step the supervisor shares the results shown on the appraisal form with the employee. This serves several vitally important purposes including communication, feedback, counseling, and planning for improvement (Figure 7–2).

Communication

If not handled properly, performance appraisal interviews can become contentious. Employees or supervisors can become angry. Employees might question ratings and

Figure 7–2
Four main purposes of
performance appraisals

make it difficult for supervisors to justify them. This potential for conflict can lead supervisors to do such things as give the completed appraisal form to the employee and leave
without any discussion or, worse yet, to send it through interoffice mail. Employees are
expected to read, sign, and return the form. This approach is more likely to lead to conflict than avoid it. The reason for this is lack of communication.

Communication is an important part of the appraisal interview. Employees need to
know not just how they have been rated, but why. On a higher level, they need to fully
understand the purpose of the performance appraisal. In addition, employees should be
given an opportunity to question, comment, explain, and generally share their views. All
of these things are part of the communication aspect of performance appraisals and they
happen during the appraisal interview.

Feedback

The appraisal interview allows supervisors to give employees specific **feedback** about
goals for improvement set during the last performance appraisal. It also gives employees
opportunities to give feedback concerning how the supervisor has helped or hindered
them in their improvement efforts. Two-way feedback is an important aspect of the
appraisal interview. It is fundamental to improved performance.

Counseling

Counseling employees is an important responsibility of supervisors. One of the most
opportune times for counseling is during the appraisal interview. In this context, **counseling** should be viewed as helping employees take a positive, mature approach in doing
their jobs and toward continually improving their performance. Supervisors should keep
in mind that the most important counseling skill is listening. Be a good listener during
the appraisal interview. Practice until the following strategies become habitual:

- Concentrate on what the employee says (verbally and nonverbally). Do not let your
  mind wander.
- Maintain eye contact with the employee.
- Continue to listen even if you do not agree with what the employee is saying.
- Let the employee say what is on his or her mind without interrupting, giving nega-
  tive nonverbal cues, or glancing at your watch.

- Follow the employee's train of thought. Do not jump ahead to where you think he or she is heading.
- When the employee has had his or her say, paraphrase what has been said, and repeat it back. This will show the employee you heard what was said.

Planning for Improvement

Supervisors should not unilaterally set goals for improvement for employees, nor should employees set their own. **Planning for improvement** should be a participatory process. Goals for improvement are more likely to be accomplished when they are mutually set by the supervisor and the employees. In addition, when supervisors and employees work together, the goals they set are more likely to be the right goals. The appraisal interview is the most appropriate occasion for mutually setting goals for improvement.

═══════ APPLICATION AND DISCUSSION ═══════

Valerie Coronita supervises seven employees. She has completed their performance appraisals for this evaluation period and has scheduled the appraisal interviews. Coronita expects all of the interviews to go well except one; and she dreads this one. Maury Extrell's performance has been mediocre during the current evaluation period. He is going to have to make improvements in several areas. Coronita has scheduled Extrell's interview first to get it out of the way.

- Put yourself in Valerie Coronita's place. What are some of the reasons you think she is dreading her interview with Maury Extrell?
- Explain in detail how you would handle this appraisal interview.

FACILITATING THE APPRAISAL INTERVIEW

This section presents several strategies supervisors can use to improve the effectiveness of the appraisal interview. These strategies will help supervisors and employees work together so that the interview is a positive experience for both.

Explain the Purpose of the Performance Appraisal

Do not assume that even the most experienced employees understand the purpose of performance appraisals. Begin the interview with a brief review of its purpose. Give employees an opportunity to share their thoughts and concerns. Take a positive attitude toward the process and stress its positive outcomes.

Discuss the Ratings

The purpose of the interview is to share the results of the appraisal. Do not prolong the employee's suspense; get right to it. Share the results openly and in a straightforward manner. A question often asked by supervisors at this point is, "Should I discuss strengths first or weaknesses?" There are proponents of both approaches. One side recommends building employees up with the positive before discussing the negative. The other side recommends getting the negative out of the way first so that the interview concludes on a positive note. Another point of view recommends intermixing the comments so that a negative is always followed by a positive. Perhaps the best advice for supervisors is to select the approach that seems to work best with the individual employee. This may take some experimenting, but over time supervisors will learn what works best with their direct reports.

Solicit Feedback

Although some employees will react angrily to ratings that do not meet their expectation, others will not react at all. It is particularly important to solicit feedback from the latter. Do not assume that no response means acceptance. Because some employees find it difficult to question the boss face to face, it is particularly important to draw out this type of employee during the interview. It is better to have employees express their opinions in the presence of the supervisor than over a cup of coffee with fellow workers. Solicit feedback and listen to it carefully.

Find Out How Employees Rate Themselves

Trouble is most likely to occur when the supervisor and employee disagree on a given rating. This is particularly true in the case of a criterion that is especially important to an employee. For example, if an employee is particularly proud of being dependable, but receives only an average rating on dependability, there is going to be a problem. For this reason some experienced supervisors ask employees to rate themselves at the same time as they are being rated. Then, during the appraisal interview, the employee and the supervisor swap evaluations. With this approach, the only criteria that need be discussed are those on which the supervisor and employee disagree. This can be an excellent way to enhance communication, and ensure that the supervisor does not inadvertently rate employees low in areas where they are actually strong.

Set Goals for Improvement

Since improved performance is the overall goal of the performance appraisal process, it is important to set goals for improvement in every category where the rating is lower than either party's expectations. Make sure goals are stated clearly, written down, and agreed to by both parties. Also, make sure they are realistic and measurable. Help employees understand that it is not always necessary to move from "needs improvement" to "excellent" in one evaluation period. Steady, incremental improvement may be more realistic. Finally, use a positive tone in setting improvement goals. For example, if an employee needs to become more independent, do not say, "I want you to stop coming to me for instructions so often." Instead say, "I would like you to work on being more of a self-starter." Then convert this into a measurable goal or goals.

Follow-Up and Feedback

The appraisal interview should be viewed as a beginning rather than an end. Once improvement goals have been set, supervisors should follow up and give employees continual feedback on their progress. This will help both parties stay focused on the goals they have set. It also shows that supervisors are interested in improved performance and want to help. Finally, follow-up allows supervisors to identify problems employees are having so that they can be dealt with immediately.

===== APPLICATION AND DISCUSSION =====

Try this experiment. Identify a friend or colleague with whom you interact frequently and who is willing to work with you. Evaluate this person according to how good he or she is at listening. At the same time, ask this person to evaluate him or herself. Make up a performance appraisal instrument that contains the following criteria to use in the evaluation:

1. When in a group of people, are you more likely to talk or listen?
2. When talking with someone, do you often interrupt?
3. When talking with someone, do you tune out and think ahead to your response?
4. When talking with someone, can you paraphrase and repeat back what has been said?
5. In a conversation, do you tend to state your opinion before the other party has made his or her case?
6. When talking with someone, do you give your full attention or continue to do other tasks simultaneously?
7. When you do not understand, do you ask for clarification?
8. In meetings do you daydream or stray from the subject?
9. When talking with someone, do you fidget and sneak glances at your watch?
10. Do you ever finish statements for people who do not move the conversation along fast enough?

- Compare your appraisal with that of your friend and discuss the results. Are there differences?
- Discuss the differences with your friend. Were your perceptions changed by the discussion?

GIVING CORRECTIVE FEEDBACK TO EMPLOYEES

If appraisals are to improve performance, supervisors must be skilled at giving corrective feedback to employees. The strategies shown in Figure 7–3 and described below will help make the process more positive and more effective:

- *Be positive.* Do not take an apologetic or negative approach. Be positive and say, "I have some feedback that might make you even more productive."
- *Be prepared.* Have your documentation readily available and be familiar with it. Also, focus only on the behavior to be corrected. Do not bring up old or undocumented problems.
- *Be realistic.* Make sure you are pointing out problems the employee is able to deal with. Do not hold an employee accountable for factors over which he or she has no control. Also, do not recommend corrective action the employee cannot possibly carry out.
- *Point out something positive.* Soften the blow for the employee by also complimenting some aspect of his or her behavior.

Figure 7–3
To be effective, corrective feedback must be given properly.

Checklist of Strategies for Giving Corrective Feedback

- Be positive
- Be prepared
- Be realistic
- Do not focus only on the negative
- Make feedback a two-way process
- Listen first

- *Make feedback a two-way process*. Let the employee have opportunities to give feedback. There may be factors with which the supervisor is not familiar. Encourage employees to give their side of the story.
- *Listen first*. Consider letting the employee give his or her side of the story first. If there are factors of which the supervisor is not aware, it is better to hear them early. This strategy may keep the employee from becoming defensive at the outset. If so, the interview will work better for both the supervisor and the employee.

APPLICATION AND DISCUSSION

Well, that didn't work," thought Monroe Dayton. He had just given an employee what he thought was constructive criticism. Rather than accept Dayton's feedback, the employee had gotten angry and stomped off. What Dayton had said to the employee was this: "If you want to go anywhere in this business, you've got to get better at processing claims. When I had your job I could process ten claims in an hour. It takes you twice that long. You need to get going!"

- Analyze Monroe Dayton's approach to giving constructive feedback. How would you have reacted if you were the employee in this situation?
- Explain how Dayton can get better results when giving feedback. How should he have proceeded?

LEGAL ASPECTS OF PERFORMANCE APPRAISALS

In today's litigious society, it is important for supervisors to be familiar with the legal aspects of performance appraisals. The **Freedom of Information Act** requires companies to approach performance appraisals carefully, objectively, and according to the book. Do supervisors need to be attorneys? No. But supervisors should be familiar with several important rules of thumb that will ensure that their performance appraisals meet the test of law. These rules are discussed in the following paragraphs.

Keep Comprehensive Records

It is important to document every rating on every performance appraisal, both good and bad. Keep accurate notes, mark dates on a calendar, and use these records when discussing performance appraisals with employees. Was an employee late several times? Counsel the employee and mark the dates on a calendar. Is an employee's attitude consistently negative? Counsel the employee and follow up with a memorandum that goes to the employee with a copy to his or her personnel file. **Documentation** takes time, but the resulting record keeping can protect supervisors and their companies if subjected to litigation. The following questions will help supervisors maintain proper documentation:

- Have you kept notes documenting your interactions with employees?
- Have you marked dates of meetings, conferences, and counseling sessions on a calendar?
- Have you kept copies of correspondence sent to employees?
- Have you retained evidence that documents good and bad behavior/performance?
- Do you have copies of previous performance appraisals showing goals for improvement?
- Have you periodically reviewed the documentation on file in the Human Resource Department?

Focus on Performance, Not Personality

Keep all comments, both verbal and written, objective and on a professional level. Criticize an employee's performance in a constructive way, but do not criticize the individual. Critiques that focus on performance are likely to pass the test of law. Critiques that appear to focus on personality or to be biased in any way may not. Good people can have a bad performance rating. Focus on the performance, not on the person.

Be Positive, Constructive, and Specific

Make sure that all comments, both verbal and written, are positive, constructive, and specific. Remember, the purpose of the performance appraisal is to improve performance, so appraisals must be positive. They should build employees up, not tear them down. Be specific in your critiques and in goals for improvement. Do not say, "This employee needs to learn how to get to work on time like everybody else." Instead say, "This employee should increase his on-time record to 98 percent." This is positive, constructive, and specific.

Be Honest and Treat All Employees the Same

Do not hold back out of fear of a lawsuit. Your job is to conduct a performance appraisal that will help improve the performance of individual employees and, as a result, that of the organization. Give an honest and straightforward appraisal of performance and make sure that you treat all employees the same. Playing favorites is an easy trap to fall into and a difficult one to get out of. If an appraisal is ever challenged by an employee, past appraisals as well as those of other employees may be examined. Supervisors who are honest, straightforward, and equitable are on solid ground legally.

Apply Objective Standards

The supervisor does not necessarily control the standards used in performance appraisals. However, by knowing that the courts expect objective standards, supervisors can at least let higher management know that potential legal problems exist if subjective standards are used. If an objective standard cannot be found for a given aspect of an employee's job, use a subjective standard (i.e., leadership, assertiveness, etc.), but give factual examples that illustrate the employee's shortcomings. For example, if a supervisor has an employee who lacks initiative, it may be necessary to comment on it as part of a performance appraisal. In such a case, do not say, "This employee needs to be a better self-starter." Instead say, "On the following occasions this employee failed to begin work until told to do so." Then list the actual dates this behavior was exhibited.

=========== APPLICATION AND DISCUSSION ===========

One of the more difficult challenges supervisors face when conducting performance appraisals is making their criticisms constructive and positive. This can be done, but it takes practice.

- Restate the following comments to make them more constructive and more positive:

  "John has a negative attitude about working overtime."

  "Mildred needs to be more productive."

  "Mark is late too often."

- Restate the following comments to make them focus on performance rather than personality:

"Jan is too chatty and talkative."

"Thomas is an introvert. He is not a team player."

THE SUPERVISOR AS A CAREER COACH

The most fundamental goal of the performance appraisal process is improved performance. When employees improve their performance, they win, the supervisor wins, and the organization wins. This is the rationale behind the philosophy that supervisors should be "career coaches" for their employees. The job of the career coach is primarily to offer direction so that the employee is able to grow on an ongoing basis.

Career management is the process through which employees take responsibility for continually developing their job-related knowledge and skills and for advancing over time. Career coaching encourages this process, thereby helping employees do a more effective job of helping themselves.

The following five-point plan can be used by supervisors to promote career management among their employees:

- *Assess*. Help employees get a clear picture of their strengths and weaknesses.
- *Investigate*. Help employees investigate all potential avenues for growth available to them within the organization (or outside the organization).
- *Match*. Help employees match their strengths and weaknesses with the appropriate opportunities available to them in the organization (or outside). Sometimes employees have to "go out to go up."
- *Choose*. Work with employees to determine if they have made appropriate choices.
- *Manage*. Help employees prepare and maintain a development plan that will result in the accomplishment of their goals.

APPLICATION AND DISCUSSION

Pam Tislecko is a good employee, but she is not happy. Tislecko has been in the same position for five years and feels "stuck." According to Tislecko, "I'm topped out. There is nowhere for me to go in this organization." Her low morale is beginning to spill over onto her teammates.

- How would you deal with the issue of Tislecko's low morale affecting other team members?
- Explain how you would use the five-point plan presented in this section to help Tislecko.

ON-THE-JOB SCENARIOS

1. Preston Manufacturing is a Department of Defense contractor. Its product line consists of airtight aluminum munitions containers of various sizes and configurations. The workforce consists of 150 employees. Key production employees are machinists and welders. CEO David Toomey likes to keep things simple. This is the reason he tried and discarded several performance appraisal forms he judged to be too complicated. In Toomey's opinion, a performance appraisal form should be easy to complete and easy for both the supervisor and the employee to understand. Out of frustration with the performance appraisal forms he had seen, Toomey decided to design his own. The result is a form that contains five simple criteria: (1) Attendance

record, (2) On-time record (also includes breaks and lunches), (3) Dependability of work, (4) Accuracy of work, and (5) Effort to improve performance.

- In your opinion, are there sufficient criteria to constitute a comprehensive evaluation? Why or why not?
- Would you add criteria? If so, what would you add?
- After completing a form with just these criteria, what would you do to get an employee to improve in each area?

2. The following scenarios simulate problems supervisors often face on the job. Apply what you have learned in this unit in solving these problems.

- You have rated an employee lower than she expected and, in spite of her protestations, you do not intend to change the rating. She is clearly upset. What should you do?
- You are having trouble being objective in evaluating an employee. You really don't like this guy. His work is mostly satisfactory, but he rubs you the wrong way. How can you perform an objective appraisal?
- During an appraisal interview you find your mind drifting. The employee has talked earnestly for five minutes, and you don't even know what she said. Before the next interview, you want to get focused. What should you do?
- A new supervisor has never conducted an appraisal interview. In an hour he will conduct his first. He is nervous and unsure of what to do. What advice or directions would you give him?
- Your company has been sued by a disgruntled former employee over performance appraisals in her personnel file. As a result, you have been asked to give a short talk to all supervisors entitled "How to Conduct a Performance Appraisal That Will Stand Up in Court." What pointers will you give your colleagues?

KEY TERMS AND PHRASES

Appraisal instrument	Job description
Appraisal interview	Objectivity
Career management	Pecking order bias
Comments section	Performance appraisal
Counseling	Performance criteria
Documentation	Performance standards
Employee's response section	Personality bias
Feedback	Planning for improvement
Freedom of Information Act	Rating methodology
Halo effect	Supervisor's report section
Improved performance	

REVIEW QUESTIONS

1. Explain the rationale for performance appraisal.
2. What is meant by effective performance appraisal?
3. List five criteria for a good job description.
4. Explain the supervisor's role in performance appraisal.
5. List the components that should be included in a performance appraisal instrument.

6. Explain four strategies for keeping performance appraisals objectives.
7. Explain the halo effect.
8. Explain pecking order bias.
9. What are the four basic purposes of the appraisal interview?
10. List five strategies for improved listening.
11. List and explain four strategies for facilitating the appraisal interview.
12. List and explain five strategies for ensuring that performance appraisals can pass the test of law.

CHAPTER EIGHT

Employee Complaints

LEARNING OBJECTIVES

After studying this chapter, you should be able to do the following:

- Explain why it is important to handle complaints properly.
- Describe the role of listening in handling complaints.
- Describe the role of questioning and confirming in handling complaints.
- List the steps in handling employee complaints.
- Describe how to handle habitual complainers.
- Explain how to involve employees in resolving complaints.
- Describe how to turn complaints into improvements.
- Know how to handle wage and salary complaints.

The process recommended in this chapter for handling employee complaints can serve three purposes. First, it can prevent complaints from escalating into problems. Second, it can help convert complaints into improvements. Finally, it can establish a mechanism to keep chronic complainers from damaging morale in the organization.

WHY COMPLAINTS MUST BE HANDLED PROPERLY

There is a saying, "Some employees aren't happy unless they are complaining." Of course some employees seem to complain habitually, and supervisors have to deal with them no matter how frustrating the process. However, most employees are not constant complainers. Complaints from most employees are evidence of a problem or a potential problem. To ignore them is to say, "I don't care about your problems," so complaint resolution is important.

> ***Complaint resolution*** *is the solving of a problem raised by an employee.*

Complaints *can* represent opportunities for improvement. The difference between a complaint being a problem or an opportunity can lie in how the supervisor handles it. Consequently, it is important for supervisors to take employee complaints seriously and handle them properly, even when they are from constant complainers.

========= APPLICATION AND DISCUSSION =========

June McCoy has been a supervisor for just six months. Before her promotion to supervisor, she had been the type of employee who worked hard and never complained. This is the type of employee she wants her direct reports to be now. In her words, "I don't whine and I don't like employees who whine." As a supervisor she refuses to listen to complaints from employees and is prone to "shoot the messenger" when employees try to complain. Consequently, her direct reports rarely complain.

- What is your analysis of June McCoy's approach to handling employee complaints? Is it a good or bad approach?
- Can you foresee any problems June McCoy might have as a supervisor because of her approach to handling complaints? If so, what are they?

ROLE OF LISTENING IN HANDLING COMPLAINTS

The first and most important step in handling employee complaints is to *listen* (Figure 8–1). No matter how rushed they may be and no matter how bogged down in the everyday details of getting the job done, supervisors should take the time to listen when an employee has a complaint. There are several reasons, all related to improving employee performance, why supervisors should listen to complaints:

- *The employee may just be frustrated and need an opportunity to vent.* In this case, a few minutes spent listening can get the employee back to normal and job performance will not suffer. On the other hand, angry or frustrated employees will not do their best work. Therefore, just listening can help maintain and even improve job performance.
- *The complaint might be evidence of a bigger problem or the potential for one.* For example, a complaint by one employee about a certain working condition might be evidence of dissatisfaction among a much larger number of employees. Listening in this case might head off employee/management problems.
- *The complaint might be the employee's way of pressing a hidden agenda.* A **hidden agenda** is a secret desire or goal an employee has but does not admit. For example,

Figure 8–1
Tips for listening to employee complaints

Listening Tips

- Maintain eye contact and assume a posture that says, "I am listening."
- Give the employee your undivided attention. Eliminate distractions.
- Do not interrupt except for clarification.
- Listen to what is said and what is not said.
- Read the employee's body language and tone of voice.
- Maintain a professional bearing. Do not become angry or hostile.
- Try to remember without taking notes.
- Paraphrase and repeat back to show you have heard and understand.

one employee's complaints about another employee might just be an attempt to cause that employee problems. By listening carefully, supervisors can identify hidden agendas and respond accordingly.

■ *The complaint might reveal a legitimate need for improvement.* This is particularly true when the complaint comes from a high-performing employee. When such employees complain about factors that are having a negative effect on the job, supervisors have an opportunity to make productivity improvements.

===== APPLICATION AND DISCUSSION =====

Cal Grant supervises a team of twelve employees in an organization that is fast-paced and busy. Consequently, his time is limited. Grant gives his direct reports an "open door" for making both suggestions and complaints. Unfortunately, he does not listen well. When an employee comes to his office to complain, Grant is prone to fidget, steal surreptitious glances at his watch, and shuffle the paperwork on his desk. Frequently, Grant will cut the employee off in mid-sentence and end the conversation by saying, "Alright. I see where you are going. I'll look into it." More times than not Grant draws the wrong conclusion when he cuts an employee off.

■ Analyze the listening skills of Cal Grant. What is he doing wrong? What advice would you give Cal Grant about how to be a better listener?

■ Assume you are Cal Grant's colleague. In a discussion about employee complaints, he asks you the following questions: "Why is listening to employee complaints such a big deal? I don't get it. Wouldn't it be better to use my time solving problems and making improvements?" What would you tell Grant?

ROLE OF QUESTIONING AND CONFIRMING IN HANDLING COMPLAINTS

In addition to listening, it is important to ask questions to clarify and enhance understanding and to avoid wasting time solving the wrong problem. Here are some tips for questioning a complaining employee:

■ *Ask questions for clarification.* If you don't understand a point the employee is trying to make, find an opening and ask for clarification. **Clarification** is the act of gaining a full and accurate understanding. For example, if an employee complains about the company's overtime policy, you might need to clarify whether she means there is too much or too little overtime.

■ *Ask questions to clear up inconsistencies.* **Inconsistencies**, differences between what the employee says and what the supervisor knows to be the case, can mean that the employee is frustrated and confused, or they can also reveal a hidden agenda or another unspoken problem. Therefore, it is important to clear them up.

■ *Ask questions to gain more complete information.* Is the employee skirting the real issue? Does he seem to be holding back? Probing questions may be necessary to gain complete information. For example, an employee who complains in general terms rather than giving specifics may have to be questioned to identify the real problem.

■ *Ask questions to determine what the employee would like you to do.* Does the employee want you to do something, or is she just blowing off steam?

■ *Paraphrase and repeat your understanding of what has been said and what action will be taken.* This will confirm that there is understanding.

===== APPLICATION AND DISCUSSION =====

Mona Desmond thinks she is a good listener. In fact, it is a point of pride with her. Employees often come to her with suggestions, complaints, and questions. In other words, Desmond is "approachable." However, in spite of her willingness to listen, Desmond frequently goes off in the wrong direction when it comes to acting on complaints and suggestions. Recently, an employee was overheard saying, "Mona Desmond listens, but I don't think she gets it."

■ Assume Desmond's problem is that she does not ask questions when listening to employees. What types of problems can you foresee happening as a result? How effective do you think Desmond is as a problem solver?

■ Have you ever had a conversation with someone and found that you did not understand what he was telling you or what he wanted you to do? Did you ask questions? If so, did the questions produce a better understanding?

■ Select a friend and have a conversation. Ask the friend to play the role of an employee who has a complaint and wants you to do something. Ask questions to clarify if necessary. At the end of the conversation, confirm your understanding by paraphrasing and repeating what has been agreed to.

HANDLING EMPLOYEE COMPLAINTS

It is important to have a structured procedure for handling complaints and to make sure that all employees are familiar with it (Figure 8–2). This will serve two purposes. First, it will reassure well-intentioned employees that their complaints will be given the attention they deserve. Second, it will discourage habitual complainers and whiners who simply use complaining as a way to get attention. The following **five-step procedure** is an effective way to handle employee complaints:

1. Listen
2. Investigate
3. Act
4. Report
5. Follow up

It is important to proceed through the steps in the order specified and to ensure that no step is left out. Each step in the process is explained in the following paragraphs.

■ *Listen*. This step was explained in the previous section; its importance is reiterated here. Remember, if you do this step well, the others may not be necessary.

Figure 8–2
Employee complaints should be handled systematically.

> **Five-Step Procedure for**
> **Handling Employee Complaints**
>
> 1. Listen
> 2. Investigate
> 3. Act
> 4. Report
> 5. Follow up

■ *Investigate*. During the listening session, you should have been able to form a thorough picture of the problem from the perspective of the complaining employee. However, every story has at least two sides. To **investigate**, talk with other employees to fill out the story. Talk with fellow supervisors to see if they have dealt with similar complaints and, if so, how they handled them. Talk with your supervisor to get his or her input and to clearly define your authority relative to the complaint. Investigating will turn off employees who complain simply to gain attention. Knowing that all sides will be heard is a deterrent to such employees.

■ *Act*. Once all of the pertinent information relating to the complaint has been collected, you can take the appropriate action: (1) correct the problem; (2) work with higher management to have the problem corrected; (3) hold the situation in abeyance while collecting additional information; or (4) take no action.

■ *Report*. It is important to **report** on the status of a complaint to keep the complaining employee fully informed as to what has been done, will be done, or will not be done. Reporting is easy when you can say the problem has been solved or will be solved. However, it can be difficult when you are forced to say that you do not intend to take any action. When this is the case, it is important to deliver the bad news in a way that does not damage the employee's morale or the supervisor-employee relationship. One way to do this is to put the employee's complaint in the context of the goals and the overall good of the organization. It is also important to thank employees for bringing complaints to your attention and to encourage them to do so in the future.

■ *Follow up*. The supervisor's job is not over once the reporting step has been accomplished. Regardless of the course of action taken and reported to the employee, supervisors should **follow up** periodically. By following up you can ensure that the good news you reported is having the desired effect or that the bad news is not having a detrimental effect.

===== **APPLICATION AND DISCUSSION** =====

You are the supervisor of a ten-person team. One of your most productive employees comes into your office and asks for ten minutes. He complains about the negative effect a new management policy is having on customer service. In desperation, he tells you, "If we don't get this policy changed, we are going to lose some of our best customers." Since this employee rarely complains, you believe his claim might be credible.

■ Explain how you would use the five-step model for handling this complaint assuming your investigation verifies the complaint.

■ How would your handling of this complaint change in each step of the model if your investigation reveals that the complaint is unfounded?

HANDLING HABITUAL COMPLAINERS

Even a well-structured process for handling complaints will not always do the job in discouraging **habitual complainers**, employees who complain constantly and about everything. This type of employee can present a difficult challenge for the supervisor. Here are some tips for handling habitual complainers:

■ *Do not give in to frustration*. This may be precisely what the habitual complainer wants you to do. Constant complaining is sometimes a sign of a deeper problem. The employee may be seeking attention, a special relationship with the supervisor, or any one of a number of items on a hidden agenda. Maintain your composure and stay with the process.

- *Ask the complainer to put it in writing.* When the habitual complainer is doing all the complaining and you are doing all the work, try turning the tables. Ask the complainer to give you, in writing, a detailed explanation of the problem. This approach will usually discourage the employee and cut the complaints down to those that are legitimate.

- *Confront the complainer with the facts.* At some point, the supervisor simply needs to confront habitual complainers with the fact that they complain too much. This should be done in an objective, professional manner. Avoid anger and judgmental statements. Point out that you appreciate the employee's input, but that he or she complains much more than other employees. Each complaint takes a significant amount of your time, and like the employee, your time is limited. You might even convey to the habitual complainer that your best employees are those who do all they can to solve problems first and then inform you of the solution, rather than those who just complain.

APPLICATION AND DISCUSSION

Invariably, supervisors will have an employee who is a constant complainer. Such people can take up an inordinate amount of a supervisor's time. This is why learning how to handle constant complainers is so important. Consider the following situation:

Mavis Stapleton complains all the time. She complains about work, about her husband, about her children, and about the weather. She practically "ambushes" her supervisor four or five times a day to complain. Stapleton's constant complaining is beginning to affect morale.

- Do you know or have you ever worked with a constant complainer? How did this individual's complaining affect you?
- If you were Stapleton's supervisor, how would you handle her constant complaining in a pro-active and positive way?

INVOLVING EMPLOYEES IN RESOLVING COMPLAINTS

If the entire team, not just one employee, has a complaint, the entire team should participate in resolving it. An advantage to involving employees in complaint resolution is that it multiplies the chances of finding an acceptable solution. However, to get employees to participate as a group, supervisors must first lay some groundwork. To prepare employees to be meaningful participants in complaint resolution, you will need to accomplish the following tasks:

- Ensure that employees know you value their participation and want their input.
- Ensure that employees understand the types of problems that are and are not appropriate for group participation.

Preparing employees to participate in group complaint resolution is half of the groundwork; the other half involves preparing for and conducting group sessions. Before scheduling a session:

- *Do your research.* Come to the meeting fully prepared and armed with information. If there is information of benefit to the entire group, copy it and provide copies to each participant at the beginning of the meeting.
- *Distribute an outline or put one on a flip chart or marker board.*

During a complaint resolution session, supervisors should accomplish the following tasks:

- *Set time limits* and hold all participants to them.
- *Listen* and encourage the other participants to listen.
- *Observe carefully.* Look for signs that participants understand or do not understand each other. Question as necessary to bring out additional information that will clarify.
- *Facilitate.* Draw everyone out to ensure maximum participation. Do not allow one or two employees to dominate the session.
- *Work for a consensus.* Then close the meeting by describing the action you will take to implement the group's recommendations. In subsequent meetings, give the group feedback about progress you have made.

=== APPLICATION AND DISCUSSION ===

Mandy Salter's team has seven members, and every one of them is upset about the new sick leave policy. Because they were all complaining about the same thing, Salter thought she would call a team meeting to deal with the situation. "Boy, was that a mistake!" thought Salter as she contemplated the debacle her team meeting had been. Everyone had talked at once, nobody would stick to the subject, and the meeting had gone on way too long.

- What did Mandy Salter do wrong?
- How should Salter have handled this meeting?

HANDLING COMPLAINTS ABOUT WAGES

Wages are likely to be a common source of complaints in any company. You will not be a supervisor long before an employee will come to you to complain about money. The same strategies used for handling any complaint apply in the case of wage problems. In addition, there are special strategies with which supervisors should be familiar:

- *Do not allow employees to draw you into* **comparison debates** (discussion in which wages are compared). Employees invariably discuss wages and make comparisons among themselves. As soon as employee X finds he is paid less than employee Y, there is likely to be a complaint. The supervisor's approach to such situations should be that individual wage rates are (1) confidential and (2) based on performance. Listen and let the employee state his case, but do not make or debate comparisons.
- *Do not discuss raises given to individual employees.* This is another case in which complaints are sure to arise. It usually happens like this. Jose and Marie, who are fellow team members, are talking during a break. Jose asks, "Did you get a raise this year?" Marie enthusiastically responds, "Yes! A good one—12 percent." Jose, whose raise was six percent, quickly finishes his coffee and marches straight to the supervisor's office. The supervisor should listen and let Jose blow off some steam, but she should not discuss anyone's raise with Jose except his.

- *Have a detailed knowledge of the wage levels and wage histories of all employees as well as the company's wage policies.* Be well enough informed to refute false claims or misconceptions. For example, if an employee demands to know "why Ethel makes twice as much as I make," the supervisor should know the salary schedule well enough to refute this claim.

=============== APPLICATION AND DISCUSSION ===============

Mark Spiceman has been a supervisor for just two weeks. Consequently, yesterday when Margaret Chase stormed into his office angry about not getting a raise, he did not handle it well. Spiceman verified that all of her teammates had gotten raises. He also discussed her salary in comparison to theirs. All of this had made Chase even more angry.

- Analyze Mark Spiceman's handling of this complaint. What did he do wrong?
- Explain how Spiceman should have handled Chase's complaint.

TURNING COMPLAINTS INTO IMPROVEMENTS

There is a natural human tendency to respond defensively to complaints. Supervisors must work to overcome this tendency for two reasons. First, complaints left unresolved may develop into bigger problems. Second, if handled properly complaints can be turned into improvements. All of the material in this chapter is intended to help supervisors turn complaints into improvements.

The most important step is deciding to take this approach. Once you have decided to view complaints as opportunities, follow the five-step procedure described earlier in this unit:

- Listen
- Investigate
- Act
- Report
- Follow up

There are no shortcuts. Undertake each step in the order specified and do so every time. Complaints are not always legitimate, but many that do not appear to be on the surface will turn out to be legitimate once you have listened and investigated. If a complaint is legitimate, act on it promptly, report results back to the employee, and follow up periodically.

An additional strategy that will help turn complaints into improvements is to maintain a complaint log. Log in every complaint that is acted on and show the final resolution. Complaints that result in positive changes such as improved productivity, quality, competitiveness, or morale should be given special recognition, as should the employee who originally brought the complaint. Supervisors who make up their minds to view complaints as opportunities; who learn to listen, investigate, act, report, and follow up; and who give appropriate recognition when complaints result in needed change will be successful in turning complaints into improvements.

=============== APPLICATION AND DISCUSSION ===============

As Myron Vermon listened, one of his direct reports lodged the following complaint. "The new software package is slowing us down. At first I thought it was because we had not yet learned to use the software well enough and that was part of the problem. But now we know how to use it, and I see the problem is the software. It's poorly designed and full of bugs. If we stay with this package, productivity is going to drop by 20 percent."

- Explain how Myron Vermon can use the five-step procedure to turn this complaint into improvements (assume the complaint is accurate and true).

- How would Vermon's actions change if his investigation revealed that the complaint was invalid?

ON-THE-JOB SCENARIOS

1. Everset, Inc.'s lunch period policy had been in effect for many years, but employees often ignored it. The policy allowed thirty-minute lunch periods, but employees often took more time and returned to work late. In an attempt to solve this problem, the company began requiring employees to punch in and out on a time clock. Angered by this decision, employees complained to their union, and the matter was referred to arbitration. Union representatives and the company attorney argued their respective cases.

   - If you were a supervisor at Everset, how would you have dealt with the employee complaints about the time clock?

   - What are some alternative solutions the company might have used instead of requiring employees to punch in and out on the time clock?

2. How would you handle the following situation? An employee bursts into your office, slams the door, and says, "I am tired of this place! It's so disorganized. It's a miracle we ever get anything done!"

3. An employee asks for an appointment to discuss a problem with you. She is calm and in control, but clearly something is wrong. Once in your office she says, "I just learned that John McCoy makes more money than I do. We both know I am a better technician than he is." How would you handle this situation?

4. Van Tram Ly is a constant complainer. He has just walked into your office with his tenth complaint of the week. How should you handle the situation?

5. Joan Gomez is one of your best employees. She rarely complains and when she does, it is usually legitimate. She has just informed you that the new four-day work week is causing morale problems among team members. How would you handle this situation?

KEY TERMS AND PHRASES

Clarification	Habitual complainers
Comparison debates	Hidden agenda
Complaint resolution	Inconsistencies
Five-step procedure	Investigate
Follow up	Report

REVIEW QUESTIONS

1. Explain briefly why it is important to handle complaints properly.

2. Give four reasons why it is important for a supervisor to listen when an employee brings a complaint.

3. What are the reasons for questioning employees who have a complaint?

4. Explain the five steps for handling employee complaints.
5. How would you handle a habitual complainer?
6. What are the steps for preparing employees for involvement in group conflict resolution?
7. Explain how to prepare for and conduct a group complaint resolution session.
8. How is handling a complaint about wages different from handling other complaints?
9. Briefly explain how you would turn complaints into improvements.

CHAPTER NINE

Conflict Management/ Workplace Violence

After studying this chapter, you should be able to do the following:

- Describe several causes of conflict in the workplace.
- Explain how people react to conflict.
- Demonstrate how supervisors should handle conflict.
- Explain how and when conflict should be stimulated.
- Demonstrate how to use communication in conflict resolution.
- Explain how to deal with angry employees.
- Explain how to overcome territorial behavior.
- Explain how to overcome negativity in employees.
- Describe how to reduce the risk of workplace violence.

Human conflict is normal and unavoidable in a highly competitive and often stressful workplace. One of the human relations skills needed by people in such a setting is the ability to disagree with fellow workers or customers without being disagreeable. However, even if most members of an organization have this skill, there is no guarantee that conflicts will not still arise. When people work together, no matter how committed they are to a common goal, human conflict is likely to occur. Consequently, supervisors must be proficient in resolving conflict. This chapter contains information supervisors need to know to be catalysts in resolving human conflict and preventing violence in the workplace.

CAUSES OF WORKPLACE CONFLICT

The most common causes of workplace conflict are predictable. They include those shown in Figure 9–1.

> **Workplace conflict** is what happens when a person's desires are frustrated or needs are threatened by another person.

Limited resources often lead to conflict in the workplace. It is not uncommon for an organization to have fewer resources (funds, supplies, personnel, time, equipment, etc.) than might be needed to complete a job. When this happens, who gets the resources and in what amounts? *Incompatible goals* often lead to conflict, and incompatibility of goals

117

is inherent in the workplace. For example, conflicts between engineering and marketing are common. The goal of engineering is to design a product that meets the customer's needs. The goal of marketing is to secure new contracts. In an attempt to win new contracts, marketing might promise a completion date that engineering cannot meet. The result? Conflict.

Role ambiguity can also lead to conflict by blurring "turf lines." This makes it difficult to know who is responsible and who has authority. *Different values* can lead to conflict. For example, if one group values job security and another values maximum profits, the potential for conflict exists. *Different perceptions* can lead to conflict. How people perceive a given situation depends on their background, values, beliefs, and individual circumstances. Because these factors are sure to differ among both individuals and groups, particularly in an increasingly diverse workplace, perception problems are not uncommon.

The final predictable cause of conflict is *communication*. Effective communication is difficult at best. Improving the communication skills of employees at all levels should be an ongoing goal of supervisors. Knowing that communication will never be perfect, communication-based conflict should be expected.

APPLICATION AND DISCUSSION

Jim Hansen and Juanita Garcia are both hardware repair technicians at Computer Dynamics, Inc. (CDI). They have worked together for three months, and things are not going well. In fact, they argue constantly. The conflict between Hansen and Garcia is having a detrimental effect on productivity and morale. They occasionally need to share one-of-a-kind tools, which usually ends up in an argument. Hansen likes to work slowly and has been heard to say, "Why rush? Repair two or repair ten. I'm paid the same." Hansen is happy as a technician and is not interested in promotions. Garcia, on the other hand, works hard to repair as many computers as possible each day. She is a single mother and needs more income. Garcia likes to talk over a repair job with Hansen before beginning her work. She also likes to solicit input from the computer's user before beginning her work. Garcia believes this saves time in narrowing down the problem. Hansen, on the other hand, does not like to talk with Garcia or users. He has been heard to snap at Garcia, "Are you going to fix this computer or talk to it?"

■ Analyze this case. What are the conflicts that actually occur or are likely to occur between Hansen and Garcia?

■ What are the sources of conflict between Hansen and Garcia?

(Use the checklist in Figure 9-1 to formulate your response.)

Figure 9–1
These factors cause conflict in the workplace.

> **Checklist of Common Causes of Workplace Conflict**
>
> - **Limited resources** (You have your needs and I have mine.)
> - **Incompatible goals** (I want this and you want that.)
> - **Role ambiguity** (Who is responsible for what?)
> - **Different values** (You and I have different beliefs.)
> - **Different perspectives** (You and I see things differently.)
> - **Communication problems** (What do you mean?)

HOW PEOPLE REACT TO CONFLICT

To deal with conflict effectively, supervisors need to understand how people react to conflict. A typical reaction to conflict is **competition** in which one party attempts to win while making the other lose. The opposite reaction to conflict is **accommodation**, in which one person puts the needs of others first, or lets them win. **Compromise** is a reaction in which the two opposing sides attempt to work out a solution that helps both to the extent possible.

Collaboration involves both sides working together to find an acceptable solution for both. **Avoidance** involves shrinking away from conflict. This reaction is seen in people who are not comfortable facing conflict and dealing with it.

In some situations, a particular reaction to conflict is more appropriate than another. Supervisors who are responsible for resolving conflict need to understand what is and what is not an appropriate reaction to conflict.

- Competing is appropriate when quick action is vital or when important but potentially unpopular actions must be taken.

- Collaborating is appropriate when it is important to work through feelings that are interfering with interpersonal relationships.

- Avoiding is appropriate when you perceive no chance of satisfying your concerns or when you want to let people cool down and have time to regain a positive perspective.

- Accommodating is appropriate when you are outmatched and losing anyway or when harmony and stability are more important than the issue at hand.

WHY CONFLICT RESOLUTION SKILLS ARE IMPORTANT

Regardless of whether employees accommodate, compromise, compete, collaborate, or avoid, they all become stressed over conflict. Conflict is a major cause of workplace stress. This is why it is important for supervisors to be skilled at resolving conflict. Workplace-related stress can have an adverse affect on the following:

- *Employee Performance.* Employees who become overly stressed will not perform at peak levels in terms of either quality or productivity.

- *Customer service/satisfaction.* Employees who are overly stressed will be unable to maintain the positive, helpful attitude needed to properly serve and satisfy customers.

- *Employee safety.* Employees who are overly stressed are more accident prone and as a result can be dangerous to other employees.

- *Employee health.* Overly stressed employees soon become sick employees. Stress can increase blood pressure and heart rate and produce gastro-intestinal problems such as ulcers.

- *Absenteeism and tardiness.* Overly stressed employees tend to be tardy and absent more often than the norm. Their absenteeism and tardiness can have a detrimental effect on the team's overall performance.

===== **APPLICATION AND DISCUSSION** =====

Cindy Andrews has twelve employees in the team she supervises. Two of them are constantly in conflict over almost any issue that comes up. They both have strong opinions, and neither is reluctant to share them. In addition, both employees are competitive by nature. At the other end of the spectrum, Andrews has two employees who go out of their way to avoid conflict, even when they are right. Andrews has seen both of these employees back down in team meetings at the first hint of a challenge to their ideas, which are usually good ideas worthy of consideration.

- What kinds of problems do you think Cindy Andrews might have in her team as a result of the competitive nature of two of her employees?
- What kinds of problems do you think Andrews might have as a result of the avoidance tendency of two of her employees?

HOW CONFLICT SHOULD BE HANDLED

Supervisors have two responsibilities regarding conflicts: **conflict resolution** and **conflict stimulation**. Where conflict is present, supervisors need to resolve it in ways that serve the organization's long-term best interests. This will keep conflict from becoming a detriment to performance. Where conflict does not exist, supervisors may need to stimulate it to keep the organization from becoming stale and stagnant. Both of these concepts, taken together, are known as **conflict management**.

The following guidelines can be used by supervisors attempting to resolve conflict:

- Determine how important the issue is to all people involved.
- Determine whether all people involved are willing and able to discuss the issue in a positive manner.
- Select a private place where the issue can be discussed confidentially by everyone involved.
- Make sure that both sides understand they are responsible for both the problem and the solution.
- Solicit opening comments from both sides. Let them express their concerns, feelings, ideas, and thoughts, but in a non-accusatory manner.
- Guide participants toward a clear and specific definition of the problem.
- Encourage participants to propose solutions while you listen carefully (Figure 9–2). Examine the problem from a variety of different perspectives and discuss any and all solutions proposed.

Figure 9–2
Good listening can help resolve conflict.

Listening Improvement Checklist

- Remove all distractions.
- Put the speaker at ease.
- Look directly at the speaker.
- Concentrate on what is being said.
- Watch for nonverbal cues.
- Make note of the speaker's tone.
- Be patient and wait.
- Ask clarifying questions.
- Paraphrase and repeat.
- No matter what is said, control your emotions.

■ Evaluate the costs versus the gains (cost-benefit analysis) of all proposed solutions and discuss them openly. Choose the best solution.

■ Reflect on the issue and discuss the conflict resolution process. Encourage participants to express their opinions as to how the process might be improved.

HOW AND WHEN CONFLICT SHOULD BE STIMULATED

Occasionally a team has too little conflict. Such teams tend to be those in which employees have become overly comfortable and the supervisor has effectively suppressed free thinking, innovation, and creativity. When this occurs, stagnation generally results. Stagnant teams need to be shaken up before they die. Supervisors can do this by stimulating positive conflict or conflict that is aimed at revitalizing the organization. A "yes" response to any of the following questions suggests a need for conflict stimulation:

■ Do team members always agree with you and tell you only what you want to hear?

■ Are team members afraid to admit they need help or that they've made mistakes?

■ Do team members focus more on reaching agreement than on arriving at the best decision?

■ Do team members focus more on getting along with others than on accomplishing objectives?

■ Do team members place more emphasis on not hurting feelings than arriving at quality decisions?

■ Do team members place more emphasis on being popular than on high job performance and competitiveness?

■ Are team members highly resistant to change?

■ Is the turnover rate usually low?

■ Do team members avoid proposing new ideas?

Each time one of these questions is answered in the affirmative, it indicates that conflict may need to be stimulated. It may be possible to have a vital, energetic, developing, improving organization without conflict, but this isn't likely to happen. Innovation, creativity, and the change inherent in continual improvement typically breed conflict. Therefore, the complete absence of conflict can also indicate the absence of vitality. Because this is the case, supervisors need to know how to stimulate positive conflict.

The techniques for stimulating conflict fall into three categories: improving communication, altering organizational structure, and changing behavior.

■ Improving communication will ensure a free flow of ideas at all levels. Open communication will introduce a daily agitation factor that will prevent stagnation and also provide a mechanism for effectively dealing with the resultant conflict.

■ Altering organizational structure to involve employees in making decisions that affect them and that empower them will help prevent stagnation. Employees in organizations that are structured to give them a voice will use that voice. The result will be positive conflict.

■ Changing behavior may be necessary, particularly in organizations that have traditionally suppressed and discouraged conflict rather than dealing with it. Supervisors who find themselves in such situations may find the following procedure helpful: (a) identify the behaviors you want employees to exhibit, (b) communicate with employees so they understand what is expected, (c) reinforce the desired behavior, and (d) handle conflict as it emerges using the procedures set forth in the previous section.

=========== **APPLICATION AND DISCUSSION** ===========

Perry Avant just transferred from another office in the XYZ Company to become the supervisor of a team of ten customer service specialists. XYZ Company is having customer service problems. Consequently, Avant is anxious to find out what is wrong and get it corrected. His first official act had been to call a team meeting to brainstorm ideas for improving the company's customer service rating. Unfortunately, the team meeting had been a waste of time. Nobody had any ideas for improvement. All team members thought everything was going just fine. Nobody had any interest in changing what they had been doing for the past several years.

■ Put yourself in Perry Avant's place. What is his problem here?

■ If you were in Avant's place, how would you handle this situation?

COMMUNICATION IN CONFLICT SITUATIONS

The point was made in the previous section that human conflict in the workplace is normal, to be expected, and, in certain instances, to be promoted. In managing conflict—which in essence means resolving conflict when it has negative effects and promoting conflict when it helps avoid stagnation—communication is critical (Figure 9—3).

The following guidelines can be used to improve communication in managing conflict:

■ *The initial attitude of those involved in the conflict can predetermine the outcome.*
This means if a person enters into a situation spoiling for a fight, he or she will probably get one. Communicating with and convincing either or both parties to view a conflict as an opportunity to cooperatively solve a problem can help predetermine a positive outcome.

■ *When possible, conflict guidelines should be in place before conflicts occur.* It is not uncommon for conflict to be exacerbated by disagreements over how it should be resolved. Before entering into a situation in which conflict might occur, make sure all parties understand how decisions will be made, who has the right to give input, and what issues are irrelevant.

■ *Assigning blame should not be allowed.* It is predictable that two people in a conflict situation will blame each other. If human interaction is allowed to get hung up on **assigning blame,** it will never move forward. The approach that says, "We have a

---

Communication Checklist

Communicate the following messages when handling conflicts or potential conflicts:

- This situation is an opportunity to solve a problem cooperatively.
- There are guidelines we will follow in handling this situation and these guidelines are. . . .
- We will not engage in blaming and finger pointing.
- "If the horse you are riding dies, get off and find another one." We will not cling to old ideas that are no longer valid.
- If you say you will do something, do it. Trust prevents conflict.

Figure 9—3
Conflict cannot be resolved without communication.

problem. How can we work together to solve it?" is more likely to result in a positive solution than arguing over who is to blame.

■ *"More of the same" solutions should be eliminated.* When a particular strategy for resolving conflict is tried but proves to be ineffective, don't continue using it. Some supervisors get stuck on a particular approach and stay with it even when the approach clearly doesn't work. Try something new instead of using "more of the same" solutions.

■ *Maintain trust by keeping promises.* Trust is fundamental to all aspects of total quality. It is especially important in managing conflict. Trust is difficult to win but easy to lose. Conflict cannot be effectively managed by someone who is not trusted. Consequently, managers in a total-quality setting must keep their promises and, in so doing, build trust among employees.

════ APPLICATION AND DISCUSSION ════

Marsha Boyington has observed an increase in the amount of conflict in her team over the past two months. People are arguing even about issues of no consequence. The type of conflict Boyington is seeing is not positive. In fact, it is petty and mean-spirited. She is concerned that a communication breakdown has occurred in her team, and she wants to fix it.

■ Decide how you would use communication to improve relations in this team if you were in Boyington's position.

■ Discuss your ideas with classmates or colleagues. Do they have any ideas you missed?

DEALING WITH ANGRY EMPLOYEES

It is critical that supervisors know how to deal with angry employees. Problems are never solved when employees or their supervisor are in a state of anger. Worse yet, angry employees can become violent employees if not handled properly. The strategies in this section are provided to help supervisors defuse angry situations before they erupt into even worse problems.

Behaviors to Avoid

When dealing with angry employees, supervisors might feel compelled to take immediate disciplinary action. While such action might be warranted, and while such action might certainly be taken at a later point, calming the angry employee should be the first priority. Supervisors must avoid the following behaviors when dealing with angry employees:

■ *Becoming angry and responding in kind.* Responding in kind to an angry employee is like pouring gasoline on a fire. Things are just going to get worse, and sooner rather than later. Getting angry and responding in kind is an option that people lose the minute they become a supervisor.

■ *Walk away or hang up the telephone.* When dealing with an angry person, there is always the temptation to think, "I don't have to put up with this," and just end it by walking away or hanging up the telephone. While this might forestall the negativity temporarily, in the long run it will probably make matters worse. It is better to deal with a negative situation immediately before it becomes even more negative.

■ *Point out that the employee is being rude.* Calling an angry employee "rude" will probably just make that employee even more angry. Remember, in a confrontational situation, few things sting worse than the obvious truth. This does not mean that the supervisor should ignore the anger. Quite the contrary. Anger should be acknowledged, but not by pointing out how rude it is. More about acknowledging anger later.

What Supervisors Should Do

The most important thing to remember when dealing with angry employees is to **remain calm and focus on the problem, not the anger**. Of course, this approach is easier to recommend than it is to do. The following strategies will help supervisors stay calm and focused when dealing with an angry employee.

- *Control your breathing.* In stressful situations, particularly those involving anger, breathing tends to become rapid and irregular, which can make you feel as if you are losing control. If this happens, take a few deep breaths and relax. This will help regulate your breathing and settle your nerves.

- *Look through the anger for the real message.* People who are upset to the point of anger often say things they don't really mean and express themselves in broad generalities as if everything and everyone is wrong. Supervisors who take such attacks personally are prone to become defensive or to want to fight back. Suppress this natural urge and try to see through the diatribe to what is really bothering the employee.

- *Be aware of your voice tone and body language.* A condescending, argumentative, or frustrated tone of voice can make an angry employee even angrier. Negative body language such as rolling the eyes, unbelieving facial expressions, or confrontational stances can also exacerbate the situation. Sit up straight, look the employee in the eye, and show that you are listening.

How to Calm an Angry Employee

The previous section provided strategies that help supervisors stay calm when dealing with angry employees. While staying calm yourself is critical, it's just the first step. The next step is to calm the angry employee. The following strategies can help supervisors calm angry employees so the problem at the heart of their anger can be dealt with.

- *Do not interrupt or disagree with the angry employee.* Sometimes the best thing to do with angry employees is to simply let them vent. Find a private place, let the employee vent, and just listen. Do not interrupt or disagree. There will be plenty of time to get the facts straight after the anger has subsided. If the employee begins to ramble and repeat himself, you can lead him back to the point in question by waiting for a convenient opening and then saying, "Excuse me. I understand your first two points, but I need you to clarify the third point for me." It might be that the employee has not actually made any points, but that doesn't matter. This technique will usually cause him to get focused. Often after letting an employee vent, supervisors will find that no action on their part is necessary. All the employee needed was someone willing to listen.

- *Paraphrase what the employee says and repeat it back.* This lets the employee know that you are listening to what she is saying. Nothing adds to the frustration of an angry employee more than not being listened to. Often employees become angry because they either feel or assume that nobody will listen to them. Another advantage of this strategy is verification. If what you paraphrase and repeat is not what the employee had tried to communicate, you will find out immediately, and you can ask the employee to clarify your understanding.

- *Acknowledge the anger.* A strategy that can be effective in calming an angry person is to simply acknowledge the anger. Just say, "I can see you are really angry about this." This is like holding up a mirror and letting the employee watch herself be angry. If we all had to look in a mirror when acting out anger, there would be fewer angry displays. In addition, acknowledgment shows understanding.

- *Encourage the angry employee to work with you in solving the problem.* This strategy does two things, both of them positive. First it subtly shows the employee that although you will work with him, you are not going to let him simply dump the problem in your lap, something disgruntled employees often want to do. Second, it moves the employee from the complaining mode to the solution mode. As soon as possible, without rushing the employee, you want to make the transition from complaining to solving the problem.

- *Arrive at a specific solution.* If the employee wants to do more than vent, it's a good idea to ask, "What solution do you propose?" If a supervisor solves a problem without involving the employee, the supervisor will be blamed if the solution doesn't work as planned. But if he is part of the solution, the employee has ownership in it and a corresponding incentive to ensure that it works. Before concluding a meeting with an angry employee, arrive at a specific solution, make sure the employee understands the solution, and make sure the employee has ownership in the solution.

=========== APPLICATION AND DISCUSSION ===========

You are a supervisor for ABC Company. While sitting at your desk returning telephone calls, an employee bursts into the office and yells "I'm sick and tired of this sorry excuse for a business. Nobody in this company knows what he is doing!"

- Explain how you intend to calm this employee.
- Once the employee has calmed down, how will you deal with the problem behind the anger?

OVERCOMING TERRITORIAL BEHAVIOR IN ORGANIZATIONS

Territory in the workplace tends to be more a function of psychological boundaries than of physical boundaries. Often referred to as "turf protection," territoriality can manifest itself in a variety of ways.

Manifestations of Territoriality

Territorial behavior can show up in a variety of ways in an organization. The most common manifestations of territoriality are as follows:

- **Occupation.** These games include actually marking territory as *mine*; playing the *gatekeeper* game with information; and monopolizing resources, information, access, and relationships.

- **Information manipulation.** People who play territorial games with information subscribe to the philosophy that information is power. To exercise power, they withhold information, bias information to suit their individual agendas (spin), cover up information, and actually give out false information.

- **Intimidation.** One of the most common manifestations of territoriality is intimidation—a tactic used to frighten others away from certain turf. Intimidation can take many different forms, from subtle threats to blatant aggression (physical or verbal).

- **Alliances.** Forming alliances with powerful individuals in an organization is a commonly practiced territorial game. The idea is to say without actually having to speak the words that "You had better keep off my turf, or I'll get my powerful friend to cause trouble."

- **Invisible wall.** Putting up an invisible wall involves creating hidden barriers to ensure that decisions, although already made, cannot be implemented. There are hundreds of strategies for building an invisible wall, including stalling, losing paperwork, forgetting to place an order, and many others.

- **Strategic noncompliance.** Agreeing to a decision up front but with no intention of carrying the decision out is called **strategic noncompliance**. This tactic is often used to buy enough time to find a way to reverse the decision.

- **Discredit.** Discrediting an individual as a way to cast doubt on his or her recommendation is a common turf protection tactic. Such an approach is called an *ad hominem* argument, which means if you cannot discredit the recommendation, try to discredit the person making it.

- **Shunning.** Shunning, or excluding an individual who threatens your turf, is a common territorial protection tactic. The point of shunning is to use peer pressure against the individual being shunned.

- **Camouflage.** Other terms that are sometimes used to describe this tactic are *throwing up a smoke screen* or *creating fog*. This tactic involves confusing the issue by raising other distracting controversies, especially those that will produce anxiety, such as encroaching on turf.

- **Filibuster.** *Filibustering* means talking a recommended action to death. This tactic involves talking at length about concerns—usually inconsequential—until the other side gives in just to stop any further discussion or until time to make the decision runs out.

Overcoming Territorial Behavior

Overcoming territorial behavior requires a two-pronged approach: (1) recognizing the manifestations described earlier and admitting that they exist and (2) creating an environment in which survival is equated with cooperation rather than territoriality. The following strategies can be used to create a cooperative environment:

- *Avoid jumping to conclusions.* Talk to employees about territoriality versus cooperation. Ask to hear their views and listen to what they say.

- *Attribute territorial behavior to instinct rather than people.* Blaming people for following their natural instincts is like blaming them for eating. The better approach is to show them that their survival instinct is tied to cooperation, not turf. This is done by rewarding cooperation and applying negative reinforcement to territorial behavior.

- *Ensure that no employee feels attacked.* Remember that the survival instinct drives territorial behavior. Attacking employees, or even letting them feel as if they are being attacked, only triggers their survival instinct. To change territorial behavior, it is necessary to put employees at ease.

- *Avoid generalizations.* When employees exhibit territorial behavior, deal with it in specifics as opposed to generalizations. It is a mistake to witness territorial behavior on the part of one employee and respond by calling a group of employees together and talking about the issue in general terms. Deal with the individual who exhibits the behavior and deal in specifics.

- *Understand "irrational" fears.* The survival instinct is a powerful motivator. It can lead employees to cling irrationally to their fears. Managers should consider this point when dealing with employees who find it difficult to let go of survival behaviors. Be firm but patient, and never deal with an employee's fears in a denigrating or condescending manner.

- *Respect each individual's* perspective. In a way, an individual's perspective or opinion is part of his or her psychological territory. Failure to respect the perspectives of people is the same as threatening their territory. When challenging territorial behavior, let employees explain their perspectives and show respect for them, even if you do not agree.

- *Consider the employee's point of view.* In addition to giving an appropriate level of respect to employees' perspectives, managers should also try to step into their shoes. How would you, as a manager, feel if you were the employee? Sensitivity to the employee's point of view and patience with that point of view are critical when trying to overcome territorial behavior.

===== APPLICATION AND DISCUSSION =====

John Markham supervises the most productive, most effective team of technicians on Microproduct Company's payroll. His team members are very proud of their record and reputation. Many are so good that the CEO of Microproduct Company would like them to serve as trainers and mentors for some of the company's less productive teams. This has caused Markham an embarrassing problem. His team members don't want to share what they know. In fact, they are being downright territorial about it. They are playing games such as *occupation, information manipulation,* and *strategic non–compliance.*

- What do you think is driving the territorial behavior for John Markham's team?
- Put yourself in Markham's place. How would you overcome your team's territoriality?

OVERCOMING NEGATIVITY IN EMPLOYEES

Negativity is any behavior on the part of any employee at any level that works against the optimum performance of the organization. The motivation behind negativity can be as different and varied as the employees who manifest it. However, negative behavior can be categorized as follows:

- Control disputes (Who is in charge?)
- Dependence/independence issues (I need/I don't need . . .)
- Need for attention/responsibility (Give me strokes/Put me in charge.)
- Authority (I am in control.)
- Loyalty issues (Support me no matter what.)

Recognizing Negativity

Supervisors should be alert to signs of negativity in the workplace because negativity is contagious. It can spread throughout an organization quickly, dampening morale and inhibiting performance. What follows are symptoms of the negativity syndrome that supervisors should watch for:

- **"I can't" attitudes**. Employees in an organization that is committed to continuous improvements must have can-do attitudes. If "I can't" is being heard regularly, negativity has crept into the organization.
- **"They" mentality.** In high-performance organizations, employees say "we" when talking about their employer. If employees refer to the organization as "they," negativity has gained a foothold.

- **Critical conversation.** In high-performance organizations, coffee-break conversation is about positive work-related topics or topics of personal interest. When conversation is typically critical, negative, and judgmental, negativity has set in. Some supervisors subscribe to the philosophy that employees are not happy unless they are complaining. This is a dangerous attitude. Positive, improvement-oriented employees will complain to their supervisor about conditions that inhibit performance, but they don't sit around criticizing and whining during coffee breaks.
- **Blame fixing.** In a high-performance organization, employees fix problems, not blame. If blame-fixing and finger-pointing are common in an organization, negativity is at work.

Overcoming Negativity

Supervisors who identify negativity in their teams should take appropriate steps to eliminate it. The following strategies can be used to overcome negativity in organizations:

- *Communicate.* Frequent, ongoing, effective communication is the best defense against negativity in organizations, and it is the best strategy for overcoming negativity that has already set in. Organizational communication can be made more effective using the following strategies: acknowledge innovation, suggestions, and concerns; share information so that all employees are informed; encourage open, frank discussion during meetings; celebrate milestones; give employees ownership of their jobs; and promote teamwork.
- *Establish clear expectations.* Make sure all employees know what is expected of them as individuals and as members of the team. People need to know what is expected of them and how and to whom they are accountable for what is expected.
- *Provide for **anxiety venting**.* The workplace can be stressful in even the best organizations. Deadlines, performance standards, budget pressures, and competition can all produce anxiety in employees. Consequently, supervisors need to give their direct reports opportunities to vent in a nonthreatening, affirming environment. This means listening supportively. This means letting the employee know that you will not shoot the messenger and then listening without interrupting, thinking ahead, focusing on preconceived ideas, or tuning out.
- *Build trust.* Negativity cannot flourish in an atmosphere of trust. Supervisors can build trust between themselves and employees and among employees by applying the following strategies: always delivering what is promised; remaining open-minded to suggestions; taking an interest in the development and welfare of employees; being tactfully honest with employees at all times; lending a hand when necessary; accepting blame, but sharing credit; maintaining a steady, pleasant temperament even when under stress; and making sure that criticism is constructive and delivered in an affirming way.
- *Involve employees.* It's hard to criticize the way things are done when you are a part of how they are done. Involve employees by asking their opinions, soliciting their feedback, and making them part of the solution. These are some of the most effective deterrents to and cures for negativity in organizations.

=========== APPLICATION AND DISCUSSION ===========

Sarah Striker had never seen a more negative bunch of people in her life. Finger-pointing, whining, complaining, and an overall defeatist attitude are all symptoms of what Striker calls her new team's "negativity disease." She has been the team's supervisor for just a week, but already Striker has had enough. She is tired of the negativity and intends to do something about it.

- Have you ever been part of an organization or a team that was infected by negativity? How did you feel about working in these conditions?
- Explain how Sarah Striker should try to overcome the negativity in her team.

WORKPLACE VIOLENCE

Workplace conflict taken to an extreme becomes **workplace violence**. Violence in the workplace no longer amounts to just isolated incidents that are simply aberrations. In fact, workplace violence should be considered a common hazard worthy of the attention of all supervisors. Consider the following facts:

- About 1,000,000 individuals are the direct victims of some form of violent crime in the workplace every year. This represents approximately 15 percent of all violent crimes committed annually in America.
- Of all workplace violent crimes reported, over 80 percent are committed by males; 40 percent are committed by complete strangers to the victims; 35 percent by casual acquaintances; 19 percent by individuals well known by the victims; and 1 percent by relatives of the victims.
- In 62 percent of violent crimes, the perpetrator is not armed; in 30 percent of the incidents, the perpetrator is armed with a handgun.
- More than 60 percent of violent incidents occur in private companies, 30 percent in government agencies, and 8 percent to self-employed individuals.
- It is estimated that violent crime in the workplace causes 500,000 employees to miss 1,751,000 days of work annually, or an average of 3.5 days per incident. This missed work equates to approximately $55,000,000 in lost wages.

Rights of Violent Employees

It may seem odd to be concerned about the rights of employees who commit violent acts on the job. After all, logic suggests that in such situations the only concern would be the protection of other employees. However, even violent employees have rights. Remember, the first thing that law enforcement officers must do after taking criminals into custody is to read them their rights. This does not mean that an employer cannot take the immediate action necessary to prevent a violent act or the recurrence of such an act. In fact, failure to act prudently in this regard can subject an employer to charges of negligence. However, before taking long-term action that will adversely affect the violent individual's employment, supervisors should follow applicable laws, contracts, policies, and procedures. Failure to do so can exacerbate an already difficult situation.

In addition to complying with all applicable laws, policies, and procedures, it is also important to apply these *consistently* when dealing with violent employees. Dealing with one violent employee one way while dealing with another in a different way puts the employer at a legal disadvantage. Consequently, it is important for supervisors to be prepared to deal both promptly and properly with violent employees.

Employee Liability for Workplace Violence

Having to contend with the rights of both violent employees and their co-workers, supervisors often feel as if they are caught between a rock and a hard place. Fortunately, the situation is less bleak than it may first appear due primarily to the **exclusivity provision** of workers' compensation laws. This provision makes workers' compensation the employee's exclusive remedy for injuries that are work-related. This means that even in cases of workplace violence, as long as the violence occurs within the scope of the victim's employment, the employer is protected from civil lawsuits and the excessive jury verdicts that have become so common.

The key to enjoying the protection of the exclusivity provision of workers' compensation laws lies in determining that violence-related injuries are within the scope of the victim's employment—a more difficult undertaking than one might expect. For example, if the violent act occurred at work but resulted from a non-work-related dispute, does the exclusivity provision apply? What if the dispute was work-related, but the violent act occurred away from the workplace?

Making Work-Related Determinations

The following guidelines can be used for categorizing an injury as being work-related:

1. If the violent act occurred on the employer's premises, it is considered an on-the-job event if one of the following criteria apply:
   - The victim was engaged in work activity, apprenticeship, or training.
   - The victim was on a break, in hallway, restrooms, cafeteria, or storage areas.
   - The victim was in the employer's parking lot while working, arriving at, or leaving work.

2. If the violent act occurred off the employer's premises, it is still considered an on-the-job event if one of the following criteria apply:
   - The victim was working for pay or compensation at the time, including working at home.
   - The victim was working as a volunteer, emergency services worker, law enforcement officer, or firefighter.
   - The victim was working in a profit-oriented family business, including farming.
   - The victim was traveling on business, including to and from customer-business contacts.
   - The victim was engaged in work activity in which the vehicle is part of the work environment (e.g., taxi driver, truck driver, and so on).

=== APPLICATION AND DISCUSSION ===

A man walks into an office and asks to see his wife. He is well known to you and other employees. Consequently, he is allowed into her work area without an escort. As soon as he sees his wife, he pulls out a gun, shoots her, two other employees, and himself.

- Is this an on-the-job event?
- Would it be an on-the-job event if this man shot his wife right after she walked off company property to her car across the street?

REDUCING THE RISK

The checklist in Figure 9-4 can be used by employers to reduce the risk of workplace violence in their facilities. A comprehensive violence prevention program has the following elements:

- Natural surveillance
- Control of access

Checklist for Risk Reduction—Workplace Violence

- Identify high-risk areas and make them visible. Secluded areas invite violence.
- Install good lighting in parking lots and inside all buildings.
- Minimize the handling of cash by employees and the amount of cash available on the premises.
- Install silent alarms and surveillance cameras where appropriate.
- Control access to all buildings (employee badges, visitor check-in/out procedure, visitor passes, etc.).
- Discourage working alone, particularly late at night.
- Provide training in conflict resolution/non-violence as part of a mandatory employee orientation.
- Conduct background checks before hiring new employees.
- Train employees how to handle themselves and respond when a violent act occurs on the job.
- Establish policies that establish ground rules for employee behavior/responses in threatening or violent situations.
- Nurture a positive, harmonious work environment.
- Encourage employees to report suspicious individuals and activities or potentially threatening situations.
- Deal with allegations of harassment or threatened violence promptly before the situation escalates.
- Take threats seriously and act appropriately.
- Adopt a *zero-tolerance* policy toward threatening or violent behavior.
- Establish a *violence hot line* so that employees can report potential problems anonymously.
- Establish a *threat-management* team with responsibility for preventing and responding to violence.
- Establish an *emergency response team* to deal with the immediate trauma of workplace violence.

Figure 9–4
Risk reduction strategies

- Establishment of territoriality
- Activity support
- Administrative controls

Natural Surveillance

Natural surveillance involves designing, arranging, and operating the workplace in a way that minimizes secluded areas. Making all areas inside and outside of the facility easily observable allows for natural surveillance.

Control of Access

One of the most common occurrences of workplace violence involves an outsider entering the workplace and harming employees. The most effective way to stop this type of incident is to **control access** to the workplace. Channeling the flow of outsiders to an access-control station, requiring visitor's passes, issuing access badges to employees, and isolating pickup and delivery points can minimize the risk of violence perpetrated by outsiders.

Establishment of Territoriality

Establishment of territoriality involves giving employees control over the workplace. With this approach, employees move freely with their established territory but are restricted in other areas. Employees come to know everyone who works in their territory and can, as a result, immediately recognize anyone who shouldn't be there.

Activity Support

Activity support involves organizing work flow and natural traffic patterns in ways that maximize the number of employees conducting natural surveillance. The more employees observing the activity in the workplace, the better.

Administrative Controls

Administrative controls consist of management practices that can reduce the risk of workplace violence. These practices include establishing policies, conducting background checks, and providing training for employees.

APPLICATION AND DISCUSSION

Much can be done to reduce the potential for workplace violence by applying strategies such as those in Figure 9-4. Using this checklist, evaluate a workplace you are familiar with (a retail store, bank, office building, manufacturing plant, or college campus).

- List some actions this organization could take to reduce its risk of workplace violence.
- Discuss your list with classmates or colleagues. Make note of the recommendations as they relate to different types of organizations (e.g. retail store as compared with a bank, etc.).

CONTRIBUTING FACTORS

Another way to reduce the risk of workplace violence is to ensure that supervisors understand the factors that can lead up to it. These factors fall into two broad categories: individual and environmental factors.

Individual Factors Associated with Violence

The factors explained in this section can be predictors of the potential for violence. Employees and individuals with one or more of the following factors may respond to anger, stress, or anxiety in a violent way.

1. **Record of violence.** Past violent behavior is typically an accurate predictor of future violent behavior. Consequently, thorough background checks should be a normal part of the employment process.
2. **Membership in a hate group.** Hate groups often promote violence against the subjects of their prejudice. Hate-group membership on the part of an employee should raise a red flag in the eyes of supervisors.

3. **Psychotic behavior.** Individuals who incessantly talk to themselves, express fears concerning conspiracies against them, say that they hear voices, or become increasingly disheveled over time may be violence-prone.

4. **Romantic obsessions.** Workplace violence is often the result of romantic entanglements or love interest gone awry. Employees who persist in making unwelcome advances may eventually respond to rejection with violence.

5. **Depression.** People who suffer from depression are prone to hurt either themselves or someone else. An employee who becomes increasingly withdrawn or overly stressed may be suffering from depression.

6. **Finger-pointers.** Refusal to accept responsibility is a factor often exhibited by perpetrators of workplace violence. An employee's tendency to blame others for his or her own shortcomings should raise the caution flag.

7. **Unusual frustration levels.** The workplace has become a competitive, stressful, and sometimes frustrating place. When frustration reaches the boiling point, the emotional explosion that results can manifest itself in violence.

8. **Obsession with weapons.** Violence in the workplace often involves a weapon (gun, knife, or explosive device). A normal interest in guns used for hunting or target practice need not raise concerns. However, an employee whose interest in weapons is unusually intense and focused is cause for concern.

9. **Drug dependence.** Perpetrators of workplace violence may be drug abusers. Consequently, drug dependence should cause concern not only for all of the usual reasons but also for its association with violence on the job.

Environmental Factors Associated with Violence

The environment in which employees work can also contribute to workplace violence. An environment that produces stress, anger, frustration, feelings of powerlessness, resentment, and feelings of inadequacy can increase the potential for violent behavior. The following factors can result in such an environment:

1. **Dictatorial supervision.** Dictatorial, overly authoritative supervision that shuts employees out of the decision-making process can cause them to feel powerless, as if they have little or no control over their jobs. Some people respond to powerlessness by striking out violently—a response that gives them power, if only momentarily.

2. **Role ambiguity.** One of the principal causes of stress and frustration on the job is role ambiguity. Employees need to know for what they are responsible, how they will be held accountable, and how much authority they have. When these questions are not clear, employees become stressed and frustrated, factors often associated with workplace violence.

3. **Partial, inconsistent supervision.** Supervisors who play favorites engender resentment in employees who aren't the favorite. Supervisors who treat one employee differently than another or one group of employees differently from another group also cause resentment. Employees who feel they are being treated unfairly or unequally may show their resentment in violent ways.

4. **Unattended hostility.** Supervisors who ignore hostile situations or threatening behavior are unwittingly giving them their tacit approval. An environment that accepts hostile behavior will have hostile behavior.

5. **No respect for privacy.** Supervisors who go through the desks, files, toolboxes, and work areas of employees without first getting their permission can make them feel invaded or even violated. Violent behavior is a possible response to these feelings.

6. **Insufficient training**. Holding employees accountable for performance on the job without providing the training that they need to perform well can cause them to feel inadequate. People who feel inadequate can turn their frustration inward and become depressed or turn it outward and become violent.

The overriding message in this section is two-fold. First, supervisors should try to establish and maintain a positive work environment that builds employees up rather than tearing them down. Second, supervisors should be aware of the individual factors that can contribute to violent behavior and respond promptly if employers show evidence of responding negatively to these factors.

APPLICATION AND DISCUSSION

Jane Martin has never had any formal supervision training. However, she works hard and wants to do a good job. Martin observes other supervisors and questions them about how they handle situations. Unfortunately, Martin is inconsistent in her treatment of employees and is seen by some as a supervisor who plays favorites. One person who feels this way is Josh McClutosh, who is intensely fond of guns, knives, and other weapons. This concerns Martin, whom McClutosh once caught rummaging through his toolbox. An embarrassed Martin had said she was just looking for a tool she wanted to borrow. McClutosh let the incident go, but relations between him and Martin have become tense.

- Analyze this situation. Do you have any concerns about the potential for workplace violence? If so, what are they and why?
- How do you think Jane Martin should have handled this situation?

Rules of Thumb for Supervisors

Supervisors can play a pivotal role in preventing workplace violence. The following rules of thumb will enhance the effectiveness of supervisors in this regard:

- *Don't* try to diagnose the personal, emotional, or psychological problems of employees.
- *Don't* discuss an employee's drinking unless it occurs on the job. Restrict comments to performance.
- *Don't* preach to employees. Counsel employees about attendance, tardiness, and job performance, *not* about how they should live their lives.
- *Don't* cover up for employees or make excuses for inappropriate behavior. Misguided kindness may allow problems to escalate and get out of hand.
- *Don't* create jobs to get problem employees out of the way. Stockpiling an employee simply gives him or her more time to brood and to allow resentment to build.
- *Don't* ignore the warning signs explained earlier. The problems that they represent will not simply go away. Sooner or later, they will have to be handled. Sooner is better. Later can be too late.
- *Do* remember that chemical dependence and emotional problems tend to be progressive. Left untreated, they get worse, not better.
- *Do* refer problem employees to the Employee Assistance Program or to the Human Resources Department.
- *Do* make it clear to employees that job performance is the key issue. They are expected to do what is necessary to maintain and improve their performance.
- *Do* make it clear that inappropriate behavior will not be tolerated.

APPLICATION AND DISCUSSION

Pete Petrocelli is not a happy person. Since his divorce, Petrocelli has become increasingly moody. At work he is either sullen and depressed or angry. He does not drink at the workplace, but his teammates can tell that Petrocelli is drinking heavily *after* work. Lately he has developed the habit of talking to himself. He does this out loud, but mumbles and growls so that his words are indistinct.

- If you were Pete Petrocelli's supervisor, how would you handle this situation?
- Discuss this case with classmates or colleagues and make note of any ideas they might offer or points they might make that you had not thought of.

ON-THE-JOB SCENARIOS

1. How would you handle the following situation? An employee bursts into your office, slams the door, and says, "I am tired of this place! It's so disorganized. It's a miracle we ever get anything done!"

2. An employee asks for an appointment to discuss a problem with you. She is calm and in control, but clearly something is wrong. Once in your office, she says, "I just learned that John McCoy makes more money than I do. We both know I am a better technician than he is." How would you handle this situation?

3. You have rated an employee in your unit lower than he expected, and, in spite of his angry protestations, you don't intend to change the evaluation. He is a good employee. He just needs to learn his job better. How can you calm him down and resolve the conflict?

4. The best way to describe the relationship between the design and manufacturing departments at Waverly Prestressed Concrete (WPC) is warfare. A typical conversation between the vice president for design and the vice president for manufacturing goes like this: "If you knew anything about manufacturing, you might design a product we can actually make every once in a while," says the vice president for manufacturing. "If you knew your job better, you could manufacture anything we design," responds the vice president for design.

   They are actually both right. The design and manufacturing departments need to work together closely and cooperatively as partners. The designers need to apply the principles of design for manufacturing (DFM) so that the product is not only functional but can be produced economically. Manufacturing personnel need to be a part of the design team so their input is part of the process from the outset. Unfortunately, both departments have built invisible walls around their domains and adopted attitudes toward each other that clearly say, "Keep off my turf!"

   What, if anything, should be done to improve relations at WPC? How can invisible walls be pulled down?

KEY TERMS AND PHRASES

Accommodation	Avoidance
Activity support	Blame fixing
Administrative controls	Camouflage
Alliances	Collaboration
Anxiety venting	Competition
Assigning blame	Compromise

Conflict management	Membership in a hate group
Conflict resolution	Natural surveillance
Conflict stimulation	Negativity
Control of access	No respect for privacy
Critical conversation	Obsession with weapons
Depression	Occupation
Dictatorial supervision	Partial, inconsistent supervision
Discredit	Psychotic behavior
Drug dependence	Record of violence
Establishment of territoriality	Role ambiguity
Exclusivity provision	Romantic obsessions
Filibuster	Shunning
Finger-pointers	Strategic noncompliance
"I can't" attitudes	"They" mentality
Information manipulation	Unattended hostility
Insufficient training	Unusual frustration levels
Intimidation	Workplace conflict
Invisible wall	Workplace violence

REVIEW QUESTIONS

1. List and explain five common causes of workplace conflict.
2. Explain the various ways people respond to conflict.
3. Explain the difference between *conflict resolution* and *conflict management*.
4. When should a supervisor stimulate conflict?
5. How would a supervisor use communication to prevent workplace conflict?
6. When dealing with angry employees there are certain things supervisors should not do. What are they? What things *should* supervisors do?
7. Explain how to calm an angry employee.
8. List and explain five manifestations of territoriality.
9. Describe five strategies supervisors can use to overcome territorial behavior.
10. What are the symptoms of negativity in an organization?
11. What can supervisors do to overcome negativity in their teams?
12. Explain why it is important for supervisors to remember the rights of violent employees.
13. Explain the exclusivity provision of worker's compensation laws as it relates to workplace violence.
14. Describe five measures for reducing the risk of workplace violence.
15. Explain five factors associated with violent people.

ENDNOTES

Annette Simmons, *Territorial Games* (New York: AMACOM, American Management Association, 1998), 6–7

CHAPTER TEN

Legal Issues: Discipline, Termination, Sexual Harassment, and Drugs

LEARNING OBJECTIVES

After studying this chapter, you should be able to do the following:

- Explain the rationale behind disciplining employees.
- Describe the fundamentals of disciplining employees.
- Describe the guidelines for disciplining employees.
- List the steps in the discipline process.
- Define *employment-at-will.*
- Define wrongful discharge.
- Define *sexual harassment.*
- Describe the EEOC guidelines on sexual harassment.
- Describe how to handle employees suspected of drug abuse.

Much of what supervisors do has legal ramifications. This is especially true when dealing with employee discipline, termination, sexual harassment, and drugs. This chapter provides prospective and practicing supervisors the information they need to do their jobs without causing legal problems.

DISCIPLINING EMPLOYEES: THE RATIONALE

> *Behavior that has a negative effect on the accomplishment of organizational goals—that is, behavior that is disruptive to the organization's performance—must be corrected. Dealing with such behavior is known as **disciplining**.*

Since some disruptive, nonproductive behavior is almost inevitable, supervisors should know how to discipline appropriately and properly. To do otherwise is to risk damaging morale, quality, productivity, and competitiveness (Figure 10-1). This is the rationale for disciplining disruptive employees. In addition, external discipline properly applied can lead to **self-discipline.** When this happens, the discipline system is a success.

Stated simply, a properly applied discipline system can lead to a self-disciplined team in which individual members know the organization's rules and regulations, abide by them, and expect co-workers to abide by them. The key to achieving self-discipline among team members is to do the following:

Figure 10–1
Failure to discipline appropriately can harm these important building blocks of competitiveness.

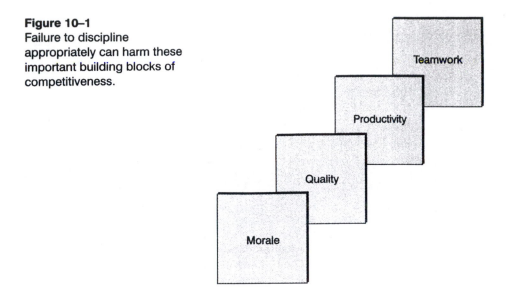

- *Personalize disruptive behavior* by helping team members see how the disruptive behavior of one is detrimental to all. Relate losses in productivity and quality to potential losses of customers and contracts. The obvious result is the potential for loss of jobs, raises, and the benefits associated with continued growth.

- *Apply discipline in a step-by-step manner.* People can be very forgiving in their attitudes toward offenders. Therefore, to dismiss an employee on the first offense is more likely to damage morale than to enhance it. Everyone is likely to err occasionally. Consequently, employees will sometimes respond to disciplinary measures applied to co-worker in the way they would want it applied to them. A step-by-step process that is reasonable and has built-in opportunities for improvement will be well received by most employees.

═══════ APPLICATION AND DISCUSSION ═══════

Mark Gracemon is not really a bad employee. In fact, at times he can be one of the most productive in the department. But he is a discipline problem. Frequently, Gracemon is argumentative and does not like to follow procedures or, in his words, "take orders." His behavior is causing morale problems.

- Explain how you would handle this situation if you were Mark Gracemon's supervisor.
- Discuss this situation with classmates or colleagues. Develop a group consensus concerning what should be said to Mark Gracemon and what should not be said.

FUNDAMENTALS OF DISCIPLINING EMPLOYEES

Regardless of the actual process set forth in company policy, supervisors should be familiar with some universal rules of thumb. Applying the following rules can enhance the supervisor's effectiveness regardless of the type of discipline process used:

- *Learn your company's rules and regulations and commit them to memory.* The company's rules and regulations translate company policy into expectations for everyday behavior. Supervisors cannot help enforce rules and regulations if they don't know them.

- *Get to know your employees and their personalities*. Prevention can be an important part of a discipline program. Supervisors who know the personalities of their employees can notice even subtle changes in behavior that might be evidence that a problem is brewing. One-on-one conferences with such employees might prevent problems that would require disciplinary measures.

- *Prevent discipline problems through education*. Make sure employees know the rules, understand the reasons for them, and know the consequences of breaking them. Rules should be posted, distributed, and periodically discussed, and the reasons for them should be emphasized. In addition, the consequences of breaking the rules should be discussed. There should be no surprises in a company's discipline program.

- *Set a positive example*. The "do as I say, not as I do" approach will not work with employee discipline. Supervisors must set a positive example of knowing the rules and abiding by them. If supervisors lose credibility, the discipline program loses credibility.

- *Consult the human resources department*. Never take disciplinary action of any kind without first consulting the human resources department. HR personnel can be "in-house consultants" for supervisors undertaking disciplinary measures.

APPLICATION AND DISCUSSION

You have just been transferred to a new location in your company and promoted to supervisor. That's the good news. The bad news is that you are about to inherit a "problem" department. Your predecessor was demoted as a consequence of his failure to properly discipline employees in the department you are about to take over. Through quiet, behind-the-scenes inquiries, you have learned that three employees cause 99 percent of the problems in the department. They arrive late, leave early, spread gossip, and complain constantly. On the other hand, all three have better than average work skills.

- Develop a plan for dealing with the discipline problems in your new department.

- Discuss your plan with classmates or colleagues. Revise your plan as appropriate based on this discussion.

GUIDELINES FOR DISCIPLINING EMPLOYEES

The following guidelines can be used for ensuring that discipline is effective, fair, and consistent:

- *Understand your authority*. Never undertake a disciplinary measure that is not within your span of authority.

- *Understand the rules and the reasons for them*. Employees want to know the parameters within which they must operate and the reasons for them. "Because I said so" is not a sufficient reason in the modern workplace.

- *Communicate the rules to all employees*. Do not assume they know. Post the rules, distribute them, and periodically discuss them.

- *Avoid negative comments about the rules*. If you don't believe in the rules, your employees won't either. Disagree with higher management in private if you must, but among employees, support the rules.

- *Follow the rules yourself*. Set a positive example and never veer from it. To your employees you should be the embodiment of the rules.

- *Never act on hearsay*. Before beginning the discipline process, make sure you have hard facts. Never act on **hearsay**, gossip, or second-hand information.

- *When rules are broken, act.* If discipline is to have the desired effect, it must be acted on. But this should be done in private. Publicity administered discipline will belittle the recipient and may damage the morale of fellow workers.

- *Discipline at the end of the day.* Employees who are disciplined probably will not be able to keep their mind on their work. Disciplining at the end of the day will give emotions time to settle down and the worker time to get his or her mind back on the job.

- *Document discipline problems and corresponding actions.* In today's litigious society, a good rule of thumb is to document, document, and document. In addition to alleviating legal concerns, documentation can help employees see where and when they have broken the rules.

- *Do not hold grudges.* Once disciplinary measures have been taken, the supervisor/employee relationship should return to normal. Do not hold grudges and do not allow employees to do so.

- *Give advance warning.* This is a matter of communicating the rules and the consequences of breaking them to all employees. There should be no surprises.

- *Discipline immediately.* For a discipline measure to work, it must be administered in a timely manner.

- *Be consistent.* Favoritism or even forgetfulness will rob the discipline program of its credibility. Consistency is fundamental to the success of the discipline process.

- *Be objective and professional.* Do not allow any step in the discipline process to be affected by personalities, yours or the employee's. Focus on the behavior, not the person.

APPLICATION AND DISCUSSION

An employee recently sued your company and won. The charge? Improperly applied disciplinary measure by a supervisor. The CEO wants to make sure that the mistakes of this supervisor are not repeated. You have been selected to serve on a committee to evaluate the situation and list the supervisor's errors. Here is what the court found.

The supervisor in question seemed to have a grudge against the employee (Burt Jones) that went way back. He overlooked tardiness in several other employees, but reprimanded Jones harshly in front of other employees for the same offense, an offense that had taken place more than a week earlier. The supervisor did not know if Jones had actually been tardy. He had only heard that this was the case from another employee in the department. When Jones had asked to see the company's policies concerning attendance, the supervisor had said, "You don't need to read the policy. Just do what I tell you."

- Analyze this case and list the supervisor's mistakes. Discuss your list with classmates or colleagues. Arrive at a group consensus concerning the list.

- Develop a report for the CEO that explains the supervisor's errors and how the situation should have been handled.

THE DISCIPLINE PROCESS

The best way to ensure that discipline measures adhere to the fundamentals and guidelines listed in this chapter is to have a step-by-step **discipline process** that takes all of these considerations into account. The following five-step approach to discipline accommodates all applicable guidelines. Steps in the process may be skipped in the case of serious or repeated offenses, but only as spelled out in company policy.

1. Informal discussion/counseling
2. Verbal warning
3. Written warning
4. Suspension
5. Dismissal

Informal Discussion/Counseling

Informal discussion/counseling should always be the first step in the process for first-time offenses or minor transgressions. It is intended to head off problems before additional measures are required. During an **informal discussion** the supervisor reminds the employee that a rule has been broken. No action will be taken. This should be explained to the employee. However, it is a good idea to mark the date and time of the informal discussion on a calendar or in a log book for future reference.

VERBAL WARNING

If the formal discussion does not stop the disruptive behavior, the next step is a **verbal warning**. Before issuing a verbal warning get the facts. What rule has been broken, when, and how? Who knows about it? Were there witnesses? Who is to blame? What action does company policy specify?

When you have all the facts, decide whether a verbal warning is in order (Figure 10–2). If so, bring the employee in for a private meeting, preferably at the end of the day. The following guidelines may enhance the effectiveness of the meeting:

Notice of Verbal Warning

Employee _____

Department _____

On this date (_____) you were issued a verbal warning for the following infraction:

_____

_____

_____

_____

_____

_____   _____
*Employee's Signature   Supervisor's Signature

_____   _____
Date   Date

*Acknowledges receipt. Does not necessarily indicate agreement.

Figure 10–2
It is important to document verbal warnings.

- *Have a definite objective and share it with the employee*. Let the employee know what rule has been broken and what the consequences of future infractions will be.

- *Have supportive material on hand and readily available*. Whatever evidence you have of an infraction plus any evidence of past problems (i.e., old warnings, material from a logbook) should be readily available to share with the employee.

- *Explain what rule has been broken and the reason for the rule*. Be specific. Keep the conversation objective, nonjudgmental, and professional. Give the employee an opportunity to offer input or to rebut any evidence you may have. At the end of the meeting, if you are still convinced a verbal warning is in order, issue it. A verbal warning should simply inform the employee that further rule breaking may result in specific consequences (as set forth in company policy). Document the verbal warning and let the employee know it has been documented. Before concluding the meeting, ask the employee the following questions:

  "Do you understand why you are receiving this warning?"

  "What can we do to prevent another infraction?"

  "Do you understand the consequences of further infractions?"

Written Warning

For most employees the informal discussion is enough to correct negative behavior. When this does not work, the documented verbal warning usually solves the problem. However, if it doesn't, a **written warning** is the next step (Figure 10–3).

Written Warning

Employee _____

Department _____

On this date (_____) you are issued this written warning for the following infraction:

_____

_____

_____

_____

_____

_____   _____
Supervisor's Signature   Date

I acknowledge receipt of this warning. However, my signature does not necessarily indicate agreement on my part.

_____   _____
Employee's Signature   Date

Figure 10–3
Sample written warning

Handle the meeting for giving the written warning in the same manner as the meeting for the verbal warning. But at the end of this meeting, give the written warning. Sign the warning and have the employee sign it. Both of you should keep a copy.

The employee should be required to acknowledge the written warning. The employee may or may not agree that the warning is justified. By signing, he or she is acknowledging only receipt of the warning, not admitting guilt. As with the verbal warning, the written warning should be specific. It is best to work with the human resources department in drafting the language that goes into the written warning.

Suspension

If verbal and written warnings do not work, the next step is **suspension**, a serious step that requires the employee to take a specified number of days off from work, usually without pay. Typically the supervisor will need the approval of higher management before suspending an employee. Before recommending a suspension, ask yourself the following questions:

- Am I overreacting?
- Am I acting in accordance with company policy?
- Has suspension ever been used for a similar infraction?
- Do I have sufficient documentation to stand up to a formal challenge?
- How will the suspension be received by the employee's co-workers?
- Does the human resources department agree with and support the suspension?

If you are not overreacting and your recommendation is clearly supported by company policy, you have a foundation for suspension. If suspensions have been used for similar infractions, a precedent has been set. If you have sufficient documentation to withstand a formal challenge, your recommendation is more likely to be well received by higher management. If the employee's co-workers will not react negatively to suspension, you have a strong case for moving forward. Finally, if the human resources department agrees that everything is in proper order, the suspension should proceed.

Dismissal

The final step in the discipline process is **dismissal**. When all other steps have failed to change the negative behavior, termination is an appropriate action. However, it should not be rushed into. Before dealing with the specifics of how to handle a dismissal, two related concepts must be explained: employment-at-will and wrongful discharge.

In the past employers could fire workers without cause or notice. This is no longer the case. Civil rights legislation provides a measure of protection for employees in protected classes and the Equal Employment Opportunity Commission (EEOC) can assist employees who feel they have been unjustly fired. Ethical reasons for the fair treatment of employees aside, susceptibility to charges of wrongful discharge is causing employers to look carefully at their dismissal practices.

The term **employment-at-will** means the employee works at the will of the employer and has no say in the matter, and no rights or protections. The concept of **wrongful discharge**, on the other hand, establishes that employees have rights relative to continued employment and should be protected from arbitrary and unjust termination.

This concept is supported by federal civil rights legislation and a steadily growing body of state legislation. The result is that employers throughout the country are being successfully sued by ex-employees who feel they were unjustly treated. The key to properly dismissing an employee is knowing why you can and cannot terminate.

An employee can be terminated for **cause**. Causes should be listed in the company's policy manual and supervisors should be familiar with them. Typical causes include the following:

■ Substance abuse on the job
■ Theft of company property
■ Fighting on the job
■ Insubordination
■ Sabotage
■ Sleeping on the job
■ Excessive absences and/or tardiness
■ Falsification of time cards or other records
■ Commission of a felony on or off the job

These examples and others may not necessarily be included in a company's policy manual, but supervisors should know what causes of termination are part of their company's approved and published policy.

It is also important to know reasons that *cannot* be used as cause for dismissing an employee. These reasons include the following:

■ Attempting to unionize fellow employees
■ Race, religion, gender, national origin, culture, or sexual preference
■ Pregnancy, childbirth, or related medical problems
■ Age (if the employee is between 40 and 70 years of age)
■ Refusal to perform unsafe tasks
■ Refusal to work in a hazardous environment
■ "Blowing the whistle" about health, safety, and environmental issues
■ Physical or mental handicap

These specific areas are protected by the same laws that prohibit discrimination in hiring practices (i.e., the Civil Rights Act and its subsequent amendments, the Pregnancy Discrimination Act, the Age Discrimination in Employment Act, the Occupational Safety and Health Act, and the Vocational Rehabilitation Act. As with hiring practices, dismissal practices should focus strictly on the job performance issues.

With this background, supervisors should be prepared to approach the termination step from a well-informed perspective. Supervisors rarely actually dismiss an employee. Typically, they recommend termination to higher management. Once approval to proceed has been secured, the employee must be properly informed. This may be done by the supervisor, by human resources personnel, or in an interview where both are present. Such procedures should be set forth in company policy and strictly adhered to.

If company policy requires the supervisor to conduct the dismissal interview, the supervisor should know the proper steps to follow:

■ Set up a private interview with the employee but have a representative of the human resources department present. This person can serve as a witness for both the supervisor and the employee.
■ Ask the employee to explain his or her side of the problem in question and listen carefully. This gives you one last opportunity to ensure that there are no relevant facts of which you are not aware. If proceeding is still appropriate, go to the next step.

- Explain that, based on the facts, you have decided to terminate the employee for cause. Explain the cause and present your documentation of the facts. Take full responsibility for the termination decision. *Do not pass the buck.*

- Inform the employee in writing of the effective date of dismissal. Be prepared for the employee to react angrily and quit on the spot. One effective way to handle such situations is to have a resignation letter prepared and dated. If the employee says, "You can't fire me, I quit!" or words to that effect, ask him or her to sign the letter. If he threatens to sue or take any other action, just listen without responding, but make mental notes of all threats. As soon as he leaves make a "Memorandum for the Record" of his threats while your memory is fresh. If he threatens violence notify higher management and law enforcement officials immediately.

- Explain or ask the human resources representative to explain the details of severance pay, vacation pay, sick leave, insurance, pensions, and other related concerns.

- Have the employee sign any exit forms required by company policy.

- Explain the company's appeal process and refer the employee to the appropriate office should he or she wish to appeal.

Once the termination has been accomplished, the supervisor must inform other members of the team. This is an important step. Do not try to make a secret of a dismissal. Co-workers will be curious and morale may suffer if they are not informed. This puts the supervisor in a touchy position. On the one hand, you must protect the right of privacy of the terminated employee. On the other hand, however, you must give remaining team members enough information to protect morale.

An effective way to do this is to call a team meeting and announce the dismissal. However, rather than disclosing details that might violate privacy, explain that the employee was terminated for continual violations and then only after an informal discussion, verbal warning, written warning, and suspension failed to correct the disruptive behavior.

Finally, check your documentation once again and make sure it is in order and readily available should the employee file a wrongful discharge suit. While you are at it, check the documentation (good and bad) maintained on all of your employees. To maintain documentation on just one employee might make termination of that employee appear to be a personal vendetta in the eyes of the court.

APPLICATION AND DISCUSSION

Assume you are a supervisor with ABC Company. You have a problem employee named Cynthia Noonan, who has been passed around from department to department by other supervisors who simply don't want the "hassle" of disciplining her. She is keenly aware of her rights and constantly threatens to sue anybody who "gives her a hard time." Consequently, other supervisors at ABC Company are afraid of her and have transferred Noonan rather than discipline her. You have decided to deal with Noonan in a straight-forward, objective manner that complies with all applicable company policies and government regulations. Within a week of arriving in your department, Noonan is up to her old tricks again (e.g., coming in late, leaving early, taking more breaks than authorized and stretching them out, failing to complete her assigned work on time, and being belligerent to her teammates).

- You have decided to have an informal discussion and counseling session with Noonan. Explain how you will handle this step in the discipline process. What will you say to her?

- Noonan's unacceptable behavior continues in spite of the informal discussion and counseling. Explain how you will handle the verbal warning step in the discipline process. Record everything about the meeting including your objective, any material you plan to have on hand, what rule (or rules) has been broken and the reason for the rule, any concluding remarks you plan to make to end the meeting, and your written notification of a verbal warning.

■ Noonan's unacceptable behavior continues even after your verbal warning. Draft a written reprimand to be given to her.

■ Two weeks after receiving your written warning, Noonan was suspended when her unacceptable behavior still continued. After consulting with your manager and the human resources department, you have decided to terminate Noonan's employment with ABC Company for cause. Develop a plan for doing so "by the book." Include enough details that it could be used effectively by someone completely unfamiliar with the process without putting the company in a compromised position legally.

SEXUAL HARASSMENT AND THE SUPERVISOR

Supervisors should be aware of the potential for sexual harassment in the workplace and understand how to prevent it. Helping men and women work together in harmony with mutual respect is a critical responsibility of the supervisor.

What is Sexual Harassment?

> ***Sexual harassment*** *is unwelcome words, actions, or conduct of a sexual nature. It can involve a man harassing a woman, a woman harassing a man, a woman harassing a woman, or a man harassing a man.*

There are two types of sexual harassment as defined by the courts (Figure 10–4). The first is *quid pro quo harassment* in which sexual favors are demanded in return for job benefits (e.g., promotion, pay increase, better working conditions, or other special considerations). The second type is *condition of work harassment* in which an offensive work environment is created. Condition of work harassment is the result of sex-related behavior that is unwelcome and/or demeaning to the extent that it creates an intimidating, offensive, or hostile work environment. Sexual harassment can come from anyone in the workplace including:

■ Managers
■ Supervisors
■ Co-workers
■ Customers
■ Suppliers

EEOC Guidelines on Sexual Harassment

The Equal Employment Opportunity Commission publishes guidelines that deal specifically with sexual harassment. These guidelines are abbreviated and summarized as follows:

■ Harassment on the basis of sex is a violation of Section 703 of Title VII of the Civil Rights Act. Unwelcome sexual advances constitute harassment when: (1) submission to the advances can be interpreted as a condition of employment; (2) accep-

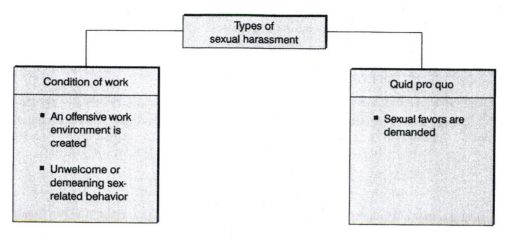

Figure 10–4
Sexual harassment can take two forms.

tance or rejection of advances is used as the basis for employment decisions; (3) this conduct affects job performance or creates a hostile work environment.

- In determining sexual harassment the EEOC examines all circumstances and facts of the case including the nature and context of the advances.

- An employer is responsible for the acts of its employees and agents, even when the behavior in question is forbidden by company policy.

- An employee may be liable for the actions of employees and nonemployees if it knows or should know of incidents of sexual harassment and does not take immediate and appropriate corrective action.

- An employer should take appropriate steps to discourage and prevent sexual harassment.

- An employer may be held liable for unlawful sex discrimination against other qualified employees who are denied an employment opportunity when another employee submits to sexual advances.

Effects of Sexual Harassment

Sexual harassment can harm both employees and the employer. Among employees it can cause the following types of problems:

- Emotional problems
- Morale problems
- Conflict
- Decline in job performance
- Personal problems
- Alienation from teammates

Anything that harms employees will eventually harm the employer. Sexual harassment can cause the following problems for employers:

- Legal costs
- Turnover, tardiness, and absenteeism
- Declining quality and productivity

- Poor morale
- Increased costs for hiring and training employees

What Is the Supervisor's Role?

The EEOC guidelines on sexual harassment plainly encourage prevention. The guidelines recommend that employers take the following action to prevent sexual harassment:

- Raise the subject of sexual harassment in an affirmative manner.
- Express strong disapproval of sexual harassment.
- Develop appropriate sanctions against sexual harassment.
- Inform employees of their rights relative to sexual harassment and how to raise the issue in accordance with Title VII of the Civil Rights Act.
- Develop methods to sensitize employees to sexual harassment concerns.

These recommendations apply to higher management. However, supervisors can play a key role in carrying them out. The supervisor's role with regard to sexual harassment can be summarized as follows:

- Set a positive example. Never make sexual advances toward an employee.
- Make sure all employees are familiar with the company's policies regarding sexual harassment.
- Make sure all employees are familiar with how to raise the issue of sexual harassment in accordance with Title VII of the Civil Rights Act.
- Help develop and participate in programs to sensitize employees to sexual harassment concerns.
- Communicate openly with employees so they feel comfortable discussing sexual harassment concerns, questions, and issues (Figure 10–5).

Figure 10–5
The supervisor's role in preventing sexual harassment in the workplace

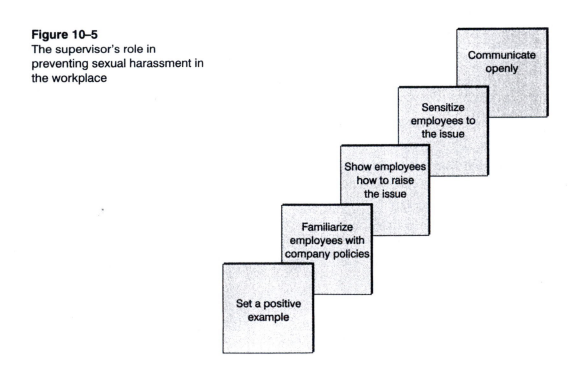

Do's and Don'ts for Supervisors

In addition to the preceding EEOC guidelines, supervisors should consider the following "do's" and "don'ts" when interacting on the job:

- Do behave professionally at all times.
- Do know and follow your employer's policy on sexual harassment.
- Do talk openly about the issue of sexual harassment.
- Don't assume that jokes and gestures will be viewed by others as harmless or inoffensive.
- Don't go along with the crowd or allow offensive behavior. When you see it, confront the offender.
- Don't make personal comments or ask personal questions. Stick to job-related comments with employees.

=== APPLICATION AND DISCUSSION ===

Mendy Wiggins supervises a team of fifteen processing clerks for ABC Company. Seven of her team members are men and eight are women. Wiggins has a good relationship with all members of her team and is comfortable telling sex-related jokes and making sex-related comments, both of which she does all the time.

Mike Anderson describes himself as a "hugger." He likes to pat the employees he supervises on the back or wrap them in a bear hug, particularly when they have done especially good job. His team is half male and half female.

- Can you foresee any problems that Mendy Wiggins might have one day relating to sexual harassment? If she were a fellow supervisor, would you advise her to continue the same pattern of behavior toward her direct reports or change it? If you think she should change her approach to interacting with employees, how should she interact?
- Can you foresee any problems that Mike Anderson might one day have relating to sexual harassment? Would you advise Anderson to continue the same pattern of behavior toward his direct reports or change it? If you think he should change his approach to interacting with employees, how should he interact?

Vernon Jones is the best computer technician on Amanda Miller's team of nine technicians. Everybody on the company who has computer problems asks Miller to send Jones if he is available. Other technicians are asked for only if Jones is tied up. In addition, he is very helpful in teaching the other technicians new techniques, troubleshooting strategies, and new technologies. Vernon Jones is widely respected. Amanda Miller has been the supervisor of the computer maintenance team for just one month, but several times she has noticed that Jones likes to kid female employees with jokes and comments that have sexual overtones. He also has a habit of putting his hand on the backs and shoulders of female employees as he shows them what he has done to correct their computer problems. Nobody has complained to her, but Miller is not comfortable with what she is seeing. She does not want to alienate Vernon Jones, but she is growing increasingly uncomfortable with his behavior.

- Put yourself in Amanda Miller's place. How would you handle this situation? Is she overreacting or should she do something?
- Discuss this situation with fellow students or colleagues. What is the consensus concerning how this situation should be handled?

DRUG ABUSE IN THE WORKPLACE

Estimates of the cost to employers of drug abuse range between $75 billion and $100 billion dollars annually. In reality, nobody knows for sure how much drug-abusing employees cost their employers. But we do know that drug abuse causes the types of problems that make it even more difficult for organizations to achieve the peak performance levels demanded by the global marketplace. Drug abuse by employees can cause the following:

- Security problems
- Safety, health, and environmental problems
- Quality problems
- Productivity problems
- Medical problems (which result in higher insurance premiums)
- Personnel problems (absenteeism, tardiness, turnover)

Supervisor's Role in Handling Drug Abuse in the Workplace

Supervisors have an important role to play in handling drug abuse on the job, a role that must be carried out with wisdom and discretion. On the one hand, the supervisor is not a police officer and should never accuse an employee of drug abuse. On the other hand, the supervisor cannot allow an employee to work while in an impaired condition. Supervisors have a responsibility to the organization, the suspected drug user, other employees, customers, and suppliers. The supervisor has a role to play in all of the following areas:

- Identifying troubled or suspicious work behavior
- Documenting troubled or suspicious work behavior
- Questioning employees who display troubled or suspicious behavior
- Participating in aftercare and follow-up as part of the organization's Employee Assistance Program (EAP).

Identifying Troubled or Suspicious Work Behavior

Supervisors represent the level of management closest to employees. Consequently, they can play an important role in detecting behavior that might indicate drug use. It needs to be said here that it is the behavior itself and not the suspected cause of it that is the supervisor's concern. Supervisors are not supposed to look for drug use. Rather, they are supposed to look for troubled or suspicious behavior that might be harmful to job performance or dangerous to other employees. The cause of the behavior is secondary, at least from the supervisor's perspective, and it is up to others to determine the cause.

In identifying troubled or suspicious behavior, supervisors should look for the following signs:

- Declines in the amount of work performed.
- Increase in errors, mistakes, or the rejection rate.
- Increased tardiness and absenteeism.
- Increase in the number of trips to the restroom.
- Sudden increase in conflict with other employees.
- Unsafe or inappropriate operation of machines and/or equipment.

These types of factors are observable. Supervisors should confront employees immediately when even one of these signs is observed. To notice such signs and not act is to potentially subject yourself and the organization to charges of negligence. However, it is important to confront the employee properly. To the supervisor this means commenting only on the less than acceptable behavior or job performance.

A SUPERVISOR SHOULD NEVER ACCUSE AN EMPLOYEE OF DRUG ABUSE.

If drug abuse is suspected, get the human resources department involved immediately and let its representatives deal with the drug-related aspects of the issue. The supervisor's concern is restricted to job performance. If the human resource personnel want to know what you have observed, what you think the problem is, or any other information, cooperate fully. But let someone with the necessary expertise determine that drugs are being used (See Figure 10–6).

Documenting Troubled or Suspicious Work Behavior

Documentation is one of the supervisor's most important tasks in situations that might require discipline, whether for drugs or any other infraction. The importance of documentation and how to maintain it has already been covered. Suffice it to reiterate here that the troubled or suspicious behavior or the unacceptable job performance is what is

---

Do's and Don'ts for Supervisors Handling
Suspected Drug Abusers

Do NOT Do the Following:

- Diagnose any employee's problem as drug abuse or alcoholism
- Tell an employee he or she has a drug or alcohol problem
- Discuss with other employees any suspicions that an employee has a drug problem
- State in writing anywhere that an employee has a drug problem
- Confront employees to try to get confessions of drug abuse
- Discipline those caught using drugs (or possessing them) unequally
- Allow unfit employees to operate dangerous machinery
- Handle the discovery of illegal drugs alone

Do the Following:

- Keep regular objective, written records
- Know employees—become familiar with skills, abilities, and normal performance and personality
- Document job performance regularly
- Take action whenever job performance fails, regardless of whether any drug or alcohol problem is suspected
- Take further action if job performance (documented) does not improve
- Know what exact steps the employer wishes taken when job performance fails and improvement efforts fail
- Know how to get help for an employee who says he or she has a problem and is ready to go for help
- Get in touch with a superior or the Human Resources Office the minute a problem is suspected, and stay in touch

Figure 10–6
Guidelines for supervisors who suspect employees of drug abuse

documented. Supervisors should never say in the documentation that this employee "is using drugs" or "this employee has a drug problem."

Questioning Employees Who Display Troubled or Suspicious Behavior

"John, I notice that your productivity has been dropping during the last two weeks. What can we do to get it back up?" "Wanda, the quality of your work has been down this week. Is there a problem?" "Martin, that's twice you've had near misses driving the forklift today. Park it and let's have a talk." Each of these is an appropriate response on the part of a supervisor who has observed trouble or suspicious behavior. With John (productivity decrease) and Wanda (quality decrease), the supervisor might just provide counseling or issue a verbal warning. With Martin (dangerous driving), the supervisor should get the human resources department involved immediately if the suspected cause is drug abuse. If Martin is just not paying attention and drug use is not suspected, counseling or a written warning would be an appropriate response.

Referring Employees to the Human Resources Department

Any time a supervisor suspects drug use on the part of an employee, the human resources department should be involved immediately. Without accusing an employee verbally or in writing, supervisors contact the human resources department and explain their concerns and suspicions in confidence. Having done so, a human resources representative will work cooperatively with the supervisor from that point forward. Often this means referring the suspected employee to the human resources department for counseling or for placement in the organization's Employee Assistance Program. Any and all referrals should be treated like a verbal or written warning and documented as such.

Participating in Aftercare and Follow-Up

Employees who choose to enter the organization's Employee Assistance Program or who are required to enter the program as a condition of continued employment will eventually be returned to work in most cases. When this happens, their behavior and work must be monitored carefully. Much of the responsibility for doing so falls to the supervisor. When the supervisor is to be involved in aftercare or monitoring an employee's progress, the human resources department will provide the necessary instructions. Supervisors should follow these instructions to the letter and work closely with both the employee and the human resources department for the duration of any prescribed rehabilitation period.

=========== APPLICATION AND DISCUSSION ===========

John Cooper is convinced that one of his direct reports, Gail Watson, is using drugs. Recently, she has been frequently late. When she is at work, Watson seems to make many more trips to the bathroom than is normal, and she has been at odds with practically every other member of the team.

- Describe how you think John Cooper should handle this situation.
- Discuss your plan with follow students or colleagues. Is there anything you missed? If so, what? What is the consensus of the group concerning how Cooper should handle this situation?

Mickey Morrison is an experienced machine operator with an excellent safety record. No one can remember his ever having an accident, damaging his machine, or having a high reject rate. But lately all of this has changed. Morrison has incurred three minor injuries in just one week. His machine has broken down twice, and his rejection rate has increased markedly.

- Put yourself in the place of Morrison's supervisor. How would you handle this situation?
- How would your handling of this situation change if Morrison approached you and admitted he was having personal problems that were causing him to drink too much?

ON-THE-JOB SCENARIOS

1. Janice Herson is the worst performing employee on your team. She is frequently late, often absent, her work is sloppy, and she is disruptive to the team. She has been bounced from team to team as one supervisor has passed her on to another. Everyone would like to see Herson fired, but so far, no supervisor has been willing to tackle the issue. The problem? Herson is well known for loudly proclaiming her rights and threatening anyone who "bothers" her with sexual harassment charges. Every time this happens, her supervisors have simply given in and had her transferred. Unfortunately for you, there is nowhere else to transfer Herson. Your team is her last stop. Explain how you plan to handle this situation.

2. You have gone through all of the steps in the discipline process with an employee except termination, but nothing has worked. He is a skilled employee, but his disruptive behavior is damaging the team's morale. As a result, absenteeism is up and productivity is down. How should you handle this situation?

3. You know Mark Peyton is using drugs and drinking heavily, as do all of his team members. You cannot prove it, but you know it. He is frequently late for work, argumentative when asked to perform work tasks, insolent to team members, and reckless in the operation of his press. Early in the morning, his speech is sometimes slurred and his eyes are often bloodshot. Lately he has lost weight. Mark Peyton has become a problem. How do you plan to handle this problem?

KEY TERMS AND PHRASES

Cause	Informal discussion
Discipline process	Self-discipline
Disciplining	Sexual harassment
Dismissal	Suspension
Documentation	Verbal warning
Employment-at-will	Written warning
Hearsay	Wrongful discharge

REVIEW QUESTIONS

1. Define the term *discipline*.
2. What is the rationale for disciplining employees?
3. Briefly explain three strategies for promoting self-discipline.
4. Explain how to ensure there will be no surprises when applying discipline.
5. Why is it important for the supervisor to set a good example?
6. List and briefly explain what you feel are the ten most important guidelines for disciplining employees.
7. What are the five steps in the discipline process?
8. Explain the proper way to issue a verbal warning.

10. What questions should you ask yourself before suspending an employee?

11. Explain the concepts of *employment-at-will* and *wrongful discharge*.

12. List five causes that might be given for terminating an employee.

13. List five reasons that *cannot* be used to justify dismissing an employee.

14. List and briefly explain the steps to follow in conducting a dismissal interview.

15. Explain how to properly inform remaining team members that one of them has been terminated.

16. Define the two categories of sexual harassment.

17. How should a supervisor respond when an employee is suspected of drug use?

CHAPTER ELEVEN

Training

=== LEARNING OBJECTIVES ===

After studying this chapter, you should be able to do the following:

- Define *training*.
- Describe the need for training.
- Discuss how to assess training needs.
- Demonstrate how to provide training.
- Explain how to evaluate training.
- Describe the role of supervisors in providing trainers.
- Explain the need for training for the supervisor.

It has always been important to have well-trained, highly skilled employees. In the age of global competition, it is more important than ever. Evidence of the importance of training can be seen in the fact that American companies spend almost $50 billion every year providing training for employees. Two factors drive the unprecedented need for training: (1) international competition that is continually more intense and (2) a workforce that is not keeping pace in terms of its capabilities. Supervisors must be proficient in assessing the need for training and for planning, coordinating, providing, and evaluating training.

TRAINING DEFINED

It is common to hear terms such as *training* and *education* used interchangeably in discussions of enhancing the competitiveness of a company's workforce. Both concepts can contribute to continual improvement, but distinctions can be drawn between them. In this book, training is defined as follows:

> ***Training*** *is an organized, systematic series of activities designed to continually enhance the work-related knowledge, skills, and performance of employees.*

Training has the characteristics of **specificity** and **immediacy**. This means that teaching and learning are geared toward the development of specific job-related knowledge and skills that have direct application on the job.

Education typically describes teaching and learning that takes place in a more formal setting where students must meet some type of entrance requirements and teachers are required to have specific credentials, certification, or accreditation. Education is typically thought of as being more theoretical than training and having less specificity, immediacy, or direct application.

The distinctions among these concepts are not black and white, however. For example, going back to school to complete a college degree in management and supervision (education) would be an educational activity for a supervisor. Additionally, college and university-based technical and business programs are always under pressure from employers to make their teaching more relevant, by which is meant more up-to-date, specific, and immediate (more like training). This unit focuses on training for employees that is specific and immediate.

APPLICATION AND DISCUSSION

The ABC Company is having trouble staying afloat. The competition is outperforming ABC on a daily basis. Its high turnover rate has caused ABC Company to lose some of its best employees. New employees don't seem to have the knowledge, skills, or attitudes the company needs to improve its performance. ABC Company's CEO, Max Bender, is at his wit's end. He sees his company floundering but does not know what to do. A consultant brought in to help solve ABC's problems told Bender that the best strategy for getting his company back on track could be summarized in just three words; *Training, Training, Training.* The consultant recommended training for new hires, retraining for experienced employees, specific training for supervisors, and several seminars for top managers. Bender's response was emphatic. Just before dismissing the consultant he said, "We don't have time for training. While we are training, the competition will be running off with our customers. Besides, training is too expensive."

■ What do you think about Max Bender's attitude toward training? Is he right or wrong?

■ If you were a supervisor at ABC Company and Bender asked for your advice, what would you tell him?

NEED FOR TRAINING

The need for training is the result of the demands on organizations to be productive and competitive. This is why employers in the United States spend almost $50 billion per year on the training, development, and education of employees at all levels. Several factors combine to intensify the need for training:

■ Intensely competitive nature of the modern workplace

■ Rapid and continual change

■ Technology transfer problems

■ Changing demographics

Unfortunately, and in spite of the huge sums spent on training every year, many employers still do not understand the role of training in continually improving performance. Less than 10 percent of U.S. employers use a flexible approach requiring better trained workers as a way to improve performance. This approach is standard practice in Japan, Germany, Denmark, and Sweden. In addition, less than 30 percent of U.S. firms have special training programs for women, minorities, and immigrants in spite of the fact that 85 percent of all new employees come from these groups. It is critical that employers understand the need for training that results from intense global competition, rapid and continual change, technology transfer problems, and changing demographics.

For an organization to succeed in a competitive global marketplace, every employee must be prepared to contribute ideas for improving performance. The best way to accomplish this is through constant training and re-training.

Competition in the Marketplace

American employers, even some of the smallest, find themselves competing in a global marketplace, and the competition is intense. A small manufacturer of automotive parts in Michigan might find itself competing with companies in the United States as well as in Korea, Japan, Taiwan, and Europe. To win the competition, this small Michigan firm must make its products both better and less expensively than the competitors. To do this every employee of this company must be better trained, better skilled, and more productive than similar employees in competing companies here and abroad. One of the key components in achieving maximum productivity levels is high-quality, ongoing training.

Rapid and Continual Change

Rapid and continual change is a fact of life in the modern workplace. Skills that were current yesterday may be obsolete today. Knowledge that is valid today may not be tomorrow. The only way working people can stay current is to undergo periodic training on a lifelong basis.

Technology Transfer Problems

Technology transfer is the movement of technology from one arena to another. There are two steps in the process. The first step is the *commercialization* of new technologies developed in research laboratories or by individual inventors. This is a business development issue and does not involve training. However, the second step does. This step, known as technology diffusion, is training dependent. **Technology diffusion** is the process of moving newly commercialized technologies into the workplace where they can be used to enhance performance.

This step breaks down unless the people who must use the technology have been trained to use it efficiently and effectively. This is critical because new technologies by themselves do not enhance performance. A computer-based word processing system is just an expensive typewriter with a screen unless one knows how to use all of its capabilities. To take maximum advantage of the capabilities of new technologies, people must know how to use them effectively. Knowing how comes from training. Two of the major inhibitors of effective technology transfer are fear of change and lack of know-how. Both of these inhibitors can be overcome by training.

Changing Demographics

The demographics of the workforce in the United States are changing. The days when the workforce consisted primarily of Caucasian males are past. The typical employee of tomorrow will be a female, a minority, or an immigrant. Approximately 85 percent of all new employees entering the labor force now come from these groups, which have their own special training needs. To compete, organizations will have to provide for these needs.

========= **APPLICATION AND DISCUSSION** =========

Mona Wilson was an excellent technician before she was promoted to supervise a team of claims processors. All of her team's work is done on computers. Because of expansion, Wilson inherited a brand new team. Her team members are eager to work and have excellent attitudes, but they just do not know how to use their computers as well as they should. To process the number of claims required of her team every hour, Wilson needs to increase their output.

Rob Beacon is a supervisor at Accu-Tech Corporation that is also expanding rapidly due to growth in its business base. Lately the job market has been so tight that Accu-Tech's CEO has decided to solve the labor shortage problems his company faces by hiring recently arrived immigrants and older people who have already retired from another career.

- Explain how Mona Wilson can use training to help improve her team's performance.
- What types of performance problems is Rob Beacon likely to experience with new employees who are recent immigrants? How about with the older employees Accu-Tech hires? How can training be used to help solve these problems?

ASSESSING TRAINING NEEDS

What knowledge, skills, and attitudes do our employees need to have to be more productive than the employees of our competitors? What knowledge, skills, and attitudes do our employees currently have? The difference between the answers to these questions represents training needs, and a **needs assessment** may be necessary to determine this difference.

Supervisors may become involved in needs assessment at both the unit or team level and the individual level. Assessing training needs at these two levels is not difficult. Supervisors work closely enough with their team members to see their capabilities first-hand. *Observation* is one method supervisors can use for assessing training needs.

A more structured way to assess training needs is to ask employees to state their needs in terms of their job knowledge and skills. Employees know the tasks they must perform every day. They also know which tasks they do well, which they do not perform well, and which they cannot do at all. A *brainstorming* session focusing on training needs is another method supervisors can use.

The most structured approach supervisors can use to access training needs is the **job task analysis** in which a job is analyzed thoroughly, and the knowledge, skills, and attitudes needed to perform it are recorded. Using this information, a survey instrument such as the one in Figure 11-1 is developed.

Employees respond by indicating which skills they have and which they need. The survey results can be used in two ways: (1) to identify unit-wide training needs, and (2) to identify individual training needs. Both types of needs are then converted into training objectives.

The following example demonstrates how supervisors might assess an organization's training needs. Keltran, Inc. manufactures low-voltage power supplies for military and civilian aircraft. Production workers at Keltran install components on printed circuit boards, wrap wires on transformers, and build up wire harnesses for cables. John Harris, production supervisor, is convinced that Keltran's production teams would benefit from specialized training aimed at improving performance. After mulling over the issue for a few days, Harris decides to assess the training needs of Keltran's three production teams: Team A (printed circuit boards), Team B (transformers), and Team C (cables). Using what he learned from reading about needs assessment, Harris proceeds as follows:

1. Harris asks himself, "What are my most persistent production problems or bottle-necks and what could be causing them?" He decides that incorrect components installed on printed circuit boards and improperly matched wires in cables are high on his list of frequently occurring problems. In his opinion, these problems are caused by a lack of blueprint reading skills and an inability to adequately read technical manuals and specifications. He lists blueprint reading and general reading improvement as potential training needs.

Job Knowledge and Skills Survey

The following is a list of tasks that are performed by some people who work in the same job as yours, or who work in related positions. In some cases, the task will be part of your job, while in other cases it will not. For each item on the list, circle the number that indicates how frequently, if at all, you perform this task yourself. If you do not understand the question indicate this by circling #5.

I perform this task

	Never	Rarely, but only as a backup or in an emergency	Sometimes as a part of my regular job	Frequently as a part of my regular job	I don't understand this question
1. Use operating manuals, repair manuals or other written instructions	1	2	3	4	5
2. Read blueprints	1	2	3	4	5
3. Interpret geometric dimensions and tolerances (e.g., true positions, datums, flatness, circularity, or perpendicularity)	1	2	3	4	5
4. Read electrical schematics	1	2	3	4	5
5. Use charts or graphs to convert from one measure to another (e.g., from inches to centimeters or calculate speed and feed rates)	1	2	3	4	5
6. Convert measures manually	1	2	3	4	5
7. Convert measures with a calculator	1	2	3	4	5
8. Use manually operated processing machines (e.g., lathes, drill presses, sewing or fabric cutters)	1	2	3	4	5
9. Use computer numerically controlled processing equipment (e.g., CNC milling machine, brake presses, or fabric cutters)	1	2	3	4	5
If yes, how many types of equipment?	1	2	3	4	5 or more

Figure 11–1
Sample training needs assessment instrument

159

2. Harris asks the lead employee in each team to undertake the same process he has completed and to do so individually without discussing the issue among themselves. The lead employees list their perceptions of the training needs of their team members and submit them to Harris.

3. Harris then calls a meeting of all production employees and explains that he is trying to assess their training needs and wants their input. After promising confidentiality, he distributes a form to each employee that has this statement typed across the top: "I could do my job better if training were provided for me in the following areas." All employees are asked to complete the statement and drop their forms into a box.

4. Harris analyzes this input from the lead employees in each team and from the employees themselves. Adding his own, Harris compiles a master list of training needs. Those needs listed most often are given the highest priority.

As a result of this process, Harris determines that the following are the highest priority training needs of Keltran's production employees:

- General reading improvement
- Interpretation of technical standards
- Proper use of specifications
- Blueprint reading

WRITING TRAINING OBJECTIVES

The first step in providing training for employees is to write **training objectives**, that is, objectives that specify in behavioral terms what skills are to be gained from training. This responsibility will fall in whole or in part to the supervisor. Some companies have training personnel who can assist; others do not. In either case, supervisors should be proficient in writing training objectives. The key to success lies in being specific and stating objectives in behavioral terms. For example, say a supervisor has identified a need for training in the area of math. She might write the following training objective: *Employees will learn mathematics*. This training objective lacks specificity and is not stated in behavioral terms. *Math* is a broad concept. What does the training objective encompass? Arithmetic? Algebra? Geometry? Trigonometry? All of these? To gain specificity, this objective must be broken down into several objectives.

To be stated in behavioral terms, these more specific objectives must explain what the employee should be able to do after completing the training. **Behavioral objectives** contain action verbs. The sample training objectives in Figure 11-2 are stated in behavioral terms, they are specific, and they are measurable. The more clearly training objectives are written, the easier it is to plan training to meet them.

Figure 11–2
Sample training objectives

> ### Sample Training Objectives
> Upon completion of the training, employees should be able to:
> 1. Add, subtract, multiply, and divide whole numbers.
> 2. Add, subtract, multiply, and divide common fractions.
> 3. Add, subtract, multiply, and divide decimal fractions.
> 4. Convert everyday shop problems into algebraic expressions.
> 5. Solve right triangles.
> 6. Solve nonright triangles.

You are the supervisor of a secretarial pool. Your team members do word processing, create spreadsheets, and create a variety of different types of graphics. Your company has just decided to give all members of the secretarial pool (your team) Internet access. This action is based on a recommendation you made three weeks ago. None of your team members has ever used the Internet. Consequently, you know that a training need exists.

■ Develop a set of specific training needs based on making your team members effective users of the Internet.

■ Compare your training objectives with those of your classmates or colleagues. Did you miss anything? Are your objectives stated in specific and behavioral terms?

PROVIDING TRAINING

Supervisors can provide training in several different ways. All fall into one of the following broad categories: *internal approaches, external approaches,* and *partnership approaches.* Regardless of the approach used, supervisors will want to maximize their training resources. Strategies for doing this are as follows:

1. *Build in quality from the start.* Take the time to do it right from the outset.
2. *Be specific.* Do not try to develop courses that are all things to all people. Develop specific activities around specific objectives.
3. *Think flexible.* Do not assume that the traditional classroom approach is automatically best. Videotapes, interactive video, one-on-one peer training, or on-line training may be more effective.
4. *Be selective.* Before purchasing training services, conduct a thorough analysis of specific job training objectives. Decide exactly what you want and make sure the provider you plan to deal with can handle it.
5. *Preview and customize.* Never buy a training product (e.g., videotape, self-paced manual) without previewing it. If you can save by customizing a generic product, do so.

Internal Approaches

Internal approaches provide training on-site in the organization's facilities. These approaches include one-on-one mentoring, computer-based training, and media-based instruction. **Mentoring** involves placing a less skilled employee under the instruction of a more skilled employee. This approach is often used when a new employee is hired. It is also an effective way to prepare a replacement for a high-value employee who plans to leave or retire.

Computer-based training (CBT) has proven to be an effective internal approach. Over the years, it has been continually improved and is now a widely used training method. It offers the advantages of being self-paced, individualized, and able to provide immediate and continual feedback to learners. Its best application is in developing general knowledge rather than in developing company-specific job skills.

Formal group instruction, in which a number of people who share a common training need are taught together, is a widely used method. This approach might involve lectures, demonstrations, multimedia use, hands-on learning, question/answer sessions, role playing, simulation, or a combination of these.

Media-based instruction has become a widely used internal approach. Private training companies and major publishing houses produce an almost endless list of turnkey media-based training programs. The simplest might consist of a set of videotapes. A more comprehensive package might include CDs and workbooks.

External Approaches

External approaches are those that involve enrolling employees in programs or activities provided by colleges, universities, professional organizations, and private training companies. The two most widely used approaches are (1) enrolling employees in short-term training (a few hours to a few weeks) during work hours, and (2) enrolling employees in short- or long-term training and paying all or part of the costs (i.e., tuition, books, fees). External approaches encompass training methods ranging from seminars to college courses.

Partnership Approaches

In recent years, community colleges, universities, and technical schools have begun to actively pursue partnerships with employers through which they provide customized training. These **training partnerships** combine some of the characteristics of the preceding two approaches.

Customized on-site training provided cooperatively by community colleges and private companies or associations have become very common. Community colleges have built extensive networks of alliances with business, industry, and government employers.

Many universities, community colleges, and technical schools have continuing education or corporate training divisions that specialize in providing training for business and industry. Supervisors should know the administrator responsible for training partnerships at colleges, universities, or technical schools in their communities.

Partnerships with institutions of higher education offer several advantages to supervisors who need to arrange training for their employees. Representatives of these institutions are education and training professionals. They know how to transform training objectives into customized curricula, courses, and lessons; how to deliver instruction; how to design application activities that simulate real-world conditions; and how to develop a valid and reliable system of evaluation and use the results to chart progress and prescribe remedial activities when necessary. They have access to a wide range of instructional support systems (i.e., libraries, media centers, and instructional design centers).

In addition to professional know-how, institutions of higher education have resources that can markedly reduce the cost of training for an organization. Tuition costs for continuing education activities are typically much less than those associated with traditional college degree coursework. If these institutions do not have faculty members on staff who are qualified to provide instruction in a given area, they can usually hire a temporary or part-time instructor who is qualified.

Other advantages institutions of higher education can offer in the training arena are credibility, formalization, standardization, and flexibility in training locations. Employers sometimes find their attempts at customized training are hampered because their employees have been conditioned to expect formal grades, transcripts, and certificates of completion. These things tend to formalize training in the minds of employees and can make it more real for them. Associating with a community college, university, or technical school can formalize a company's training program and give it credibility.

Another problem employers sometimes experience when providing their own customized training is a lack of standardization. The same training provided in three different divisions might produce markedly different results. Professional educators can help standardize the curriculum and evaluation systems. They can also help standardize instruction by providing train-the-trainer workshops for employees who serve as in-house instructors. Figure 11–3 lists the advantages of training partnerships.

Regardless of the approach used in providing training, supervisors should be familiar with the following rule of thumb: *People learn best when their learning involves seeing, hearing, speaking, and doing.*

Educators hold that the following percentages apply regarding what learners are able to retain:

10 percent of what is read

20 percent of what is heard

30 percent of what is seen

50 percent of what is seen and heard

70 percent of what is seen and spoken

90 percent of what is said while doing what is being talked about

Clearly, for learning to be effective, it must involve activity on the part of learners, must be interactive in nature, and must involve reading, hearing, seeing, talking, and doing.

APPLICATION AND DISCUSSION

As the supervisor of ten employees for Anderson Services, Inc. you have been asked to arrange a training program on the subject of dealing with angry customers. Conduct a thorough search of potential training programs available on the market. Also contact a university, community college, or technical school in your area and investigate the possibility of a partnership.

■ In your area, for this particular need, what is the best option? Why?

■ Develop a proposal for your manager explaining how you think the training should be provided. Include your rationale and the total cost of the training.

EVALUATING TRAINING

Did the training provided satisfy the training objectives? This can be a difficult question to answer. Evaluating training requires that supervisors begin with a clear statement of purpose. What is the overall purpose of the training? This broad purpose should not be

Figure 11–3
Training partnerships offer several advantages.

Checklist

Advantages of Training Partnerships with Colleges, Universities, and Technical Schools

- Training professionals in colleges, universities, and technical schools know how to:

  - Transform training objectives into customized curricula, courses, and lessons.

  - Design learning activities that simulate real-world conditions.

  - Develop valid systems of evaluation.

  - Use the results of evaluations to chart progress and plan remedial activities.

- Colleges, universities, and technical schools have access to instructional support systems, including libraries and media centers.

- Colleges, universities, and technical schools can offer credibility, formalization, credentialing, and standardization.

confused with training objectives. The objectives translate this purpose into more specific, measurable terms.

The purpose of training is to improve the individual productivity of employees and the overall productivity of the organization so that the organization becomes more competitive. In other words, the purpose of training is to improve performance.

To know if training has improved performance, supervisors need to answer the following questions: (1) Was the training provided valid? (2) Did the employees learn? (3) Has the learning made a difference? Valid training is training that is consistent with the training objectives.

Evaluating training for validity is a two-step process. The first step involves comparing the written documentation for the training (i.e., course outline, lesson plans, curriculum framework, etc.) with the training objectives. If the training is valid in design and content, the written documentation will match the training objectives. The second step involves determining if the actual training provided is consistent with the documentation. Training that strays from the approved plan will not be valid. Student evaluations of instruction conducted immediately after completion of training can provide information on consistency and the quality of instruction. Figure 11-4 is an example of an instrument for evaluating instruction.

Determining if employees have learned is a matter of building an evaluation into the training. If the training is valid and employees have learned, the training should result in

---

Organization of Workshop

1. Objectives — *Clear to Unclear*
2. Requirements — *Challenging to Unchallenging*
3. Assignments — *Useful to Not Useful*
4. Materials — *Excellent to Poor*
5. Testing Procedures — *Effective to Ineffective*
6. Grading Practice — *Explained to Unexplained*
7. Student Work Returned — *Promptly to Delayed*
8. Overall Organization — *Outstanding to Poor*

Trainer _____

Workshop Title _____

Date: Month____ Day ____ Year ____.

Instructions: On a scale from 5 to 1 (5=highest rating to 1=lowest rating) rate each item. Leave blank any item which does not apply.

Comments:

Teaching Skills

9. Class Meetings — *Productive to Nonproductive*
10. Lectures/Demonstrations — *Effective to Ineffective*
11. Discussions — *Balanced to Unbalanced*
12. Class Proceedings — *To-the-Point/Wandering*
13. Provides Feedback — *Beneficial/Not Beneficial*
14. Responds to Students — *Positively/Negatively*
15. Provides Assistance — *Always to Never*
16. Overall Rating of Trainer's Teaching Skills — *Outstanding to Poor*

Comments:

Substantive Value of Workshop

17. The course was — *Intellectually Challenging/Too Elementary*
18. The trainer's command of the subject was — *Broad and Accurate/Plainly Defective*
19. Overall substantive value of the course — *Outstanding to Poor*

Comments:

Figure 11–4
Form for evaluating instruction (to be completed by students)

improved performance. Supervisors can determine if performance is improved using the same indicators that told them training was needed in the first place.

"Can employees perform tasks they could not perform before the training? Has quality improved? Is customer satisfaction improved? Is the production rate up? Is the throughput time down?" Supervisors can ask these types of questions to determine if training has improved performance. The following questions can be used to evelute purchased training programs:

- Does the program have specific learning objectives?
- Is there a logical sequence for the program?
- Is the training relevant for the trainees?
- Does the program allow trainees to apply the training?
- Does the program accommodate different levels of expertise?
- Is the philosophy of the program consistent with that of the organization?
- Is the trainer credible?
- Does the program provide follow-up activities to maintain the training on the job?

APPLICATION AND DISCUSSION

Mohammed Jakur has been asked to develop a proposal for training all of his team members on a new desktop publishing software package his company would like to purchase. His team of technicians specializes in the layout and word processing of corporate newsletters. They take in rough copy, photographs, and artwork from corporations and convert this into camera-ready newsletters that are ready for the printer. The new software will revolutionize how Jakur's team works and how much work it is able to do. But first his team members must be trained.

- Put yourself in Mohammed Jakur's place and develop the training plan by writing training objectives and explaining the approach to be used.
- Add a section to your plan that justifies the approach you have selected.

THE SUPERVISOR AS A TRAINER

It is not unusual for supervisors to serve as instructors in a company-sponsored training program. In fact, this is becoming so common that it is important for supervisors to have at least basic instructional skills and to understand the basic principles of learning and the basic four-step teaching approach.

Principles of Learning

The **principles of learning** summarize what is known and widely accepted about how people learn (Figure 11–5). Trainers can do a better job of facilitating learning if they understand the following principles:

- *People learn best when they are ready to learn.* You cannot make employees learn anything, but you can help them learn what they want to learn. Therefore, time spent motivating employees to *want* to learn will be time well spent. Explain why they need to learn and how they will benefit personally from learning.
- *People learn more easily when what they are learning can be related to something they already know.* Build today's learning on what was learned yesterday and

Figure 11–5
Basic principles of learning

Basic Principles of Learning

1. People learn best when they are ready to learn.
2. People learn more easily when what they are learning can be related to something they already know.
3. People learn best in a step-by-step manner.
4. People learn by doing.
5. The more often people use what they are learning, the better they will remember and understand it.
6. Success in learning tends to stimulate additional learning.
7. People need immediate and continual feedback to know if they have learned.

---

tomorrow's learning on what was learned today. Begin each new learning activity with a brief review of the activity that preceded it.

■ *People learn best in a step-by-step manner.* An extension of the preceding principle, this means that learning should be organized into logically sequenced steps that proceed from the concrete to the abstract.

■ *People learn by doing.* This is probably the most important principle for trainers to understand. Inexperienced trainers tend to confuse talking (i.e., lecturing or demonstrating) with teaching. These things can be part of the teaching process, but they do little good unless they are followed up with application activities that require the learner to do something. To illustrate this point, consider the example of teaching employees how to roller-skate. You might present a thorough lecture on the principles of roller-skating and give a comprehensive demonstration on how to do it. However, until the employees put on the skates and begin taking those first tentative steps, they have not begun to learn how to skate. They learn by doing.

■ *The more often people use what they are learning, the better they will remember and understand it.* How many things have you learned in your life that you can no longer remember? People forget what they do not use. Trainers should keep this principle in mind. It means that repetition and application should be built into the learning process.

■ *Success in learning tends to stimulate additional learning.* This principle is a restatement of a principle of management that success breeds success. Organize learning into short enough segments to allow learners to see progress, but not so short that they become bored.

■ *People need immediate and continual feedback to know if they have learned.* Did you ever take a test and get the results back a week later? That was probably a week later than you wanted them. People in a learning setting want to know immediately how they are doing. **Feedback** can be as simple as a nod, a pat on the back, or a comment such as "Good job!" It can also be more formal, such as a progress report or a graded paper. Regardless of the form it takes, trainers should concentrate on giving immediate and continual feedback.

Four-Step Teaching Approach

Regardless of the setting, teaching is a matter of helping people learn. One of the most effective approaches for facilitating learning is not new, innovative, or high tech in nature. It is known as the **four-step teaching approach**, and it is an effective approach to use in a corporate training setting (Figure 11–6). The four steps are explained in the following paragraphs.

- **Preparation** encompasses all tasks necessary to get students prepared to learn, trainers prepared to teach, and facilities prepared to accommodate the process. Preparing students means motivating them to want to learn. Personal preparation involves planning lessons and preparing all the necessary instructional materials. Preparing the facility involves arranging the room for both function and comfort, checking all equipment to ensure it works properly, and making sure that all tools and other training aids are in place.

- **Presentation** is a matter of presenting the material students are to learn. It might involve giving a demonstration, presenting a lecture, conducting a question/answer session, helping students work with a computer or interactive videodisk system, or assisting students who are proceeding through self-paced materials. Regardless of the format, certain rules of thumb apply. The following strategies will help strengthen a presentation:

  - Begin dramatically (get their attention).
  - Be brief.
  - Be organized (use an outline and distribute copies).
  - Use humor (laugh at yourself, not the audience).
  - Keep it simple.
  - Take charge (be confident, but don't be arrogant).
  - Be sincere.
  - Be enthusiastic (let them see that you care).
  - Tell stories (to illustrate key points).

- **Application** refers to arranging for learners to use what they are learning. Application might range from simulation activities in which learners role-play to actual hands-on activities in which learners use their new skills in a live format.

- **Evaluation** means determining the extent to which learning has taken place. In a training setting, evaluation does not need to be a complicated process. If the training objectives are written in measurable, observable terms, evaluation is simple. Employees are supposed to learn how to do X, Y, and Z. Have them do X, Y, and Z and observe the results. In other words, have employees demonstrate proficiency and observe the results.

APPLICATION AND DISCUSSION

Assume that you are a supervisor for XYZ Company. You have been asked to train twenty new employees on how to perform CPR (you have the necessary CPR certification). Develop a comprehensive plan for providing the training. It should contain two parts. The first part is the four-step teaching approach. Explain everything you intend to do in

Figure 11–6
The four-step teaching approach

Four-Step Teaching Approach

1. Preparation
2. Presentation
3. Application
4. Evaluation

each of the steps (preparation, presentation, application, and evaluation). The second part of the plan is the principles of learning. In this part, explain what you will do to ensure that the presentation, application, and evaluation steps will accommodate the principles of learning. Discuss your plan with fellow students or colleagues.

TRAINING THE SUPERVISOR

In addition to ensuring that their employees are trained, supervisors should be attentive to their own training needs. Training for supervisors is more important than it has ever been. It should be comprehensive and continual. Supervisory training can be summarized as the table of contents of this book.

Supervisors must be leaders. This means they must develop communication and motivation skills. They must also understand the role ethics plays in leadership. These things can be learned.

Training for supervisors should also cover planning, staffing, and decision-making skills. The counseling aspects of a supervisor's' training should focus on how to conduct effective performance appraisals, how to properly handle problem employees and employee complaints, and how to discipline properly.

Training for supervisors should focus on helping them learn how to arrange, develop, present, and evaluate training; improve productivity; enhance quality; ensure safety; and make better decisions. Finally, supervisory training should focus on the legal concerns of the job including sexual harassment, termination, discipline, and drug abuse.

APPLICATION AND DISCUSSION

Mandy Denison is the new supervisor of nurses for Beltway Medical Center (BMC). She was a nurse for twelve years before being promoted to her current position. Denison attends seminars, workshops, and college courses to stay current in her nursing field, but she has not had supervision training. Nor does she see the need for such training. However, after being a supervisor for just one month, problems are beginning to occur in her team.

- What types of problems might Mandy Denison experience as a result of having no supervision training?
- Discuss the following issue with fellow students or colleagues: Supervisors are critical to the success of organizations that must compete in the global marketplace. Why do you think so few receive supervision-related education or training?

ON-THE-JOB SCENARIOS

1. At Morlon Company you are the only supervisor with formal education and training in the field. Consequently, you have been asked to confidentially assess the training needs of the company's other supervisors. Develop a survey instrument for making the assessment.

2. Select a unit from this book and develop a presentation about that unit. Make the presentation to your fellow students or a group of colleagues.

3. Develop a form students in your presentation from Scenario #2 can use to evaluate the quality of your instruction. Distribute the form and ask participants to complete it without attribution and return it to you. Analyze the results. What shortcomings do you need to work on? Where are your strengths?

=== **KEY TERMS AND PHRASES** ===

Application

Behavioral objectives

Computer-based training

Education

Evaluation

Feedback

Four-step teaching approach

Immediacy

Job task analysis

Mentoring

Needs assessment

Preparation

Presentation

Principles of learning

Specificity

Technology diffusion

Technology transfer

Training

Training objectives

Training partnership

=== **REVIEW QUESTIONS** ===

1. Define the term *training*.
2. Distinguish between *education* and *training*.
3. Why do organizations in the United States spend about $50 billion each year on education, training, and development?
4. Explain the impact of international competition on the training needs of organizations in the United States.
5. Explain the term *technology transfer* and the impact it has on training needs.
6. What is *technology diffusion* and how does it relate to training needs?
7. Explain the most structured approach for assessing training needs.
8. Write a sample training objective that can be readily measured.
9. Explain briefly the following approaches to providing training: internal, external, and partnership.
10. List four principles of learning.
11. Explain the four-step teaching approach.

CHAPTER TWELVE

Health and Safety

LEARNING OBJECTIVES

After studying this chapter, you should be able to do the following:

- Discuss the legal foundation of health and safety programs.
- Explain the policy aspects of health and safety.
- Practice safety training methods.
- Explain accident prevention techniques.
- Demonstrate how to conduct accident investigations.
- Define *workers' compensation*.
- Describe the impact of bloodborne diseases on health and safety in the workplace.

LEGAL FOUNDATION OF HEALTH AND SAFETY PROGRAMS

The Occupational Safety and Health Act represents the federal government's attempt to ensure a safe and healthy working environment for the broadest possible base of employees. It applies to most employers in the United States and its various possessions including the federal government. State and local governments and industries covered by other federal acts (e.g., Federal Mine/Safety and Health Act) are exempt. The Act clearly establishes that workplace health and safety is a responsibility of management.

Administration and Enforcement

Administration and enforcement of the Act are the responsibility of the U.S. Secretary of Labor and the Occupational Safety and Health Review Commission. Administrative and enforcement duties are divided as follows:

- The U.S. Secretary of Labor conducts investigations of suspected wrongdoing and prosecutes alleged violators as necessary.
- The Occupational Safety and Health Review Commission arbitrates cases of wrongdoing that are challenged and rules in such cases as necessary.

In addition to investigations, prosecutions, and arbitration, there is a need for an agency to carry out the day-to-day tasks required in the act. This agency is the **Occupational Safety and Health Administration, or OSHA.** (See Figure 12–1 for contact information.) OSHA is responsible for the following duties:

Figure 12–1
How to contact OSHA

Contact Information
U.S. Department of Labor
Occupational Safety and Health Administration (OSHA)
200 Constitution Avenue, N.W.
Washington, DC 20210
1-800-321-6742
http://www.osha.gov

Setting health and safety standards

Revising health and safety standards

Revoking health and safety standards

Inspecting companies

Issuing citations

Assessing penalties

Petitioning for court action against flagrant violators

Providing training for employers and employees

Awarding grants to promote health and safety

OSHA has regional offices for carrying out its responsibilities, and within each region are smaller area offices that bring OSHA services to the local level. When OSHA takes action against an employer, the employer has the right to contest the action. Such challenges are heard and acted on by the Occupational Safety and Health Review Commission. Penalties assessed by OSHA are held in abeyance until the commission issues a final ruling, which can be appealed within sixty days to the U.S. Court of Appeals.

Employer and Employee Rights Under OSHA

Employers are responsible for complying with OSHA's regulations. Employers can stay abreast of the most recent regulations by monitoring OSHA's website (http://www.osha.gov) which, among other information, contains the latest edition of the **Code of Federal regulations (CFR)**. The CFR is divided into 50 parts or titles. Title 29 contains the regulations set forth by the U.S. Department of Labor and is the title with which supervisors should be familiar.

Both employers and employees have clearly defined rights. The rights of employers include the following:

1. Seek off-site consultation from the nearest OSHA office.
2. Receive free on-site consultation service from OSHA to help identify hazardous conditions and take corrective measures.
3. Receive proper identification from the OSHA compliance officer before an inspection takes place.
4. Receive advice from the OSHA compliance officer concerning the reason for the inspection.
5. Receive opening and closing sessions with the OSHA compliance officer if an inspection takes place.
6. Receive protection of proprietary trade secrets observed by an OSHA compliance officer.

7. Request a conference with the area director when a citation is issued. A notice of intent to challenge can be filed within fifteen working days from receipt of a citation.

8. If unable to comply with a standard within the required time, a request for an extension can be filed with OSHA. This is called a petition for modification of abatement (PMA).

9. Assist in developing safety and health standards through participation with OSHA Standards Advisory Committees, through standards writing organizations, and through public comment and public hearings.

10. Use Small Business Administration loans to bring the company into compliance, if applicable.

The rights of employees with regard to health and safety are also clearly set forth by OSHA. Examples of employees' rights are as follows:

1. An employer cannot be punished, harassed, or reassigned for job safety or health activities, such as complaining to the union or OSHA or participating in union or OSHA inspections or conferences.

2. Employees can privately confer with and answer questions from an OSHA compliance office in connection with a workplace inspection.

3. During an OSHA inspection, an authorized workers' representative may be given an opportunity to accompany the compliance officer to aid the inspection. An authorized worker has the right to participate in the opening and closing inspection conferences and be paid his or her normal wage for the time.

4. Employees can contact OSHA to make an inspection when employers fail to correct a hazard. OSHA will not tell the employer who requested an inspection without the employee's permission.

5. An employee can notify OSHA or a compliance officer in writing of a potential violation before or during a workplace inspection.

6. An employee can give OSHA information that could influence proposed penalties by OSHA against the employer.

7. If OSHA denies the inspection request of an employee, the employee must be informed of the reasons in writing by OSHA. The employee may request an OSHA hearing should he or she object to the OSHA decision.

8. If an OSHA compliance officer fails to cite an employer concerning an alleged violation submitted in writing by an employee, OSHA must furnish the employee with a written statement of the reason for the disposition.

9. Employees have the right to review an OSHA citation against their employer. The employer must post a copy of the citation and identify where the violation took place.

10. Employees can appear to view or be a witness in a contested enforcement matter before the Occupational Safety and Health Review Commission.

11. If OSHA fails to take action to rectify a dangerous hazard and an employee is injured, that employee has the right to bring action against OSHA to seek appropriate relief.

12. If an employee disagrees with the amount of time OSHA gives the employer to correct a hazard, he or she can ask for review by the Occupational Safety and Health Review Commission within fifteen days of when the citation was issued.

13. Employees may ask OSHA to adopt a new standard or to modify or revoke a current standard.

14. Employees may take action for or against any proposed federal standards and may appeal any final OSHA decision.

15. An employer must inform employees when applying for a variance of an OSHA standard.

16. Employees must be given the opportunity to view or take part in a variance hearing and have a right to appeal OSHA's final decision.

17. Employees have the right to access all information available in the workplace pertaining to employee protections and obligations under OSHA and standards and regulations.

18. Employees involved in hazardous operations have a right to information from the employer regarding toxicity, conditions of exposure, and precautions for safe use of all hazardous materials in the establishment.

19. The employer must inform an employee who might be overexposed to any harmful material, and the employee must be told of corrective action undertaken.

20. If an OSHA compliance officer determines that an imminent danger exists, he or she must tell affected employees of the danger and further inform them that prompt action will be taken if the employer fails to eliminate the danger.

21. If an employee requests access to records covering his or her exposure to toxic materials or harmful physical agents that require monitoring, the employer must comply with the request.

22. Employees must be given the opportunity to observe the monitoring or measuring of hazardous materials or harmful physical agents, if OSHA standards require monitoring.

23. An employee can make a request in writing to NIOSH (National Institute for Occupational Safety and Health) for a determination of whether or not a substance used in the workplace is harmful.

24. If an employee asks to review the Log and Summary of Occupational Injuries, the employer must comply with the request.

25. An employee is entitled to a copy of the Notice of Contest and to participate in hearings on contested hearings.

OSHA Violations

An employer can be cited for four types of violations during an OSHA inspection:

- **Imminent danger violation.** An imminent danger violation is issued when an OSHA inspection reveals a condition that is so unsafe or so unhealthy that serious injury or death might result, and the employer does not correct it immediately. Imminent danger violations can result in court action to shut a company down.

- **Serious violation.** A serious violation citation is issued when a condition exists that might result in death or serious injury, and the employer knew or should have known of the condition.

- **Nonserious Violation.** A nonserious violation citation is issued when a hazard exists that the employer legitimately did not know about.

- **De minimis violation.** A de minimis violation citation is issued when an OSHA standard is violated, but there is no danger of injury, death, or illness.

APPLICATION AND DISCUSSION

Supervisors play a critical role in making sure the workplace is safe, healthy, and conducive to peak performance. OSHA can be helpful to supervisors in carrying out their responsibilities in this area. Consequently, supervisors should be familiar with applicable OSHA standards and services.

- Visit OSHA's website and find the office that serves your region of the country. Contact your regional office and find out what services are available to supervisors.

■   While at its website, call up OSHA's "General Industry Standards." Go to Subpart D
(1910.25). What do the standards say about the safe use of portable wooden ladders?

POLICY ASPECTS OF HEALTH AND SAFETY

The supervisor's role with regard to health and safety in the workplace should be defined
by management policy. Organizations should have written health and safety policies that
clearly define the supervisor's responsibilities and authority.

A safety policy, regardless of the type and size of company, should have the following
characteristics:

■   Be developed with input from employees at all levels and in all departments.

■   Have the full support of top management and reflect the attitude of management
toward health and safety.

■   Be put in writing, shared with all employees, and widely publicized throughout the
organization.

■   Should be simply stated and easy to understand.

■   Clearly delineate responsibility for health and safety.

■   Provide the foundation for the development of a plan for creating and maintaining a
safe working environment.

There are two fundamental reasons for having a comprehensive health and safety
policy. The first has to do with legislative mandates and the second with economics.
These reasons are explained as follows:

■   *Legislative mandates and policy*. The OSHA Act sets forth specific health and safety
standards. In addition to the specific standards, the Act contains an all-encompass-
ing general-duty clause that covers conditions not specifically covered by the minimum standards. Complying with the Act begins with the development of a written
health and safety policy.

■   *Economics and policy*. It has been well established that good health and safety are
good business. A safe and healthy working environment is the most economical and
most productive environment. Accidents resulting in injuries or death cost the
employer. The costs fall into two categories: direct costs and hidden costs. **Direct
costs** include medical treatment, direct payments to the injured employee, workers'
compensation costs, and the cost of lost time of the injured employee. **Hidden costs**
include the cost of temporarily replacing the injured employee, the cost of paperwork associated with the accident, the cost of repairing damaged equipment, and
the cost of reworking damaged products (Figure 12-2).

Direct Costs	Hidden Costs
• Medical treatment	• Temporarily replacing the employee
• Payment to the injured employee	• Paperwork
• Workers' compensation	• Repairs to damaged equipment
• Lost time	• Reworking damaged products

Figure 12–2
Direct costs and hidden costs of accidents

Assigning Responsibility for Health and Safety

Health and safety in the workplace are the responsibility of management and employees. Management is responsible for providing a safe working environment, and employees are responsible for working in a safe manner.

Supervisors should be assigned responsibility for the work environment in their units and for the safety of their employees. This means supervisors should also have the authority necessary to make decisions about safety, disciplining employees, and correcting unsafe conditions in their units. In addition, management must back decisions made by the supervisor concerning safety.

═══ APPLICATION AND DISCUSSION ═══

A safety policy gives supervisors the guidance they need to help maintain a safe and healthy workplace and to insist that their direct reports work safely. Identify an organization that will cooperate with you in completing this activity. Then, do the following:

- Obtain a copy of the organization's safety and health policy. (If your organization does not have one, find an organization that does.)
- Compare the policy you obtained with those obtained by classmates or colleagues. How are they similar? How do they differ?

SAFETY TRAINING

A written health and safety policy accompanied by principles that operationalize it set the tone. Once this step has been taken, the next step is to provide health and **safety training**, which builds on the foundation and gives employees the knowledge they need to be safe workers.

It is important to train new employees so they learn to work safely from the outset. When beginning a safety program in an established organization that has not trained previously, treat all employees as new employees. It is also important to provide training that is appropriate to the level of employee and the type of work performed.

OSHA specifies minimum requirements for safety training in Parts 1910 through 1926. OSHA's guidelines for training recommend a model consisting of the following steps:

- Determining if training is needed
- Assessing training needs
- Setting training goals and objectives
- Developing learning materials
- Conducting the training
- Evaluating the training
- Using evaluation data to improve training

Supervisors are interested primarily in the type of training that is appropriate for their employees. Generally speaking, such training should cover the following subjects:

- Orientation to the organization's safety policy and principles
- General housekeeping procedures
- Emergency procedures
- Proper use of applicable equipment

- Orientation to hazardous materials present in the organization and proper handling of these materials
- Accident reporting procedures
- Accident follow-up procedures

The method of instruction used can range from simple one-on-one conversations between supervisor and employee to discussion groups to formal instruction. As explained in chapter 11, it is important to combine both visual and verbal material when presenting instruction. There is an important message in this for supervisors regarding how safety instruction should be presented. Just reading safety materials, hearing safety lectures, or seeing safety videos is not sufficient. Employees need to participate in active learning that involves seeing, hearing, speaking, *and* doing.

APPLICATION AND DISCUSSION

You are a supervisor at ABC, Inc. As such, you have been asked to develop a seminar for all of ABC's other supervisors on the subject of "Accident Reporting Procedures."

- Visit OSHA's website (http://www.osha.gov) and learn what you need to know about accident reporting. Also determine if there is such a seminar already available from OSHA.
- Develop a lesson plan for your seminar. You may develop your own or use material available from OSHA.

ACCIDENT PREVENTION TECHNIQUES

Accident prevention requires an ongoing program consisting of a variety of techniques. Here are some techniques supervisors can use to prevent accidents in their units:

- *Involve all employees in an ongoing hazard identification program.* Employees should be empowered to identify hazards associated with their work and to make recommendations for eliminating them.
- *Involve employees in developing safe job procedures.* Once hazards are identified, supervisors and employees should work together to find productive but safe ways to perform the job in question.
- *Teach employees how to properly use personal protective equipment and monitor to make sure they do.* It is important to ensure that employees learn how to use appropriate personal protective equipment before beginning a job. Supervisors should also make sure that employees follow through and apply what has been learned. When pressed to meet a deadline, the natural human tendency is to take shortcuts. Shortcuts taken with personal protective equipment can cause accidents. Therefore, supervisors must monitor as well as train.
- *Teach employees good housekeeping practices and require their use.* One of the most effective ways to prevent accidents is to maintain a clean, organized, orderly workplace. These things result from good housekeeping. Supervisors should teach good housekeeping and monitor to ensure it is practiced.
- *Teach employees the fundamentals of safe work practices (i.e., safe lifting, proper dress, safety glasses, etc.).* General safe work practices are perhaps the most important practices to remember. Some of the most frequently occurring accidents result from simple mistakes such as improper bending and lifting. Supervisors should monitor general work practices closely.

====== **APPLICATION AND DISCUSSION** ======

A tale of two supervisors. Lois Bridges is known as a supervisor who "takes care" of her employees. This includes their safety on the job. Bridges' employees have worked for three years straight without lost time due to an injury. Vicky Morecraft, on the other hand, is known as a supervisor who expects employees to "cut corners" to meet work quotas and deadlines. Lost time due to injuries is common in Morecraft's department. Yesterday Morecraft received a verbal warning about the increasing numbers of accidents in her department. Today she asked her good friend, Lois Bridges, for help. "I've got to stop these accidents and injuries in my department," said Morecraft to her friend. "What can I do?"

- In the long run, what do you think will happen to the productivity of Morecraft's team if things don't change?
- Put yourself in the position of Lois Bridges. What would you tell Vicky Morecraft to do?

ACCIDENT INVESTIGATION AND REPORTING

In spite of your best prevention efforts, an accident may still occur. It is important to determine the cause. Why did the accident happen? Answering this question is the purpose of an accident investigation. By investigating the cause of an accident, supervisors may be able to prevent a recurrence. For this reason, it is also important to conduct the investigation immediately. Time can obscure the facts, the accident scene can change, witnesses can forget what they saw, or unrelated factors can creep in and obscure what really happened.

Figure 12-3 contains a checklist supervisors can use as a guide in conducting on-the-spot accident investigations. This checklist will help supervisors determine if the accident was caused by factors that could have been prevented and what those factors are. Occasionally the causal factor will be the failure of employees to observe mandatory safety precautions. When this is the case it should be noted, but the purpose is to prevent future accidents, not assign blame.

Writing the Accident Report

Once the investigation has been completed, an accident report should be written.

> An **accident report** is a comprehensive summary of all of the pertinent facts about an accident.

The report format can follow the investigation checklist unless the company uses a standard accident report form. Regardless of the format, supervisors should remember several rules when writing accident reports. Prominent among these are the following:

- Be brief and stick to the facts.
- Be objective and impartial.
- Be comprehensive; leave out no facts.
- State clearly what employees and what equipment were involved.
- List any procedures, processes, or precautions that were not being observed at the time of the accident.

Checklist for On-the-Spot Accident Investigations

- What was the injured employee doing at the time of the accident?
- Had the injured employee received proper training in the task before being asked to perform it?
- Was the injured employee authorized to use the equipment or perform the process involved in the accident?
- Were other employees present at the time of the accident? If so, who are they and what were they doing? (Interview them *separately* as soon as possible after the accident.)
- Was the task in question being performed according to properly approved procedures?
- Was proper personal protective equipment being used and were work procedures being followed at the time of the accident?
- Was the injured employee new to the job in question?
- Was the process/equipment/system involved new? Old? Properly maintained?
- Was the injured person being supervised at the time of the accident?
- Has a similar accident occurred before? If so, were corrective measures recommended? Were they implemented?
- Are there obvious factors that led to the accident or that could have prevented the accident?

Figure 12–3
Guidelines for conducting on-the-spot accident investigations

- List causal factors and any contributing factors.
- Make brief, clear, concise recommendations for corrective measures.

=========== APPLICATION AND DISCUSSION ===========

Assume you are the supervisor of a team in which an accident has occurred. You are required to conduct an investigation and write an accident report. Use an accident with which you are familiar or make up a hypothetical (but realistic) accident.

- Conduct a simulated accident investigation.
- Write an accident report based on your investigation.

WORKER'S COMPENSATION

Workers' compensation is a concept with which supervisors should be familiar. Unlike OSHA, workers' compensation is not a federal law. Rather, it is based on state laws that vary from state to state. The purpose of **workers' compensation** is to give injured workers recourse without the need for lengthy, expensive court action, a purpose that has not been fully achieved due primarily to claims of psychological injuries such as stress. Regardless of the form they take, all workers' compensation laws are designed to finance the rehabilitation of injured employees and to minimize the employee's loss of ability to work.

- *Income replacement.* **Income replacement** is the money paid to an injured worker to replace income lost due to injury or disease. This applies to both present and future income. Replacement should be prompt and approximately equivalent to the amount of income lost. This is typically the first objective of a workers' compensation law.

- *Rehabilitation of the worker.* **Rehabilitation** refers to restoring the injured worker's ability to participate competitively in the workplace. The compensation should cover the cost of both medical and vocational rehabilitation. This is typically an objective of workers' compensation laws.

- *Accident prevention.* Like any health and safety program, one of the objectives of workers' compensation laws is to prevent accidents. As with insurance, worker's compensation rates assessed employers are affected by accident rates. Therefore, workers' compensation laws provide a strong incentive for employers to maintain high safety standards. This is an objective of most workers' compensation plans.

- *Cost distribution.* **Cost distribution** motivates employers to make continual safety improvements because it allocates cost based on safety performance. In other words, the better an industry's safety record, the lower its workers' compensation rates, at least in theory. In reality, rates are typically based on the type of employee in question (e.g., rates for roofing contractors are higher than those of retail stores regardless of experience).

Workers' Compensation Benefits

Employers are required to carry workers' compensation insurance. It is typically obtained through one of three options: (1) a private insurance company, (2) self-insurance, or (3) state insurance funds. Benefits typically include the following:

- Payment for medical treatment.
- Income for the injured worker during the period of disability.
- Funeral and burial costs in the event of death.
- Income for dependents of the injured worker as appropriate.
- Income to cover the costs of in-home medical care (available in some states).
- Payment of the cost of a prosthesis (available in some states).

Employer Liability Beyond Workers' Compensation

One of the main objectives of the enactment of workers' compensation laws has been to make appropriate recourse to injured workers without the need for court action. In most cases involving physical rather than psychological injuries, this works. However, there are instances in which employers can be liable beyond the coverage of workers' compensation.

> ***Employer liability*** *refers to the employer's legal obligation to the employee to provide a safe working environment.*

Supervisors should be familiar with instances in which the employer might be liable. The potential areas of employer liability are summarized as follows:

- **Criminal liability**. Employers can be held criminally liable if they fail to train employees in how to properly handle on-the-job hazards, fail to provide personal protective equipment, or fail to respond appropriately to employees' complaints about hazardous conditions.

- **Aggravation of injuries**. Employers can be held liable if they aggravate injuries suffered by a worker. This is particularly important to supervisors because an injury that is aggravated by personnel attempting to help an injured employee can result in the employer being held liable.

- **Product liability**. An employer can be held liable if a product it produces causes an injury to an employee who uses it.

- **Intentional assault**. Employers can be held liable if a supervisor or higher level manager attacks and injures an employee.

- **Losses to the immediate family**. Employers can be held liable for losses felt by members of the immediate family as a result of the worker's injuries. Losses to immediate family members may include loss of consortium, companionship, or peace of mind.

APPLICATION AND DISCUSSION

Miriam Webster, a supervisor for ABC, Inc., had been right there when Kay Scampella slipped and fell down a flight of stairs while delivering a report to the Accounting Department. Anxious to help, she ran down the stairs and pulled Scampella to her feet. Scampella complained of back pain, so Webster had her sit down while she called for help.

- Evaluate Miriam Webster's handling of this accident from the perspective of workers' compensation. Were her actions appropriate or ill advised?

- How would you handle this situation?

BLOODBORNE PATHOGENS AND EMPLOYEE HEALTH AND SAFETY

AIDS, hepatitis C, and hepatitis B have become significant health and safety issues for supervisors. It is critical that supervisors know how to deal properly and appropriately with these controversial diseases. The major concerns of supervisors with regard to bloodborne pathogens are (1) legal considerations and (2) employee education.

Legal Considerations

The legal considerations relating to bloodborne pathogens in the workplace grow out of several pieces of federal legislation, including: the Rehabilitation Act, the Occupational Safety and Health Act, and the Employee Retirement Income Security Act.

The *Rehabilitation Act* was enacted to protect handicapped people, including handicapped workers. Section 504 of the Act makes discrimination on the basis of a handicap unlawful. Any agency, organization, or company that receives federal funding falls within the purview of the Act. Such entities may not discriminate against handicapped individuals who are otherwise qualified. Through various court actions, this concept has been well defined. A handicapped person is **otherwise qualified** when he or she can perform what the courts have described as the **essential functions** of the job. When the worker's handicap is a contagious disease such as AIDS or hepatitis, it must be shown that there is no significant risk of the disease being transmitted in the workplace. If there is a significant risk, the infected employee is not considered otherwise qualified. Employers and the courts must make these determinations on a case-by-case basis.

There is one final concept associated with the Rehabilitation Act with which supervisors should be familiar: the concept of **reasonable accommodation**. In determining if a handicapped worker can perform the essential functions of a job, employers are required to make reasonable accommodations to help the employee. This concept applies to workers with any type of handicapping condition including a communicable disease. What constitutes reasonable accommodation, like what constitutes otherwise qualified, must be determined on a case-by-case basis.

The concepts growing out of the Rehabilitation Act give the supervisor added importance when dealing with infected employees. The supervisor's knowledge of the various jobs in his or her unit will be essential in helping make an "otherwise qualified" decision. The supervisor's knowledge of the job tasks in question will be helpful in determining the likelihood of a bloodborne disease being transmitted to other employees. Finally, the supervisor's knowledge of the job tasks in question will be essential in determining what constitutes reasonable accommodation and what the actual accommodations should be (Figure 12–4).

In arriving at what constitutes reasonable accommodation, supervisors should be aware that employers are not required to make fundamental changes that alter the nature of the job or result in undue costs or administrative burdens. Clearly, good judgment and a thorough knowledge of the job are required when attempting to make reasonable accommodations for an infected employee. Supervisors should expect to be actively involved in such efforts.

The Occupational Safety and Health Act requires that employers provide a safe workplace free of hazards. The Act also prohibits employers from retaliating against an employee who refuses to work in an environment he or she believes may be unhealthy (Section 654). This poses a special problem for supervisors of infected employees. Other employees may attempt to use Section 654 of the Act as the basis for refusing to work with such employees. For this reason, it is important that organizations educate their employees concerning how bloodborne diseases are transmitted. If they know how a disease is transmitted, they will be less likely to exhibit an irrational fear of working with an infected colleague.

Even when a comprehensive education program is provided, employers should not automatically assume that an employee's fear of working with the infected individual is irrational. Employers have an obligation to treat such cases individually. Does the complaining employee have a physical condition that puts him or her at greater risk of contracting a disease than other employees? If so, the fears may not be irrational. However, a fear of working with an infected co-worker is usually irrational, making it unlikely that Section 654 could be used successfully as the basis for refusing to work.

The Employee Retirement Income Security Act (ERISA) protects the benefits of employees by prohibiting actions taken against them based on their eligibility for benefits. This means that employers covered by ERISA cannot terminate an employee with a bloodborne disease or one who is suspected of having such a disease as a way of avoiding expensive medical costs. Under ERISA, it is irrelevant whether the employee's condition is considered a handicap since the Act applies to all employees regardless of condition.

APPLICATION AND DISCUSSION

You are the supervisor of a team of truck drivers who make long cross-country trips using the "buddy system." One person drives while the other sleeps on eight-hour rota-

Figure 12–4
Key components of the Rehabilitation Act relating to bloodborne pathogens

Rehabilitation Act
✓ Essential Functions
✓ Reasonable Accommodation
✓ Otherwise Qualified

tions. You have twenty drivers on your team who are mixed and matched so that over time everyone works with everyone else. This morning nineteen of your team members submitted a petition demanding that Ed Stuart be fired. They had just learned that Stuart has AIDS. As a result, nobody wants to drive with him.

- How should you handle this situation?
- Discuss your plan with classmates or colleagues. Are there any concerns or issues you did not think of?

========== ON-THE-JOB SCENARIOS ==========

1. Before his automobile accident, Ron Marin had been the most senior security guard at Southeastern Electric Company's "Big Bend" Plant (a nuclear-powered electricity-generation facility). Federal laws governing the operation of facilities such as the Big Bend Plant make security an important issue. In a word, security at the Big Bend Plant is "tight." Ron Marin's colleagues patrol carefully and constantly every square inch of the rugged terrain that makes up the plant's property, which is heavily wooded and swampy. Ron Marin recently returned to work after a long period of healing and physical rehabilitation, but he can now walk for only limited periods of time and then only with a special walker. The company has offered Marin the job of dispatcher at the same salary he earned as the senior security guard, but Marin is adamant. He wants his old job back. "I'm an outdoors type. I don't want a desk job," was Marin's response to the offer of the dispatcher position. He wants the company to purchase a specially designed four-wheeler he can use to make his rounds. But even with such a vehicle, about 25 percent of the patrolling area would still be inaccessible to Marin.

   - Does Ron Marin's request constitute "reasonable accommodation"? Why or why not?
   - If you were Marin's supervisor, how would you handle his request?

2. ABC Company uses the concept of the self-directed workforce to promote safety. Employees are responsible for developing safety standards, conducting inspections, and working with OSHA personnel. The self-directed workforce concept is based on the philosophy that well-trained employees make the best decisions concerning how employees as a group do their work. Consequently, ABC trains employees to make decisions, solve problems, and take the initiative.

   The self-directed concept was originally initiated at ABC to improve productivity, but it worked so well that the concept was extended to be used to reduce accident rates and lower accident–related costs. ABC wants its employees to understand the need for safety and feel ownership in the company's safety policies and practices.

   A key part of the self-directed safety program at ABC is the participative safety management team. Each team chooses its own leader. Team members are trained to conduct walk-through inspections using the same criteria and methods used by OSHA inspectors. Workers observed in the act of an unsafe practice are handed a wallet-sized safety awareness card that carries the following message:

Safety Awareness

The Best Accident Prevention

I just noticed you doing something that could have caused an accident. Think about what you've done in the last few minutes and you will probably recall what I saw. I am giving you this card as a part of our campaign to make all of us safety conscious. Keep it until you see someone doing something in an unsafe way and then pass it on. P. S. I hope I don't get it back!

Safety problems discovered with machines, equipment, or facilities are recorded and the list of corrective actions needed is given to higher management for action. The list is monitored until all corrective actions have been accomplished. The result has been that workers know management places a high priority on safety and that their voice is heard.

A safety incentive program originally developed by one participatory safety management team reduced injuries from 8 or 8 per week to an average of 2.4, with a number of weeks in which only one injury occurred.

However, even these excellent results did not completely solve all safety problems. Ninety-five percent of ABC's employees went along with the self-directed safety program, but a hardcore 5 percent still worked unsafely. This group was always comprised of the same employees.

One participatory safety management team took the initiative and developed a safety performance policy that established standards for allowable numbers and types of injuries. Three recordable injuries are allowed per year. On the occasion of the fourth injury, the employee is required to meet with the supervisor to discuss safety. The supervisor can recommend additional safety training that must be done on the employee's time. The training is optional, but if the employee waives it he or she can be removed from the workplace and placed on layoff status. Analyze these approaches to safety carefully. Discuss them with classmates or colleagues. Do you see weaknesses? How would you improve these approaches?

3. You are the most senior supervisor at Gulf Coast Electrical Power Company. Each year for the past five years your company's accident rate has increased markedly. The company has no written health and safety philosophy statement, no principles, no education and training, and only haphazard record keeping. You have been asked to chair a committee of workers, supervisors, and higher level managers to recommend what the company should do to stem the increasing flow of accidents. Formulate the recommendations you will make to your committee.

4. Your company has a health and safety program. However, it does not seem to be working well and it is not popular with the employees. Develop a plan for evaluating the program and making recommendations for improvement.

5. You have been selected to chair a committee of employees that will be responsible for developing health and safety training goals and objectives for the organization. Select any type of organization and develop a comprehensive set of training goals and objectives for that organization in the area of health and safety.

6. You have recently been appointed as the new supervisor of the packaging and shipping unit of Microtech Computer Company. The accident rate in your unit is the highest in the company. Develop a plan for preventing future accidents.

7. A serious accident has occurred in your unit and you did not witness it. However, as the supervisor, you are required to write an accident report. Develop an accident report that meets all the criteria of a well-written report. You may create the circumstances of the accident.

8. You are the shift supervisor in a plastics recycling plant. One of your employees approaches you at the shift change and asks to speak with you in private. The employee tells you confidentially that he has just tested positive for AIDS. How should you handle this situation with regard to the employee, the other employees in your unit, and your company?

KEY TERMS AND PHRASES

Accident report

Aggravation of injures

Cost distribution

Criminal liability

CFR   Nonserious violation
De minimis violation   OSHA
Direct costs   Otherwise qualified
Employer liability   Product liability
Essential functions   Reasonable accommodation
Hidden costs   Rehabilitation
Imminent danger violation   Safety training
Income replacement   Serious violation
Intentional assault   Workers' compensation
Losses to immediate family

REVIEW QUESTIONS

1. Explain briefly what prompted the U.S. government to pass the Occupational Safety and Health Act.

2. Explain how the Occupational Safety and Health Act is administered and enforced.

3. The Occupational Safety and Health Administration has several specific responsibilities. List at least four of these.

4. The Code of Federal Regulations is updated annually and contains a list of employer rights under the Occupational Safety and Health Act. List four of these rights.

5. Explain what rights a worker has if he or she disagrees with the amount of time OSHA gives the employer to correct a hazard.

6. Explain the following types of OSHA violations: imminent danger violation, serious violation, nonserious violation, and *de minimis* violation..

7. There are two fundamental reasons for having a comprehensive health and safety policy. Explain these two reasons from the perspective of an industrial supervisor.

8. Differentiate between *direct costs* and *hidden costs*.

9. What is the supervisor's responsibility with regard to health and safety in the workplace?

10. Why is it important to have a written health and safety policy that is operationalized by health and safety principles?

11. List the seven steps recommended by OSHA for health and safety training.

12. What are the general subject areas that should be covered in any health and safety education program?

13. List and explain three accident prevention techniques that can be used by modern industrial supervisors.

14. List four rules to apply when writing accident reports.

15. Explain the specific objectives of workers' compensation legislation.

16. List the types of benefits typically provided by worker's compensation insurance.

17. Explain three potential areas of employer liability beyond workers' compensation.

18. How do the following concepts contained in the Rehabilitation Act apply to AIDS-infected workers: otherwise qualified, essential functions, and reasonable accommodation?

CHAPTER THIRTEEN

Staffing

LEARNING OBJECTIVES

After studying this chapter, you should be able to do the following:

- Definite the term *staffing.*
- Describe the staffing process.
- Discuss the legal considerations related to staffing.
- Define *forecasting* and discuss job analysis techniques.
- Explain the recruiting component of staffing.
- Explain the interviewing component of staffing.
- Describe the controversies involved in employment testing.
- Explain the selection component of staffing.
- Explain the orientation component of staffing.
- Describe other staffing concerns such as handling layoffs.

In today's workplace, employees are viewed as valuable resources rather than simply as laborers as was often the case in the past. This attitude has resulted in many modern organizations changing what used to be called *personnel* to **human resources**. Such companies see people as critical resources who have a vested interest in the organization's success and, as a result, should be full participants in the overall enterprise.

Staffing is a critical aspect of human resources management, and supervisors have a key role to play in the staffing process. This chapter should help supervisors understand their role in staffing and help them become proficient in all aspects of the process

STAFFING DEFINED

> **Staffing**, *a critical component in an organization's overall resource management program, is the process through which employees are recruited, interviewed, selected, and oriented.*

Effective staffing results in filling an accurately forecasted number of positions with the best qualified people when they are needed.

OVERVIEW OF THE STAFFING PROCESS

Staffing is a process consisting of six steps, which sometimes are given different names. In this book, the six steps in the staffing process are named as follows:

1. Analyzing and specifying
2. Forecasting
3. Recruiting
4. Interviewing
5. Selecting
6. Orienting

Analyzing and Specifying

This step involves **analyzing** the needs of the company to determine what types of job positions are required and in what numbers. Typically, these needs are displayed on an organizational chart. There must be clear-cut specifications that delineate the job requirements and minimum qualifications. These specifications are set forth in a job description. Supervisors typically are not responsible for this task, although they may participate in it along with human resources professionals.

Forecasting

Forecasting involves predicting the number of employees that will be needed to achieve the organization's goals. Supervisors play a key role in this step since they are in the best position to know how many employees will be needed on their teams. This step is covered in greater detail later in this unit.

Recruiting

Recruiting involves undertaking those activities necessary to bring in applicants, such as advertising job openings, and screening applications, which may come from inside the organization or from outside. These tasks are usually accomplished by the human resources department. Supervisors do not play a major role, if any, in this step. However, it is not uncommon for a supervisor to need to fill a vacancy on short notice. How can the process be speeded up in these occasional emergency situations? The following strategies can help:

- Keep an updated list of all positions for which you are responsible. Note the positions you have had to fill most frequently.
- Determine how long the high turnover positions remain filled on the average and the reasons employees give for quitting. Is there something you can do in response to these reasons?
- Determine whether high turnover positions typically have been filled from inside the company or outside.
- Using this information, develop a chart that forecasts likely turnover in your unit for the next twelve months.
- Decide in advance from where you plan to attract new applicants. For example, will it be local vocational schools, community colleges, or other sources? Keep an updated directory of telephone contacts for quick reference. Stay in touch with your contacts and nurture your relationship with them so that when needed on short notice they will respond.

Interviewing

Once the applicants have been narrowed down to those who appear to be qualified, interviews are arranged, usually by the human resources department. A human resources specialist may even participate in the interviews to ensure that all applicable policies and regulations are observed. However, the key role in **interviewing** is played by the supervisor, who typically asks the job-related questions that help determine which applicant is the best qualified. This step is covered in more detail later in this unit.

Selecting

When filling a job opening there are numerous factors to consider in **selecting** an applicant: Which applicant has the best technical skills? Which applicant appears to have the most growth potential? Which applicant appears to have the best generic work skills (i.e., dependability, loyalty, personality)? Which applicant will best fit into the team? Supervisors play a key role in answering these types of questions. Human resources personnel help ensure that all factors considered are fair, equitable, and legal. This step is covered in more detail later in this chapter.

Orienting

Too often, the staffing process stops with the selection step. Once selected, new employees are put to work and expected to fend for themselves. This inevitably leads to problems that could have been prevented had the new employees been given a thorough orientation.

Orienting new employees involves making them familiar with their new employer, their fellow employees, their new job, and what is expected of them. It also involves clearing up unknowns that might inhibit their productivity. The purpose of orienting employees is to give them the information they need to succeed in their new jobs and to help them break down the barriers inherent in being new. This step is covered in more depth later in this unit.

APPLICATION AND DISCUSSION

Identify an organization that will work with you and schedule an appointment with their Human Resources Director.

- Determine how the organization handles all aspects of the staffing process (i.e., analyzing and specifying, forecasting, recruiting, etc).
- Determine what role supervisors play in the staffing process.
- If you were a supervisor with this company, would you want to play more or less of a role in the staffing process? Why?

LEGAL CONSIDERATIONS OF STAFFING

Staffing has evolved over the years into a complex and potentially litigious activity for organizations. Gone are the days when supervisors could hire whomever they wanted without concern for legal, ethical, or equity considerations. Society now insists that staffing practices be fair and equitable, as they should be. To ensure this is the case, numerous laws relating to staffing have been enacted over the years. Some of these are summarized in the following list:

- Equal Pay Act
- Civil Rights Act, Title VII
- Age Discrimination in Employment Act
- Occupational Safety and Health Act
- Equal Employment Opportunity Act
- Vocational Rehabilitation Act
- Employee Retirement Income and Security Act
- Freedom of Information Act
- Privacy Act
- Vietnam Era Veterans Readjustment Act
- Minimum Wage Law
- Pregnancy Discrimination Act
- Civil Service Act, Title VII
- Americans with Disabilities Act

From this list, you can see that the legal considerations of staffing have become too complex for supervisors alone to keep up with. This is one of the reasons the human resources department has become so important. Human resources specialists are responsible for staying up to date with the legal aspects of staffing and for developing in-house procedures that translate applicable laws into everyday practice.

However, even with the assistance of human resources personnel, supervisors are still actively involved in the staffing process. Consequently, this section discusses the legal considerations with which supervisors should be familiar. More specifically, supervisors should be familiar with legal issues relating to equal employment opportunity, employee compensation, health and safety, and employee relations.

Equal Employment Opportunity

Staffing policies, procedures, and practices must ensure equal employment opportunity for all people. More specifically, they cannot discriminate based on race, gender, age, national origin, handicapping conditions, religion, or marital status in any aspect of the staffing process or in guiding any employment decision. The equal employment opportunity provisions of staffing grow out of two pieces of federal legislation: (1) the **Civil Rights Act** (Title VII) and (2) the **Equal Employment Opportunity Act**, two statutes that establish the responsibilities of employers in the critical area of hiring, promoting, paying, and disciplining employees.

Since these legislative initiatives were enacted, the courts have heard thousands of cases relating to discrimination in the workplace. A percentage of these worked their way up through the system to the U.S. Supreme Court. Two concepts have evolved from these cases for challenging an organization's staffing practices: (1) disparate impact and (2) disparate treatment. **Disparate impact** involves discrimination that affects a protected class of people (i.e., minorities, women, the handicapped). **Disparate treatment** involves discrimination against individuals.

In a case in which disparate impact is alleged, the courts apply a three-step process:

- **Step 1:** The employee who feels wronged (complainant) files a suit alleging discrimination that has resulted in disparate impact against a protected class.
- **Step 2:** The employer is required to show how the staffing practice in question relates to the job. The concept of *job relatedness* is critical. For example, an individual cannot be required to pass a heavy-lifting test unless it can be shown that heavy-lifting is an integral part of the job.

- **Step Three:** The employee is required to show that the employer's justification in step two is unacceptable or that the employer could have implemented a practice that would be less likely to have a negative impact.

Cases alleging disparate treatment focus on the intent of the employer. The key question is, "Did the employer implement a staffing practice with the intent to discriminate?" The burden of proof shifts from the complainant to the employer if the following conditions exist:

1. The complainant is a member of a protected class.
2. The complainant applied for the job, was qualified for the promotion, was eligible for the raise, etc.
3. The complainant did not get the job, promotion, raise, etc.
4. The employer continued the job search, gave another person the promotion, gave another person the raise, etc.

At this point, the burden shifts to the employer to provide nondiscriminatory reasons for its staffing or employment-related decision. The court rules on the viability of these reasons. The development of the disparate impact and disparate treatment concepts have given any person (or group) who feels discriminated against in the workplace an avenue for resolving the situation.

The handbook used by human resources personnel for ensuring compliance with equal opportunity laws is *Uniform Guidelines on Employee Selection Procedures*, published by the Equal Employment Opportunity Commission (EEOC). Prospective and practicing supervisors can benefit from familiarizing themselves with this document, which is available in most college and university libraries.

In addition to the Civil Rights Act (Title VII), several other federal laws prohibit discrimination against specific protected classes of people. The **Age Discrimination in Employment Act** singled out people between the ages of forty and sixty-nine for special protection in the workplace. The **Vocational Rehabilitation Act** made people with mental and/or physical handicaps a protected class. The U.S. Supreme Court has ruled that employees who have a contagious disease may be considered handicapped and therefore are protected under the Vocational Rehabilitation Act. For example, employees with AIDS are covered by the act and are therefore protected from discrimination. The **Vietnam Era Veterans Readjustment Act** extended special protection in the workplace to Vietnam veterans.

Some states have established their own equal employment opportunity agencies. These agencies may supplement and extend the efforts of the EEOC, but they cannot supersede them. The EEOC is traditionally deferred to by the U.S. Supreme Court in equal employment questions.

Compensation and Benefits

The United States has a long history of enacting laws to regulate **compensation** (wages, salaries) and **benefits** (insurance, paid leave, retirement). One of the principal laws that still governs the behavior of employers in this regard was passed in 1938: the **Fair Labor Standards Act** (FLSA). This act established minimum wages, maximum hours, overtime guidelines, and child labor standards. Enforcement of the FLSA is the responsibility of the U.S. Department of Labor.

Two key concepts in the FLSA are those of exempt and nonexempt employees. Nonexempt employees are those to whom all the provisions of the law apply. Exempt employees are those in executive, administrative, and professional positions to whom certain provisions in the law do not apply. One provision that does not apply to exempt employees is the overtime pay provision. This is why companies are not obligated to pay overtime pay to their salaried managers and professionals.

The **Equal Pay Act (EPA)** was enacted to ensure that men and women receive equal pay for equal work. For example, male and female machine operators doing the same job must receive the same pay under the provisions of this Act. To determine if two jobs constitute equal work and therefore must receive equal pay the following criteria are used:

1. Does the work require equal skill?
2. Does the work require equal effort?
3. Does the work involve equal responsibility?
4. Is the work performed under similar working conditions?

The EPA is administered by the EEOC. It has come into play frequently in recent years in suits in which women allege that they are paid less than men who do the same job. In a few exceptional cases equal pay for equal work is not required. Most of these cases fall into the following three categories:

1. **Seniority**-based pay systems (based on length of employment)
2. **Merit pay systems** (based on clearly measurable distinctions such as a higher degree)
3. **Incentive systems** (based on performance)

Other systems that can be shown to discriminate on any basis other than gender may be allowed under the EPA. However, such programs will be carefully scrutinized.

In addition to the FLSA and the EPA, several other laws govern compensation and benefit plans. Prominent among these are the **Employee Retirement Income and Security Act** (ERISA), the Pregnancy Discrimination Act, and the Federal Insurance Contribution Act (FICA). ERISA protects employee retirement pensions from misuse or poor management, and it ensures pensions against the potential bankruptcy of employers.

The **Pregnancy Discrimination Act** protects pregnant employees from discrimination by requiring employers to treat pregnancy as they would a disability. This allows pregnant employee to draw the same benefits they would receive for a disability resulting from an accident. The **Federal Insurance Contribution Act** requires that employers pay at least half of an employee's social security contribution for each pay period.

Health and Safety

Individual states enact workers' compensation laws to protect employees who are temporarily or permanently disabled on the job. Typical legislation requires employers to pay medical costs and premiums that are used to pay injured employees a percentage of their normal pay.

Perhaps the most comprehensive and far-reaching piece of health and safety legislation is the **Occupational Safety and Health Act**, which is federal legislation that requires employers to open their doors to federal health and safety inspectors. The OSHAct is administered by the Occupational Safety and Health Administration (OSHA).

The purpose of the Act is to assure as far as possible every working man and woman in the nation safe and healthful working conditions. Section 5(a) of the Act reads as follows:

Each employer

1. shall furnish to each of his employees employment and a place of employment which are free from recognized hazards that are causing or are likely to cause death or serious physical harm to his employees;
2. shall comply with occupational safety and health standards promulgated under the Act.[1]

OSHA inspections may occur unannounced at any time. Employers are also required to keep comprehensive health, safety, and accident records and file periodic reports.

Employee Relations

Employee relations laws were born during the worst years of the Depression. Consequently, the earliest legislation was tilted heavily in favor of organized labor. The most significant piece of legislation passed at this time was the **National Labor Relations Act**, sometimes referred to as the Wagner Act.

The **Wagner Act** made unionization of employees legal. The act is credited with being the foundation upon which the union movement in the United States was built. For the first time employees were allowed to organize, use the court system to resolve differences with employers, and bargain collectively for higher wages, better working conditions, and more reasonable hours.

The Wagner Act also defined a set of unfair labor practices employers are prohibited from engaging in and established the **National Labor Relations Board** (NRLB) to oversee employer-employee relations. The NLRB is empowered to conduct union elections, schedule hearings, conduct investigations into alleged unfair labor practices, and issue injunctions when unfair practices are discovered.

In 1947, the **Taft-Hartley Amendment** was attached to the Wagner Act. Taft-Hartley was put in place to balance what had come to be seen, at least by employers, as labor relations legislation slanted too heavily in favor of labor. It identified unfair labor practices on the part of unions, protected the free speech of employers, and provided a mechanism for employees to vote out or decertify a union.

The Labor-Management Reporting and Disclosure Act—also called the **Landrum-Griffin Act**—was enacted in 1959 to rid unions of corruption. It established a bill of rights for individual union members, enacted controls on union dues, and put in place reporting requirements with which unions must comply.

APPLICATION AND DISCUSSION

Joe and John applied for the same job at ABC, Inc. Joe is twenty-five years old and has an employment record and recommendations that show he is the "best in the business" at the job in question. John is fifty-six years old. He meets all of the qualifications for the job, but his recommendations indicate that his performance is typically "average" or "slightly above average." He is also a minority.

■ Who should ABC, Inc. hire in this case — Joe or John? (You might want to locate a copy of the *Uniform Guidelines on Employee Selection Procedures* before answering.)

■ Assume Joe was hired and John files an age discrimination complaint, making the point that very few people in the company are over forty years old. Does John have a good case? Why or why not?

Marsha Waylon is an executive secretary with XYZ, Inc. She is upset because the company's long distance truck drivers are paid more than executive secretaries. She has threatened to file a complaint under the Equal Pay Act (EPA).

■ Analyze her complaint and the relative skill and effort required by the two jobs.

■ Defend or refute Waylon's claim.

■ Make a list of problems you face in trying to pin down "comparable" skills when comparing vastly different jobs (e.g., secretary versus truck driver).

FORECASTING STAFFING NEEDS

Forecasting staffing needs is a major responsibility of supervisors. Forecasting is the process through which supervisors determine their personnel needs for a given period or for a specific project. Supervisors are called on to forecast staffing needs on two occasions.

The first occasion is when an organization has a given amount of work and needs to know how many of what type of employee will be needed to complete it. The second occasion is when a company is preparing for a contract it hopes to win. In both cases, it is critical that the company have accurate personnel forecasts.

Forecasting staffing needs is both an art and a science. The key to effective forecasting is the ability to accurately estimate the amount of time that will be needed to accomplish a specified amount of work. What follows is an annotated list of the steps involved in developing a staffing forecast:

1. *Clearly identify the amount of work to be done during the period in question.* You will typically be given a specified amount of work to be completed within a specified amount of time (e.g., process 250 packages in 60 days).

2. *Compute the direct labor needs.* This step involves both the art and the science of forecasting. The art is in determining the total number of employee hours needed to complete the work. Experienced supervisors have an advantage here. They can look back at previous projects and base their estimates on these. The cost accounting department might be able to help if the work is of the type that has been done before. If the project is new to your organization, be sure to allow for preparation time.

   - Divide the estimated total employee hours by 8 to determine how many employee days will be needed. For example, if you estimated 3,200 employee hours, dividing by 8 will convert this to 400 employee days.

   - Divide the employee days figure by the number of workdays in the period of time in question. Continuing our example, if there are 90 workdays in the period in question, divide the 400 employee days by 90. This computation reveals the need for 4.44 employees.

   - Complete this step by adjusting your calculations to accommodate absenteeism. Attendance records for your unit will provide a weekly or monthly absentee rate per employee. Multiply that rate times the projected number of employees (4.44). For example, if the monthly absentee rate in your unit is one-quarter of a day (2 hours) per employee, multiply 4.44 employees times 2 hours. The result is a loss of 8.88 hours to absenteeism per month.

   - To continue our example, using 20 workdays per month as the conversion factor, 90 working days converts to 4.5 months. Multiplying 4.5 months times 8.88 hours per month results in 39.96 hours that must be added to the total employee hours estimate (3,200 + 39.96) for a new total of 3,239.96 employee hours.

   - Dividing the adjusted total of employee hours (3,239.96) by 8 results in a new workdays total of 405. Dividing the adjusted workdays total (405) by 90 workdays results in an adjusted direct labor need of 4.5 employees.

3. *Compute the indirect labor needs.* In addition to the people who will actually produce the product or provide the services (**direct labor**) new support personnel (**indirect labor**) may also be needed. Will you need additional clerical help? If so, their position must be added to the forecast.

4. *Add the direct figures to the indirect figures to get a total **labor** figure.* Suppose you determine that a part-time employee will be needed to work half-time. This indirect position (.5) is added to the adjusted direct figure (4.5) for a total forecast of 5 employees to complete the projected work in a 90-day period.

To see how these steps are actually applied, consider the example of Harrison Washington, senior supervisor for Military Clothing Manufacturers, Inc. MCM has just won a contract to produce field jackets for the U. S. Army. The contract gives MCM 6 months or 120 workdays to complete the project. Already working at capacity, MCM will need to add personnel. Harrison Washington has been asked to forecast the personnel needed for his unit. Harrison's calculations are as follows:

Step 1: Identify the Work

Produce 10,000 field jackets in 120 workdays.

Step 2: Compute the Direct Labor

Total work hours = 40,000
(4 hours per jacket x 10,000)

Total work days = 5,000
(40,000 ÷ 8)

Employees needed (nonadjusted figure) = 42
(5,000 ÷ 120)

Total absentee hours = 504
(2 hours per month x 42 x 6 months)

Adjusted total work hours = 40,504
(40,000 + 504)

Adjusted total workdays = 5,063
(40,504 ÷ 8)

Adjusted direct labor need = 42.19
(5,063 ÷ 120)

Step 3: Compute the Indirect Labor

Need two material runners and one warehouse worker.

Step 4: Add the Direct and Indirect Figures

42.19 direct labor + 3 indirect labor = 45.19

By these calculations, Harrison Washington is forecasting a need for 45 new workers to complete the contract in 120 workdays. These calculations represent the science of forecasting. The art comes into play when taking into account such intangible factors as the expected level of competence for new hires. Will MCM be able to find 45 fully trained, experienced employees or will the company have to provide on-the-job training? Will MCM's current workforce remain stable? How will these factors affect the contract? Such considerations become part of the forecasting process for experienced supervisors. Supervisors learn to increase their forecasts by a percentage depending on the relative capabilities of applicants.

================= APPLICATION AND DISCUSSION =================

As supervisor of the shipping department, you have been asked to forecast the number of temporary employees that will be needed as the result of an increased workload. Your department will have to prepare 1,500 more boxes for shipping than usual over a period of 50 workdays. This comes to 30 extra boxes per day. Each box requires 45 minutes of preparation time for a total of 67,500 minutes or 1,125 hours of work over and above the normal workload. How many full-time temporary employees will be needed?

INTERVIEWING

Interviewing is an important part of the staffing process for supervisors. In this step the supervisor's experience and expertise come into play. The human resources department can be very helpful in making sure that equal opportunity guidelines are adhered to, that open positions are advertised, that applicants are screened, and that interviews are scheduled. But during an interview, the supervisor is in the best position to determine whether an applicant is really qualified. Because of this, supervisors should be prepared to play an active role in interviews.

The purpose of an interview is to determine the real qualifications of people who, from their applications, appear to be qualified. The best way to do this is in a face-to-face conversation involving the applicant and one or more persons who can determine from interacting through questions and answers if someone really knows a given job. The interview also gives supervisors an opportunity to explain the realities of the job to applicants and gauge their reactions.

Interviewing is a process that can be learned. To be effective interviewers, supervisors need to know what to look for when conducting an interview, the types of questions to ask, the types of questions that should not be asked, and some general interviewing guidelines.

General Interviewing Guidelines

What follows are some guidelines supervisors should observe when conducting or participating in an interview.

1. *Be relaxed but businesslike.* Being overly formal will make the applicant nervous, and nervous applicants are not at their best. You do not want to lose a well-qualified employee simply because he or she became nervous and did not interview well.

2. *Ask open-ended questions* that let the applicant do most of the talking. Instead of asking "Do you know how to use XYZ software?" say "Tell me about your experience with XYZ software." This approach will cause the applicant to reveal more information than will the use of closed-ended questions. Remember, the more an applicant talks, the more you will learn.

3. *Listen intently* to the applicant and do not create distractions. Do not fiddle, fidget, flip through the applicant's resume, or take notes. These things can be distracting to an applicant. Sit still, listen, and look the applicant in the eyes.

4. *Prepare* before the interview. Familiarize yourself with the applicant's paperwork. Prepare a list of questions you plan to ask. In today's litigation-prone society, it can be important to ask all applicants the same list of questions.

5. *Do not hurry.* Avoid stealing glimpses at your watch or appearing to be rushed in any way. It is important for applicants to feel they are being given ample time to present their best case.

6. *Remain neutral.* Do not communicate agreement or disagreement verbally or non-verbally. The time to comment, favorably or unfavorably, on an applicant's response is after the interview has concluded and the applicant has departed.

Questions to Ask in an Interview

The primary purpose of an interview is to elicit information. Information is obtained through questioning. This section sets forth the types of questions that will elicit the most information.

As we stated in the previous section, an **open-ended question** is one that does not predetermine the answer or the nature of the answer. Rather, it lets applicants formulate their own answers and define for themselves the breadth and depth of their responses. Counselors use open-ended questions to get their clients talking. Open-ended questions typically begin with terms or phrases such as the following:

Tell me about . . .

Describe for me . . .

Explain . . .

Expound on . . .

The types of questions that should be asked in an interview elicit information relating to the job. These include questions about education and training, experience, specific or special skills, past jobs, past attendance records, references, earliest possible date of availability, and health. Questions in these areas can be asked using the open-ended approach. For example:

"Explain your educational background for me."

"Tell me about your work experience."

"Expound on your reasons for leaving your last job."

Besides using open-ended questions to elicit more complete information, ask only questions that elicit information that is directly related to the job. Remember, if a selection is questioned by an unsuccessful applicant, you may be called upon to show how your questions relate to what the courts call a **bona fide occupational qualification**, that is, a genuine job-related qualification.

Questions to Avoid in an Interview

In today's litigious society, it is almost as important to know what questions to avoid as it is to know which to ask. This is important because a supervisor can unwittingly violate an equity statute simply by asking the wrong type of question. Questions that do not relate to a bona fide occupational qualification should be avoided. Questions in the following areas are prohibited:

Race, color, or culture

National origin, ancestry, lineage

Pregnancy

Gender

Personal preferences (sexual or otherwise)

Religion

Credit rating

Age

Birthplace

Marital status

Citizenship

Children

Relatives

Place of residence

Membership in organizations or clubs

Criminal record

Disability

Military service (type of discharge)

Physical ability

If physical ability, such as the ability to lift a specified amount of weight, can be shown to be a bona fide occupational qualification, the human resources department can arrange an appropriate physical test. Let the results of such a test speak for themselves.

Certain questions about a person's criminal record can be asked, but these are limited. Again, it is best to let the human resources department deal with inquiries about an applicant's criminal record.

Characteristics to Look for in an Interview

Is this person right for the job? This question should be answered by the interviewing process. Although the questions you may ask are limited, you are not limited with regard to listening and observing. This is another reason for asking open-ended questions. They may elicit information about which you are not allowed to ask.

As you listen and observe, try to determine if the applicant has a positive attitude. Will this person fit in and be a contributing member of the team? If the position is physically demanding, you can observe if the applicant is clearly in poor condition. Did the applicant discuss his or her personal interests or hobbies? How do these relate to the job? What was the applicant's attitude toward previous employers? What does this attitude suggest to you? As you listen and observe, be a detective. Look for spoken and unspoken clues that give you more insight into the suitability of applicants.

Contacting References

Society's propensity for litigation has made contacting **references**, or people who have worked with a job applicant, more complicated than it used to be. You may find that references are reluctant to give information beyond verifying employment dates. This is because references have been sued by applicants for making negative statements and by employers for being unrealistically positive.

When you contact references, ask whatever you want. If references respond, make a mental note of the information and use it in the selection process. One question is always safe for references to answer, and it will tell you much of what you want to know. That question is, "Is this applicant eligible for reemployment with your company?" Even without further details, knowing the answer to this question can tell you a great deal.

=========== **APPLICATION AND DISCUSSION** ===========

Identify a human resources director who will work with you in completing this activity. Using a job description as the starting point, develop a list of open-ended questions that could be used when interviewing applicants for this position.

- ■ Show your list to the human resources director you are working with and ask for a critique. Are the questions appropriate from a technical perspective? How about from a legal perspective? Should questions be added? Eliminated? Revised?

- ■ Discuss the critique you received with colleagues and classmates. How does your critique compare to theirs?

THE EMPLOYMENT TESTING ISSUE

Employment testing as a part of the staffing process is an issue with which the modern supervisor should be familiar. Some companies test applicants and claim it is an effective part of the process; other companies avoid testing. Proponents claim it can be an effective way to predict future behavior on the job. Opponents claim testing can discriminate unfairly and violate the right to privacy.

It is not the purpose of this book to recommend for or against employment testing. Rather, prospective and practicing supervisors should be aware of the issue so they can be informed participants regardless of their company's policy on tests.

The first point to understand is that a distinction must be drawn between tests that attempt to measure knowledge and/or skills that are directly related to the job and tests that attempt to predict a person's integrity. Although both can be challenged, the latter type of testing is particularly controversial.

Job Knowledge Skills

Testing for job-related knowledge and skills is a procedure with a long history. Once the practice was quite common. However, over time such tests began to be challenged as unfair and discriminatory. The courts have upheld the viability of this type of testing only when it can be clearly shown that (a) the tests are **valid** (they measure what they were designed to measure and not some unrelated factor); (b) the tests are **reliable** (they produce similar results over and over when administered to similar groups); and (c) the tests measure knowledge and skills that are directly related to doing the job in question.

Because it can be difficult to establish the validity and reliability of employment tests, many employers have stopped using them. Others have turned to professional testing firms or educational institutions for assistance, especially as the illiteracy problem continues to persist.

Employers who need workers with at least basic literacy skills are beginning to administer or contract for the administration of professionally produced tests. Several such tests that have withstood validity and reliability challenges are now available. Tests and testing methodologies must themselves pass the test of adverse impact. Tests that have an **adverse impact** on protected classes of people are not allowed. Testing companies have responded to this in a number of ways. One way has been to compare test results among like groups. For example, test results for Hispanics are compared only with those of other Hispanics.

As more and more companies started using **integrity tests**, job applicants began to challenge them. At the heart of the controversy over such tests is the nature of the questions asked. Following are examples of the types of questions found on integrity tests:

Cheating a little on your income tax is not really all that wrong. (true or false)

Office workers don't work as hard as shop workers. (true or false)

Have you ever taken something that did not belong to you? (yes or no)

Do you ever borrow things and forget to bring them back? (yes or no)

If you found a wallet in the street and it contained a lot of money, would you return it and the money? (yes or no)

Proponents of integrity tests say they can predict whether employees are likely to lie and steal on the job. Opponents claim they discriminate unfairly, invade the privacy of test takers, and are not valid predictors of behavior. This is an issue that is likely to continue to be controversial.

The American Bar Association (ABA) sets forth the following parameters concerning employment testing:[2]

Lie detector testing. Lie detector testing is allowable in only a limited number of situations (i.e., government work, company security, national security). Even in these cases the use of lie detectors is strictly controlled and tightly regulated.

Preemployment screening test. Preemployment screening tests are allowable only if they are job-related. No matter how fair a screening test might appear to be, if it has an adverse impact on the protected group it is not allowable. This is determined by comparing the pass rate of minorities (including women) with that of the majority group. The pass rate for minorities should be at least 80 percent of that for the majority group.

Drug testing and medical examinations. Drug testing and medical examinations are allowable as long as the employer keeps the results confidential and does not use them to discriminate against protected classes.

APPLICATION AND DISCUSSION

Jones Processing Company (JPC) has a "drug-free workplace" policy. Consequently, pre-employment drug tests and periodic retesting are required. In addition, all applicants are required to take the "Test of Adult Basic Education," also called the TABE test. JPC's human resources director justifies using the TABE test claiming that all employees must be able to read at the eighth grade level or higher to understand their process manual and work procedures. JPC does not compare test scores within minority groups. Instead they set the cut-off score at eighth grade and enforce it consistently across the board.

■ Is the company's use of preemployment drug tests appropriate? Why or why not?

■ Is JPC's use of a literacy test appropriate? Why or why not?

SELECTION

Having conducted interviews, how do you select the best applicant? This section provides several pointers that will help supervisors increase their chances of selecting the best applicant, a more difficult task than one might expect. These pointers are as follows:

1. Put aside personal bias.
2. Make a checklist of skills, qualities, and characteristics you are looking for.
3. Require a physical examination.
4. Check references.

Put Aside Personal Bias

You are not looking for a buddy. You are looking for a person who can do a job. It is important to keep this in mind. All people have personal biases. Consequently, it is easy to fall into the trap of recommending the applicant who is most like you, or whose background is similar to yours, or who has characteristics you are comfortable with, but that might have little or nothing to do with the job in question.

Before recommending an applicant for employment, ask yourself if the recommendation is affected by personal bias. If it is, step back and take a second look. Remember, you will be held accountable if the new employee does not work out.

Make a Checklist

One of the best ways to enhance the effectiveness of the selection process is to sit down and make a comprehensive checklist before asking that a position be advertised. This checklist should contain all the qualities you are looking for in an applicant. Making such a checklist is an effective way to eliminate bias from the process.

Physical Examination

A physical examination should be part of the selection process because it offers two important benefits. First, it answers questions about the applicant's health that might be out of order in an interview. Second, it ensures that any preexisting health conditions are identified before an applicant becomes an employee. Such prior knowledge could be important if the employee ever files a workers' compensation claim. It can also ensure that an applicant is not employed in a position that is likely to exacerbate a preexisting condition.

Check References

This strategy has already been discussed, but is included again to emphasize its importance. Candid comments from people who have worked with an applicant will sometimes tell you more than all the paperwork, test results, and interview questions combined. It is said that in personal relationships you don't really know people until you have lived with them. Similarly, you don't really know an individual's skills and work habits until you have worked with him. For this reason, talking not just with past employers but also with past fellow employees can be helpful.

In talking with past employers and supervisors, make sure you determine the applicant's reemployment status. Would they hire this person again? If not, why not? In talking with past colleagues, two questions can help you gain valuable insight into the likelihood of an applicant being a positive, contributing employee. Those questions are:

"How would you feel about having this person for a supervisor?"
"How would you feel about supervising this person?"

The first question provides insight into how well the applicant works with other people. Is he or she bossy? cooperative? pushy? helpful? The second question will provide insight into the applicant's work habits. Fellow workers would want to supervise a person who has good job skills, is a team player, and is willing to put forth extra effort when it is called for. Staffing is not an exact science, but the procedures set forth herein can help make the process more effective and help make supervisors a more effective part of the process.

=== APPLICATION AND DISCUSSION ===

Select a job with which you are familiar. You do not need to have held the job yourself, but you do need to know it well enough to complete this activity.

- ■ Develop a checklist of the qualities you would look for in people applying for this job.
- ■ Discuss your list with classmates or fellow participants. How are the various lists similar? Different? What changes would you make to your list as a result of this discussion of other lists?

ORIENTATION

Too often the staffing process stops after the selection step. The successful applicant is put to work and expected to begin producing results. This approach is not sufficient in today's workplace. New employees will face too many potential inhibitors to get a good start without some special attention and organized assistance. The final step in the selection process is orientation, and it is critical.

Orientation involves helping new employees gain acceptance as a member of the team, gain a full understanding of where they fit in and what is expected of them, and learn the practical information all employees need to know. The orientation process can be divided into two parts: organizational orientation and departmental orientation.

The **organizational orientation** makes new employees familiar with the company, its products, and its history. It also familiarizes them with policies, rules, and regulations they need to know as well as key personnel, health and safety, and compensation/benefits information. **Departmental orientation** helps them gain a foothold in becoming a fully accepted member of the team, an understanding of what is expected of them, and practical knowledge about day-to-day functioning. The human resources department typically provides the organizational orientation. Supervisors should provide the departmental orientation.

Information that is old hat to the supervisor may be brand new to the employee. Therefore, it is important to pace the orientation so new employees have time to take it all in. Overloading new team members can be just as bad as failing to orient them. Once the orientation process has been completed, supervisors should follow up periodically to ensure that the information provided has been digested and understood. Ask for feedback, encourage questions, and clarify where necessary.

APPLICATION AND DISCUSSION

Nancy Matson started work in the administration department of BELCO, Inc. on the same day she was hired. She soon found herself awash in an ocean of uncertainty. In a word, she didn't know what she was supposed to do. After her first week with BELCO, Matson told a friend, "I feel like a person assigned to take a trip without a roadmap or a destination." A week later, out of frustration, Matson resigned. She is now an outstanding employee for one of BELCO's competitors, which gave her the orientation she needed.

■ Assume that you were Nancy Matson's supervisor before she left BELCO, and you want to avoid any further loss of new employees. Explain how you plan to orient future new hires.

■ Discuss your plan with classmates or colleagues. Did you miss anything in your plan? How would you change your plan as a result of this discussion?

OTHER STAFFING CONCERNS

In addition to the topics covered so far in this chapter, several other staffing issues are of concern to supervisors. Prominent among these are how to find employees during labor shortages, the benefits of checking references, how to handle layoffs, and termination by discharge.

Finding Employees During Labor Shortages

With the first decade of the new millennium came labor shortages that were the result of a lower birthrate and a thriving economy. These circumstances forced employees to think about new approaches to staffing. Five strategies for overcoming labor shortages are as follows:

1. Hire immigrants.
2. Hire ex-convicts.
3. Hire older workers.

4. Hire the handicapped.

5. Hire temporary or part-time employees.

It is against the law to hire illegal aliens. However, immigration restrictions have been liberalized somewhat, and the U. S. Immigration and Naturalization Service is the agency to contact for information on hiring immigrants.

More than a million ex-convicts are repentant first-time offenders in the United States. As the prison system continues to overflow, more and more will be returned to society. Evidence suggests that such people can make excellent employees. However, when you hire ex-convicts, it is important to do a thorough background search so the company does not become involved in a negligent hiring suit.

Older people can be excellent employees. More than other groups, they tend to have good work habits and a positive work ethic. Participation in the workforce drops off sharply in the fifty-five to sixty-seven age group. Many people who retire during this period soon become restless and want to return to work. Income restrictions enforced by the Social Security Administration have been relaxed, making this group an excellent potential labor pool.

The handicapped represent another source of good employees. At the same time, there is a great deal of positive pressure on employers to hire the handicapped, particularly employers doing government work. Consequently, employers can benefit doubly by hiring handicapped workers.

Part-time and temporary employees represent another good source of workers. They can help you meet your needs less expensively than full-time employees. Most cities have companies that specialize in placing temporary and part-time workers. Supervisors should be familiar with these companies, which are listed in the yellow pages of the telephone directory.

Reference Checking

Reference checking is more important than it has ever been. It has become increasingly difficult to terminate even incompetent employees. Therefore it is critical to ensure that applicants can do the job before hiring them. One way to do this is through extensive reference checking. Unfortunately, too often reference checks are not done or are done in only a cursory manner.

The lack of reference checking is typically the result of two misconceptions about the process: (1) you check only the references supplied by the applicant and (2) applicants list only good references anyway. The first misconception is simply not true. Supervisors can always contact additional references. It is a good idea to talk with the applicant's previous supervisors. What they tell you, as well as what they *don't*, can be invaluable in determining an applicant's real abilities.

The second misconception can be overcome using two simple strategies. First, ask references open-ended questions. Listen to what they say as well as what they don't say. Long pauses, unnatural caution, and evasiveness are all signs of potential problems. Second, always conclude the discussion by asking if the employee is eligible for rehire. Some references will be reluctant to say much for fear of litigation, but the rehire question is both legal and ethical. How it is answered may tell all that you need to know. These strategies can turn even hand-picked references into sources of valuable information. Reference checking can ensure that an applicant who looks good on paper or does well in an interview performs equally well on the job.

Handling Layoffs Effectively

The other side of staffing involves reducing staff. When layoffs are necessary, higher management typically decides how many must go, but supervisors may decide *who*. A number of different criteria can be applied when making layoff decisions. Prominent among these are length of service, current performance, and proximity to retirement age. Regardless of the method used, layoff decisions should be objective, consistent business decisions.

A good strategy is to develop a set of objective job-related criteria that can be consistently applied, including current performance, productivity, quality of work, ability to work independently, past performance, willingness to follow directions, current/future need for a given skill, ability to perform multiple jobs, customer relations ability, and knowledge of the product or system. Weights should be applied to each criterion so that all employees can be assessed and given a score.

Keep actual documentation for each employee's rating for each criterion. This approach will bring at least three benefits: (1) it identifies the employees who can best serve the company; (2) the objectivity built into the process puts the company on a better legal footing; and (3) the objective approach is more likely to be received well by employees than would a subjective approach.

Termination by Discharge

A final staffing concern is **termination by discharge** or as it is more commonly known, firing an employee. It is dealt with only briefly here to make the point that termination by discharge is an important consideration relating to staffing.

Termination by discharge is one of the most potentially problematic situations a supervisor must deal with. Increasingly, discharged employees are seeking redress in the courts claiming *wrongful* discharge. In addition, how the discharge is handled can affect the morale of employees who remain on the job. Correspondingly, if a problem-causing or nonperforming employee is removed appropriately, it can actually improve morale. "Appropriately" in the eyes of other employees is likely to mean that they view the process as being objective, impersonal, and humane.

To discharge an employee, supervisors must first establish and document **cause.** Generally acceptable causes include: absence without appropriate leave, nonperformance of job duties, disobedience, poor discipline, disruptive behavior, lying, falsification, theft, damaging company property, and conduct off the job that is detrimental to the company. Before a determination of cause can be made, supervisors must have valid documentation and must have warned the employee about the unacceptable behavior and negative behavior. This is known as **progressive discipline**. Every step in the process should be fully documented. When this has been done, the final step is discharge.

═══════ APPLICATION AND DISCUSSION ═══════

Assume you are a new supervisor with ABC, Inc. ABC's president calls a meeting of all supervisors and says: "I am asking each of you to serve on an ad hoc committee to assist our human resources director in developing a plan for downsizing our workforce by 25 percent. Layoffs will begin in one week. I suggest you get started."

- ■ Select a job classification with which you are familiar (e.g., mechanic, driver, secretary, bookkeeper, engineer, network technician, etc.). Assume you are the supervisor of sixteen employees in this type of job at ABC, Inc. Develop a set of job-related criteria for ensuring that layoffs in your department are objective, consistent business decisions.

- ■ Discuss your plan with classmates or colleagues. Do they have any ideas you did not think of before the discussion? Revise your plan as appropriate.

═══════ ON-THE-JOB SCENARIOS ═══════

1. After being rejected for a promotion four times, Clara Watson, an African American employee, sued her employer under the provisions of Title VII of the Civil Rights

Act. This Act prohibits discrimination in employment on the basis of race, religion, gender, or national origin. Ms. Watson had a compelling case.

In all four instances the promotions had gone to white employees. Her employer had relied primarily on subjective evaluations in ruling Ms. Watson unfit for promotion. During the trial, evidence was presented showing that the employer had no minority directors, only one minority supervisor, and paid minorities lower wages. The employer did not challenge the claim that it based promotion decisions on subjective judgments.

Ms. Watson invoked the theory of disparate impact in charging her employer with discrimination. However, the court required her to claim disparate treatment instead because the employer had used subjective evaluation procedures.

The court denied Ms. Watson's claim, saying she had failed to prove intentional discrimination, a criterion for disparate treatment. The appellate court reviewed the case and upheld the lower court's ruling. However, the U.S. Supreme Court vacated the appellate court's decision and returned the case to the lower court to be retried on the basis of disparate impact. The Supreme Court ruled that subjective evaluations can be submitted to the test of disparate impact.

- Do you think the case will be ruled differently using disparate impact as the basis? Why or why not?
- Could the employer have handled this situation differently and avoided litigation? How? What do you see as the supervisor's role in this situation?

2. You are the floor supervisor in a manufacturing plant. You have been asked to forecast the staffing needs for a job that will involve producing 5,000 metal backpack frames over a period of just sixty days. Assume it takes one hour and fifteen minutes to make one backpack frame. Forecast your staffing needs. Now, assume that you will hire temporary full-time employees. Identify an agency in your community you might work with.

3. You are about to begin the selection process to fill two positions: a word processing specialist and a supervisor to replace you so that you can accept a promotion. Develop two separate checklists, one for each position. Make sure each checklist contains all the characteristics and experience you want applicants to have. Now develop a standard list of questions to be used for each position during interviews.

KEY TERMS AND PHRASES

Adverse impact

Age Discrimination in Employment Act

Analyzing

Benefits

Bona fide occupational qualification

Cause

Civil Rights Act

Compensation

Departmental orientation

Direct labor

Disparate impact

Disparate treatment

Employee Retirement Income and Security Act

Equal Employment Opportunity Act

Equal Pay Act

Fair Labor Standards Act

Federal Insurance Contribution Act

Forecasting

Human resources

Incentive system

Indirect labor

Integrity testing

Interviewing

Labor

Landrum-Griffin Act

Merit pay system

National Labor Relations Act

National Labor Relations Board

Occupational Safety and Health Act

Open-ended question

Organizational orientation

Orienting

Pregnancy Discrimination Act

Progressive discipline

Recruiting

References

Reliable

Selecting

Seniority

Staffing

Taft-Hartley Amendment

Termination by discharge

Valid

Vietnam Era Veterans Readjustment Act

Vocational Rehabilitation Act

Wagner Act

REVIEW QUESTIONS

1. Define the term *staffing*.

2. What are the five steps in the staffing process?

3. What role do supervisors play in recruiting?

4. What role do supervisors play in selecting the best applicant?

5. Why is it so important to have the assistance of human resources personnel in the staffing process?

6. What are these protected classes of people with regard to equal employment opportunity?

7. What legislation established today's equal employment opportunity mandates?

8. Explain *disparate treatment*.

9. Explain *disparate impact*.

10. Explain the three-step process the courts use in handling cases of alleged disparate impact.

11. What is the key in determining disparate treatment?

12. What conditions must exist in a disparate treatment case before the burden of proof shifts to the employer?

13. What is the handbook used by human resources personnel to ensure compliance with equal opportunity laws?

14. Explain the major tenets of the following laws: Age Discrimination in Employment Act, Vocational Rehabilitation Act, and Vietnam Era Readjustment Act.

15. Explain the concepts of *exempt* and *nonexempt* as set forth in the Fair Labor Standards Act.

16. List the four steps used to forecast staffing needs.

17. List six general guidelines for conducting interviews.

18. Give an example of an open-ended question.

19. What is a bona fide occupational qualification?

20. List five areas in which questions should *not* be asked in an interview.

21. If references are reluctant to give you information, what is the best question you can ask?

22. How are professional testing companies handling the issue of disparate impact in literacy testing?

23. What are the main complaints about integrity testing?

24. List four pointers for improving your chances of selecting the best qualified among a group of apparently qualified applicants.

ENDNOTES

1. U.S.C. Section 654(A).

2. American Bar Association, *You and the Law* (Lincolnwood, IL: Publications International, 1990), pp. 384-385.

CHAPTER FOURTEEN

Total Quality

After studying this chapter, you should be able to do the following:

- Define *quality*.
- Define *Total Quality*.
- Describe the key elements of *Total Quality*.
- Explain the supervisor's role in quality improvement.

The **Total Quality** concept as a way to continually improve competitiveness has gained wide acceptance in the United States. In fact, elements of the concept, such as the use of statistical data, teamwork, and employee involvement, have been used by visionary organizations for years. The pulling together and coordinated use of these and other previously disparate elements gave birth to the comprehensive concept known as Total Quality. This chapter provides an overview of the concept of continuous quality improvement and the role supervisors play in it.

WHAT IS QUALITY?

To understand Total Quality, one must first understand quality. Although few consumers can define quality as a concept, they know it when they see it. Quality is in the eye of the beholder, and the beholder is the customer. This is why customer-defined quality is essential to competitiveness.

People deal with the issue of quality every day. Consumers are concerned with quality whenever they shop for groceries, eat in a restaurant, and make purchases. Perceived quality is a major factor by which people make distinctions in the marketplace. Whether consumers openly articulate these distinctions or simply have them in mind, they all apply a number of criteria when making a purchase. The extent to which the purchase meets these criteria determines its quality in the consumer's eyes.

One way to understand quality as a consumer-driven concept is to consider the example of eating out at a restaurant. How is the quality of the restaurant judged? Most people apply criteria such as service, response time, food preparation, atmosphere, price, and selection.

This example speaks to one aspect of quality: results. Does the product or service meet or exceed customer expectations? While this is a critical aspect of quality, it is not the only one. Total Quality is a much broader concept that encompasses not only the results, but also the quality of the people involved and the quality of the processes employed. For the purpose of this book, quality is defined as follows:

> ***Quality*** *is a dynamic state associated with products, services, people, processes, and environments that meet or exceed current expectations.*

The **"dynamic state"** element of this definition refers to the fact that what is considered quality can and often does change as time passes and circumstances are altered. For example, gas mileage is an important criterion in judging the quality of modern automobiles. However, in the days when gasoline cost 20 cents per gallon, consumers were more likely to be concerned with an automobile's horsepower, engine size, and acceleration rate than with gas mileage.

The "products, services, people, processes, and environments" element of quality is critical. It makes the point that while quality certainly applies to products and services, it also applies to the people and processes that provide them and the environments in which they are provided. There is an important reason for this; it's called longevity. In the short term, two competitors who focus on continual improvement might produce a product of comparable quality. But the competitor who looks beyond just the quality of the finished product and also focuses on the continual improvement of the people who produce the product, the processes they use, and the environment in which they work will win in the long run. This is because quality products are produced most consistently by quality organizations.

APPLICATION AND DISCUSSION

We all consider quality issues every day, even without thinking. When shopping we notice the quality of the service provided and the quality of the products purchased. We either feel that we got our money's worth or that we did not. We are either pleased with the service and, as a result, will do return business or we are displeased and want to find another place to do business. As customers, we can all think of times when the quality of service received was excellent, and we can all tell horror stories about service that was even worse than bad.

- Think of an instance in which you shopped, ate out, or called on a business for help and received excellent service. What did you like about the service? Why? Now think of the opposite situation. What did you dislike about the poor service? Why? Discuss your examples with classmates or colleagues and listen as they discuss theirs.

- Think of an instance in which you purchased a product (anything from the smallest item to the largest) and were really pleased with its quality. What impressed you about this product? Now think of the opposite situation. What did you dislike about the product? Discuss your examples with classmates or colleagues and listen as they discuss theirs.

TOTAL QUALITY DEFINED

Just as there are different definitions for quality, there are also different definitions for Total Quality. For the purpose of this book, the definition in Figure 14-1 is used.

How Is Total Quality Different?

The elements that distinguish Total Quality from traditional ways of doing business can be found in how it is achieved. The distinctive characteristics of Total Quality include customer focus (internal and external), obsession with quality, use of the scientific approach in decision making and problem solving, long-term commitment, teamwork,

---

What It Is

Total quality is an approach to doing business that attempts to maximize the competitiveness of an organization through the continual improvement of its products, services, people, processes, and environments.

How It Is Achieved

The total quality approach has the following characteristics:

- Customer focus (internal and external)
- Obsession with quality
- Scientific approach to decision-making and problem-solving
- Long-term commitment
- Teamwork
- Continual process improvement
- Education and training
- Freedom through control
- Unity of purpose
- Employee involvement and empowerment

Figure 14–1
Total Quality defined

employee involvement and empowerment, continual improvement, bottom-up education and training, freedom through control, and unity of purpose.

=========== APPLICATION AND DISCUSSION ===========

Total Quality is sometimes referred to as "Big Q," while traditional quality control is referred to as "Little Q." Quality control typically involves after-the-fact inspections of finished products or services that have already been provided. Total Quality, on the other hand, involves focusing all of an organization's efforts on continually improving people, processes, and products so that rejected work is corrected during the process and waste is reduced to the absolute minimum.

- Consider the two concepts, Big Q and Little Q. What role do you see supervisors playing in each?
- Discuss your conclusions with classmates or colleagues. Did you miss anything?

KEY ELEMENTS OF TOTAL QUALITY

The Total Quality approach defined in Figure 14-1 has two components: the "what" and the "how" of Total Quality. What distinguishes Total Quality from other approaches to doing business is the "how" component. Each element of this component is explained in the following sections.

Customer Focus

Customer focus drives a Total Quality setting. This applies to both internal and external customers. External customers define the quality of the product or service delivered.

Internal customers help define the quality of the people, processes, and environments associated with the products or services.

Obsession with Quality

In a Total Quality organization, internal and external customers define quality. With quality defined, the organization must then become obsessed with meeting or exceeding this definition. This means all personnel at all levels approach all aspects of the job from the perspective of "How can we do this better?" When an organization is **obsessed with quality**, good enough is never good enough.

Scientific Approach

Detractors of the Total Quality concept sometimes see it as nothing more then "mushy people stuff." While it is true that people skills and employee empowerment are important in a Total Quality setting, they represent only part of the equation. An equally important part is the use of the **scientific approach** in structuring work and in decision making and problem solving relating to that work. This means that hard data are used in establishing benchmarks, monitoring performance, and making improvements.

Long-Term Commitment

Organizations that have a history of implementing management innovations after attending short-term seminars often fail in their initial attempt to adopt the Total Quality approach. This is because they approach Total Quality as just another management innovation rather than as a whole new way of doing business that requires a whole new corporate culture. Too few organizations begin the implementation of Total Quality with the **long-term commitment** to change that is necessary for success.

Teamwork

In traditionally managed organizations, the best competitive efforts are often between departments within the organization. Internal competition tends to use up energy that could and should be focused on improving quality and, in turn, external competitiveness. Total Quality organizations perform work in teams that are continually improved. Job descriptions, training, performance appraisals, and reward/recognition systems should all promote **teamwork**.

Continual Improvement of Systems

Products are developed and services are delivered by people using processes and systems within environments. To continually improve the quality of products or services—which is a fundamental goal in a Total Quality setting—**continual improvement** of systems is also necessary.

Education and Training

Education and training are fundamental to Total Quality because they represent the best way to improve people on a continual basis. Through education and training people who know how to work hard learn how to also work smart.

Freedom through Control

Involving and empowering employees is fundamental to Total Quality as a way to simultaneously bring more minds to bear on the decision-making process and increase the ownership employees feel in decisions that are made. Detractors of Total Quality sometimes mistakenly see employee involvement as a loss of management control, when in fact control is fundamental to Total Quality. The freedoms enjoyed in a Total Quality setting are actually the result of well-planned and well-carried-out controls.

Unity of Purpose

Historically, management and employees have had an adversarial relationship in U.S. businesses. One could debate the reasons behind this discord *ad infinitum* without achieving consensus. Such is not the purpose here. Suffice it to say that there is probably wrong and right on both sides of the issue. From the perspective of Total Quality, who or what is to blame for adversarial management-employee relations is irrelevant. What is important is that to apply the Total Quality approach, organizations must have **unity of purpose**.

A question frequently asked about this element of Total Quality is, "Does unity of purpose mean that unions will no longer be needed?" The answer is that unity of purpose has nothing to do with whether unions are needed. Collective bargaining is about wages, benefits, and working conditions, not corporate purpose and vision. While employees should feel more involved and empowered in a Total Quality setting than in a traditionally managed situation, the goal is to enhance competitiveness, not eliminate unions. For example, in Japan where companies are known for achieving unity of purpose, unions are still very much in evidence. Unity of purpose does not necessarily mean that employees and management will always agree on wages, benefits, and working conditions.

Employee Involvement and Empowerment

This is one of the most misunderstood elements of the Total Quality approach and one of the most misrepresented by its detractors. The basis for **employee involvement** is twofold. First, it increases the likelihood of a good decision, a better plan, or a more effective improvement by bringing more minds to bear on the situation—and not just any minds, but the minds of the people closest to the work in question. Second, it promotes ownership of decisions by involving the people who will have to implement them.

Employee empowerment means not just involving people, but involving them in ways that give them a real voice. One way this can be done is by structuring work that allows employees to make decisions concerning the improvement of work processes within well-specified parameters. Should an employee be allowed to unilaterally drop a vendor if the vendor delivers substandard material? No. However, the employee should have an avenue for offering her input into the matter. Should the same employee be allowed to change the way she sets up her machine? Yes, if by doing so she can improve her part of the process without adversely affecting someone else's. Having done so, the next step should be to show other members of her team the innovation so that they might try it and so that this better way she has discovered can be standardized.

=========== **APPLICATION AND DISCUSSION** ===========

Marsha Maddox and her best friend, Susan Larrabie, are both supervisors for XYZ Corporation. They have known each other for years and are close both on and off the job, but there is one issue on which they disagree. Maddox involves her employees in every decision she makes unless it has to be a split-second decision. She asks for their input, invites them to punch holes in her logic, and solicits better ideas from them. In short, Maddox is an advocate of employee involvement and empowerment. Larrabie, on the other hand, makes all of her own decisions without consulting employees. She decides and then tells her employees what the decision is.

- Compare these two approaches to decision making. What are the relative merits of these approaches? What do you see as potential problems with each?
- Which approach comes closest to being your natural inclination? Discuss this case with classmates or colleagues and pay special attention to areas of agreement and disagreement.

SUPERVISOR'S ROLE IN QUALITY IMPROVEMENT

Supervisors can play a key role in quality improvement regardless of whether their organization uses the traditional approach to quality or the Total Quality approach. Strategies supervisors can use are as follows:

- *Do not accept normal levels of delay, mistakes, or defects*. Work with employees to do better. Improve on what is considered acceptable quality levels by striving for zero quality problems.
- *Continually improve processes*. Supervisors are in an excellent position to see an overall process as well as individual operations within it. Use this simultaneously broad and focused view to identify and correct process problems on a continual basis.
- *Focus supervision efforts on helping employees do a better job*. Because of pressure to produce both output and quality, supervisors can sometimes emphasize the wrong things. Supervisors who focus their efforts on helping employees do a better job will, as a result, improve both productivity and quality.
- *Empower through two-way communication*. Make sure that employees are empowered to make suggestions for improving performance. Communicate with employees continually and *listen, listen, listen*.
- *Eliminate barriers among departments*. Quality is everybody's responsibility. Establish a close working relationship with supervisors in other departments. Communicate with them frequently and encourage mutual support. Quality cannot be achieved as long as it is someone else's problem.
- *Provide ongoing education and training* aimed at simultaneously improving quality, productivity, and competitiveness.
- *Emphasize quality* among employees and make sure they know it is your top priority.
- *Make the quality commitment visual* by displaying examples of good and poor quality, displaying quality awards or records, and displaying quality reminders such as "Quality First" posters. If posters are used, however, make sure they are changed and updated regularly so that they don't begin to blend into the wall.
- *Make sure that all employees understand the expectations* and then encourage them to exceed the standards.
- *Personally conduct periodic inspections* beyond those normally done by quality control personnel or individual employees and conduct them at critical points in the process.
- *Take the necessary action to correct problems* or defects immediately.
- *Make sure all employees are aware of their role* in quality improvement and work with them to build a commitment to this role.

APPLICATION AND DISCUSSION

The quality of work coming out of Department B has gone from bad to worse. You have been sent in to improve the department's performance. After just one week of investigating, you have decided that team members are poorly trained and don't care. They seem to be angry at higher management and at odds with other departments in the company.

- Develop a plan for improving the performance of Department B.
- Discuss your plan with those of classmates or colleagues. Did the discussion reveal anything you had not thought of? If so, adjust your plan accordingly.

ON-THE-JOB SCENARIOS

1. Your company is in the process of developing a new quality philosophy. During a meeting a fellow supervisor says, "We can't afford all the money it's going to take to have that level of quality." Explain how you would refute this argument.

2. Higher management has formed an ad hoc task force of supervisors to develop supervisory strategies for enhancing quality. You have been elected chair of the committee. What strategies will your committee recommend? Put your strategies in the form of a checklist.

3. You have been asked by your manager to get your employees involved in quality. Develop a plan for doing so.

4. Develop a plan for implementing a company-wide suggestion program and explain your strategies.

KEY TERMS AND PHRASES

Continual improvement	Obsession with quality
Customer Focus	Quality
Dynamic state	Scientific approach
Employee empowerment	Teamwork
Employee involvement	Total Quality
Long-term commitment	Unity of purpose

REVIEW QUESTIONS

1. Define the term *quality*.
2. What is the "dynamic state" element of the definition of quality?
3. What is the definition of *Total Quality*?
4. How is Total Quality different?
5. What are the key elements of Total Quality?
6. What is the supervisor's role in quality improvement?

CHAPTER FIFTEEN

Team Building and Teamwork

After studying this chapter, you should be able to do the following:

- Explain the rationale for teamwork.
- Explain the four-step approach to team building.
- Explain the coaching aspect of supervision.
- Demonstrate how to handle conflict in teams.
- Explain the supervisor's role in rewarding team and individual performance.
- Explain the supervisor's role in recognizing teamwork and team players.

OVERVIEW OF TEAMWORK

Teamwork is fundamental to success in the modern workplace.

> A **team** *is a group of people with a common, collective goal.*

The collective goal of teams is critical. This point is evident in the performance of athletic teams. For example, a basketball team in which one player hogs the ball, plays the role of the prima donna, and pursues his or her own personal goals (a personal high point total, MVP status, publicity, e.g.) will rarely win against a team of players, all of whom pull together toward the collective goal of winning the game. A well-coached (supervised) team will be better than the collective talents of the individual members. This is as true of work teams as it is of sports teams.

Rationale for Teams

On a well-coached team, the team's ability is more than the sum of the abilities of individual members. This is the primary rationale for teamwork. **Teamwork** is what occurs when employees put aside their personal goals and preferences and work together cooperatively to achieve the team's goal. Other reasons for promoting teamwork are as follows:

- Two or more heads are better than one.
- People in teams get to know each other, build trust, and as a result, want to help each other.

- Teamwork promotes better communication.
- Teams give employees a support base and a sense of belonging. A group of individuals becomes a team when the following conditions exist:
  - When all members understand and agree on the mission.
  - When members adhere to team ground rules established for teamwork.
  - When fair distribution of responsibility and authority exists.
  - When people adapt to change. People in teams should help each other adapt to change in a positive way.

Learning to Work Together

A group of people does not a team make. People in a group do not automatically or magically find ways to work together. One reason teams sometimes fail is the supervisor's failure to deal with human factors that can work against success. These factors are as follows:

- *Personal identity of team members*. People naturally wonder where they fit into an organization. People worry about being an outsider, getting along with other team members, having a voice, and developing mutual trust among team members. The work of the team cannot proceed effectively until team members feel as if they fit in. Helping employees see where they fit in is the supervisor's responsibility.
- *Relationships among team members*. Before people in a group can work together, they have to get to know each other and form relationships. When people know and care about each other, they will go to greater lengths to support each other. Time spent by supervisors helping team members get acquainted and establish common ground is time invested well. This point is especially important now that the modern workforce has become so diverse that common ground among team members can no longer be assumed.
- *Identify within the organization*. How does the team fit into the organization? Is its mission a high priority in the company? Does the team have support at the highest management levels? Helping employees understand where their team fits into the organization is the supervisor's responsibility.

Team Performance

Teamwork is not a magic cure-all. Poorly run teams can do more damage to an organization's performance and competitiveness than having no teams at all. For this reason, it is critical that excellence in team performance be an overriding goal of the organization. Supervisors are key players in determining the performance of teams.

Dennis King, personnel manager for Proctor & Gamble, recommends the following strategies, which he calls the Ten Team Commandments:[1]

- *Interdependence*. **Interdependence** means that team members should be mutually dependent on each other for information, resources, task accomplishment, and support. Interdependence is the glue that will hold a team together.
- *Stretching tasks*. Teams need to be challenged or stretched. Responding to a challenge or a **stretching task** as a team builds team spirit and instills pride and unity.
- *Alignment*. A team with **alignment** is one in which all members not only share a common mission, but are also willing to put aside individualism to accomplish it.
- *Common language*. Teams sometimes consist of members from different departments that typically have their own terminology that may be foreign to people from other departments. Consequently, it is important for supervisors to establish a **com-**

mon language to ensure that department-specific terms and phrases are used minimally and fully explained in common terms when used.

- *Trust/respect.* For team members to work well together, there must be **trust and respect**. Time and effort spent building trust and respect among team members is time invested well.

- *Shared leadership/followership.* Some team members tend to emerge as more vocal while others sit back and observe. If a few members are allowed to dominate, the team will not achieve its full potential. A better approach is to draw out the special talents of each individual team member so that leadership and followership are shared.

- *Problem-solving skills.* Time invested in helping team members become better problem solvers is time well spent. Much of the business of teams is problem solving.

- *Confrontation/conflict-handling skills.* Human **conflict** is inevitable in a high-pressure, competitive workplace. Even the best teams have disagreements. Learning to disagree without being disagreeable and to air disagreements openly and frankly—attacking ideas, issues, and proposed solutions without attacking the people proposing them—are critical skills in a team setting.

- *Assessment/action.* **Assessment** is a matter of asking and answering the question "How are we doing?" The yardsticks for answering this question are the group's mission statement and corresponding action plan. The **action plan** contains goals, objectives, timetables, and assignments of responsibility. By monitoring these continually, group members can assess how the team is doing.

- *Celebration.* An effective team reinforces its successes by celebrating them. Recognition of a job well done with a **celebration** can motivate team members to work even harder and smarter to achieve its next goal.

==== APPLICATION AND DISCUSSION ====

Martha Furlong was recently promoted to supervisor of a twelve-person team that has already caused two previous supervisors to resign in frustration. There is a great deal of conflict among team members over who does what. In addition, team members complain constantly about not knowing where they or the team fit in.

- What "human factors" do you see at work here?
- What will Martha Furlong have to do to turn things around in her team?

FOUR-STEP APPROACH TO TEAM BUILDING

Effective team building is a four-step process (Figure 15–1):

1. Assess
2. Plan

Figure 15–1
Team building is a systematic process.

Four Steps to Team Building
1. Assess
2. Plan
3. Execute
4. Evaluate

3. Execute

4. Evaluate

To be more specific, the **team-building** process proceeds along the following lines: (a) assess the team's developmental needs (e.g., its strengths and weaknesses), (b) plan team-building activities based on the needs identified, (c) execute the planned team-building activities, and (d) evaluate results. The steps are spelled out further in the next sections.

Assessing Team Needs

If you were the coach of a baseball team about which you knew very little, what is the first thing you would want to do? Most coaches in such situations would want to begin by assessing the abilities of their new team. Can we hit? Can we pitch? Can we field? What are our weaknesses? What are our strengths? With these questions answered, the coach will know how best to proceed with team-building activities.

This same approach can be used in the workplace. A mistake commonly made by supervisors is beginning team-building activities without first assessing the team's developmental needs. Resources are usually limited in organizations. Consequently, it is important to use them as efficiently and effectively as possible. Organizations that begin team-building activities without a **needs assessment** in which they first assess strengths and weaknesses run the risk of wasting resources in an attempt to strengthen characteristics that are already strong, while overlooking characteristics that are weak. For work teams to be successful, they should have at least the following characteristics:

- Clear direction is given to and understood by all members.
- "Team players" are members of the team.
- Accountability measures are fully understood and accepted by the team members.

Supervisors can use the following criteria to assess the team-building needs of work teams. The criteria are arranged in three broad categories: *Direction and Understanding, Characteristics of Team Members,* and *Accountability.* Individual team members record their perceptions of the team's performance and abilities relative to the specific criteria in each category by answering "yes," "no," or "somewhat."

Direction and Understanding

- The team has a clearly stated mission.
- All team members understand the mission.
- All team members understand the scope and boundaries of the team's charter.
- The team has a set of broad goals that support its mission.
- All team members understand the team's goals.
- The team has identified specific activities that must be completed to accomplish team goals.
- All team members understand the specific activities that must be completed in order to accomplish team goals.
- All team members understand projected time frames, schedules, and deadlines relating to specific activities.

Characteristics of Team Members

- All team members are open and honest with each other all the time.
- All team members trust each other.

- All team members put the team's mission and goals ahead of their own personal agendas all of the time.
- All team members are comfortable that they can depend on each other.
- All team members are enthusiastic about accomplishing the team's mission and goals.
- All team members are willing to take responsibility for the team's performance.
- All team members are willing to cooperate to get the team's mission accomplished.
- All team members will take the initiative in moving the team toward its final destination.
- All team members are patient with each other.
- All team members are resourceful in finding ways to accomplish the team's mission in spite of difficulties.
- All team members are punctual when it comes to team meetings, other team activities, and meeting deadlines.
- All team members are tolerant and sensitive to the individual differences of team members.
- All team members are willing to persevere when team activities become difficult.
- The team has a mutually supportive climate.
- All team members are comfortable expressing opinions, pointing out problems, and offering constructive criticism.
- All team members support team decisions once they are made.
- All team members understand how the team fits into the overall organization.

Accountability
- All team members know how team progress/performance will be measured.
- All team members understand how team success is defined.
- All team members understand how ineffective team members will be dealt with.
- All team members understand how team decisions are made.
- All team members know their respective responsibilities.
- All team members know the responsibilities of all other team members.
- All team members understand their authority within the team and that of all other team members.
- All team goals have been prioritized.
- All specific activities relating to team goals have been assigned appropriately and given projected completion dates.
- All team members know what to do when unforeseen inhibitors impede progress.

Team-building activities should be developed and executed based on what this assessment reveals. Activities should be undertaken in order of the assessment findings. "No" responses are worked on first and "somewhat" responses second.

Planning Team-Building Activities

Team-building activities should be planned around the results of the needs assessment conducted in the previous step. Consider the example of a newly chartered team. Say the team in question has a "No" response to "All team members understand the mission." Clearly, part of the process of building this team must be explaining the team's mission more clearly. This solution might be as simple as the supervisor sitting down with the team, describing the mission, and responding to questions from team members.

On the other hand, if the assessment produces a "No" response to the criterion "All team members are open and honest with each other all the time," more extensive trust-building activities may be needed. In any case, what is important in this step is to (a) plan team-building activities based on what is learned from the needs assessment and (b) provide team-building activities in the priority indicated by the needs assessment, beginning with the "No" responses.

Executing Team-Building Activities

Team-building activities should be implemented on a just-in-time basis. A mistake made by many organizations is rushing into team building. Like any kind of training, teamwork training will be forgotten unless it is put to immediate use. Consequently, the best time to provide teamwork training is after a team has been formed and given its charter. In this way, team members will have opportunities to apply immediately what they are learning.

Team-building is an ongoing process. The idea is to make a team better and better as time goes by. Consequently, basic teamwork training is provided as soon as a team is chartered. All subsequent team-building activities are based on the results of the needs assessment and planning process.

Evaluating Team-Building Activities

If team-building activities have been effective, weaknesses pointed out by the needs assessment process should have been strengthened. A simple way to evaluate the effectiveness of team-building activities is to re-administer the appropriate portion of the needs assessment document. The best approach is to reconstitute the document so that it contains the relevant criteria only, which focuses the attention of team members on the specific targeted areas.

If the evaluation shows that sufficient progress has been made, nothing more is required. If not, additional team-building activities are needed. If a given team-building activity appears to have been ineffective, get the team together and discuss it. Use the feedback from team members to identify weaknesses and problems and use the information to ensure that team-building activities become more effective.

=========== APPLICATION AND DISCUSSION ===========

Chances are you have been a member of a work team. Maybe you are new. Using the criteria listed in this section, assess the needs of a team you are familiar with for team building.

■ What are the most pressing needs of your team?
■ What types of team-building activities are needed?

"COACHING" WORK TEAMS

If employees are expected to work together as a team, supervisors have to realize that teams are not bossed—they are coached. Supervisors need to understand the difference between bossing and coaching. Bossing, in the traditional sense, involves planning work, giving orders, monitoring programs, and evaluating performance. Bosses approach the job from an "I'm in charge—do as you are told" perspective. Coaches, on the other hand, are facilitators of team development and continually improved performance. **Coaching** involves leading the team in such a way that it achieves peak performance on a consistent basis. This philosophy is translated into everyday behavior as follows:

- Coaches give their teams a clearly defined charter.
- Coaches make team development and team building a constant activity.
- Coaches are mentors.
- Coaches promote mutual respect between themselves and team members and among team members.
- Coaches make human diversity within a team a plus.

Clearly Defined Charter

Picture this. A basketball, soccer, or track coach calls her team together and says, "This year we have one overriding purpose—to win the championship." In one simple statement, this coach has clearly and succinctly defined the team's charter. All team members now know that everything they do this season should be directed at winning the championship. The coach didn't say the team would improve its record by twenty-five points, improve its standing in the league by two places, or make the playoffs, all of which would be worthy missions. This coach has a higher vision. This year the team is going for the championship. Coaches of work teams should be just as specific in explaining their team's mission to team members.

Team Development/Team Building

The most constant presence in an athlete's life is practice. Regardless of the sport, athletic teams practice constantly. During practice, coaches work on developing the skills of individual team members and the team as a whole. Team development and team-building activities never stop. Supervisors of work teams should follow the lead of their athletic counterparts. Developing the skills of individual team members and building the team as a whole should be a normal part of the job—a part that takes place regularly, forever.

Mentoring

Good coaches are mentors, which means they establish a helping, caring, nurturing relationship with team members. Developing the capabilities of team members, improving the contribution individuals make to the team, and helping team members advance their careers are all **mentoring** activities. Supervisors can be mentors by helping team members in the following ways:

- Develope their job skills.
- Build character.
- Teach them the organization's mission and where the team fits in.
- Teach them how to get things done in the organization.
- Help them understand the viewpoints of other team members.
- Teach them how to behave in unfamiliar settings or circumstances.
- Give them insight into differences among people.
- Build teamwork skills.

Mutual Respect and Trust

It is important for team members to respect their coach, for the coach to respect the team members, and for team members to respect each other. **Trust building** is achieved by (a) setting the example, (b) sharing information, (c) explaining personal motives, (d) avoiding both personal criticisms and personal favors, (e) handing out sincere rewards and recognition, and (f) being consistent in disciplining. Respect for teammates is shown by (a) respecting their thoughts, feelings, values, and fears; (b) respecting their desire to lead and follow; (c) respecting their individual strengths and differences; (d) respecting their desire to be involved and to participate; (e) respecting their need to be winners; (f) respecting their need to learn, grow, and develop; (g) respecting their need for a safe and healthy workplace that is conducive to peak performance; and (h) respecting their personal and family lives.

Human Diversity

Human **diversity** is an advantage in any organization. Sports and the military have typically led American society in the drive for diversity, and both have benefited immensely as a result. To list the contributions to either sports or the military made by people of different genders, races, religions, and so on, would be a big task. Many organizations in the United States have followed the positive example set by sports and the military. The smart ones have learned that most of the growth in the workplace will be among women, minorities, and immigrants. These people bring new ideas and different perspectives, precisely what an organization needs to stay on the razor's edge of competitiveness. However, in spite of steps already taken toward making the American workplace both diverse and harmonious, wise supervisors understand that people—consciously and unconsciously—tend to erect barriers between themselves and people who are different from them. This tendency can quickly undermine the trust and cohesiveness on which teamwork is built. To prevent this, supervisors can take the following steps (Figure 15–2):

- *Conduct a cultural audit.* Become familiar with personal characteristics, cultural values, and individual differences among team members.

- *Identify the specific needs of different groups.* Ask women, ethnic minorities, and older workers to describe the unique inhibitors they face. Make sure all team members understand these barriers and then work together as a team to eliminate, overcome, or accommodate them.

- *Confront cultural clashes.* Wise supervisors meet conflict among team members head-on and immediately. This approach is particularly important when the conflict is based on issues of diversity. Conflicts that grow out of religious, cultural, ethnic, age and/or gender-related issues are potentially more volatile then everyday disagreements over work-related issues. Consequently, conflict that is based on or aggravated by human differences should be confronted promptly. Few things will polarize a team faster than diversity-related disagreements that are allowed to fester and grow.

- *Eliminate institutionalized bias.* A company that had historically been predominantly male now has a workforce in which women are the majority. However, the facility still has ten men's restrooms and only two for women. This imbalance is an example of **institutionalized bias** (bias that has become ingrained in an organiza-

Figure 15–2
Cultural barriers among individuals can undermine teamwork.

Promoting Cultural Harmony In Teams

- Be familiar with the cultural values of team members.

- Identify the specific barriers individual team members face.

- Deal with cultural clashes within the team directly and immediately.

- Identify and eliminate institutionalized bias.

tion's culture). Teams may find themselves unintentionally slighting members simply out of habit or tradition. This is the concept of *discrimination by inertia*. It happens when the demographics of a team change, but its habits, traditions, procedures, and work environment do not. An effective way to eliminate institutional bias is to circulate a blank notebook and ask team members to record—without attribution—instances and examples of institutionalized bias. After the initial circulation, repeat the process periodically. Supervisors can use the input collected to help eliminate institutional bias. By collecting input directly from team members and acting on it promptly, supervisors can ensure that discrimination by inertia is not creating or perpetuating quiet but debilitating resentment.

=========== APPLICATION AND DISCUSSION ===========

The A Team at Bentwell, Inc. is anything but an "A" Team. In fact, it is falling apart. Once the highest performing team in the company (hence the name), it has become a group of disgruntled individuals. Because of turnovers and transfers, only two of the team's original members remain. All of the original members were of the same gender, sex, race, and background. They were also of the same generation. The new team has male and female members, a broad range of ages, and representation from several different racial groups.

■   If you were the supervisor of the new A team, how could you use mentoring to help pull the team together?

■   How would you deal with the issue of human diversity?

HANDLING CONFLICT IN TEAMS

The following conversation took place in a meeting the author once attended: A supervisor called together employees on his team to deal with issues that were disrupting work. Where the supervisor wanted teamwork, he was getting conflict. Where he wanted mutual cooperation, he was getting bickering. The conversation started something like this:

Supervisor: We all work for the same company, don't we?

Employees: [Nods of agreement.]

Supervisor: We all understand that we cannot do well unless the company does well, don't we?

Employees: [Nods of agreement.]

Supervisor: Then we want the company to do well, don't we?

Employees: [Nods of agreement.]

Supervisor: Then we are all going to work together toward the same goal, aren't we?

Employees: [Silence. Employees stare uncomfortably at the floor.]

This supervisor made a common mistake. He thought that employees would automatically work together as a team because this approach is so obviously the right thing to do. In other words, just give employees a chance, explain things to them, and they'll work together. Unfortunately, this is not always the case. Human beings are individuals with their own wants, needs, ambitions, and goals. To work as a team member, individuals must be willing to put aside some of their personal needs for the overall good of the team. This kind of self-sacrifice is hard to do.

In addition to these personal inhibitors of teamwork, there is the *example* issue. Supervisors who advocate teamwork while not contributing to the team themselves and undercutting the performance of other teams in the organization will find it difficult to persuade their employees to be team players. To promote teamwork, supervisors must be good team players themselves.

Resolution Strategies for Team Conflicts

Conflict will occur in even the best teams. Even when team members agree on a goal, they can still disagree on how best to accomplish it. Lucas recommends the following strategies for preventing and resolving team conflict.[2]

- Plan and work to establish a culture where individuality and dissent are in balance with teamwork and cooperation.
- Establish clear criteria for deciding when decisions will be made by individuals and when they will be made by teams.
- Don't allow individuals to build personal empires or to use the organization to advance personal agendas.
- Encourage and recognize individual risk-taking behavior that breaks the organization out of unhelpful habits and negative mental frameworks.
- Encourage health and productive competition and discourage unhealthy, counter-productive competition.
- Recognize how difficult it can be to ensure effective cooperation and spend the energy necessary to get just the right amount of it.
- Value and encourage constructive dissent.
- Assign people of widely differing perspectives to every team or problem.
- Reward and recognize both dissent and teamwork when they solve problems.
- Reevaluate the project, problem, or idea when no dissent or doubt is expressed.
- Avoid hiring people who think they don't need help, who don't value cooperation, or who are driven by the desire to be accepted.
- Ingrain into new employees the need for balance between the concept of cooperation and constructive dissent.
- Provide ways for employees to say what no one wants to hear.
- Realistically and regularly assess the ability and willingness of employees to cooperate effectively.
- Understand that some employees are going to clash, so determine where this is happening and remix rather than waste precious organizational energy trying to get people to like each other.
- Ensure that the organization's value system and reward/recognition systems are geared toward cooperation with constructive dissent rather than dog-eat-dog competition or cooperation at all costs.
- Teach employees how to manage both dissent and agreement. Don't let either get out of hand.
- Quickly assess whether conflict is healthy or destructive, and take immediate steps to encourage the former and resolve or eliminate the latter.

APPLICATION AND DISCUSSION

Team X is not producing at the desired level. The supervisor, Mahammed Nasier, does not like dissent. He is proud of "running a tight ship" in which his word is final and not open for discussion. Unfortunately, Team X is being torn apart by conflict, dissent, and bickering among its members. Nasier refuses to get involved. His typical response is, "Bickering is for children; do what I say and work your differences out on your own time."

■ What do you think of Nasier's handling of team conflict? Why?
■ If you replaced Nasier as supervisor of Team X, how would you handle the problem of conflict within his team?

STRUCTURAL INHIBITORS OF TEAMWORK

One of the primary reasons that teamwork fails to gain a foothold in certain organizations is that those organizations fail to remove built-in structural inhibitors. A **structural inhibitor** is an administrative procedure, organizational principle, or cultural element that works against a given change—in this case, the change from individual work to teamwork. Organizations often make the mistake of espousing teamwork without first removing the structural inhibitors that will guarantee failure. Structural inhibitors that are commonly found in organizations are as follows:[3]

■ *Accountability.* In a traditional organization, employees feel accountable to management. This perception can undermine teamwork, because teams work best when they feel accountable to customers. Supervisors in a team setting should view themselves as internal emissaries for customers.
■ *Unit goals.* Traditional organizations are task oriented, and their unit goals reflect this orientation. A task orientation can undermine teamwork. Teams work best when they focus on overall process effectiveness rather than individual tasks.
■ *Responsibility.* In a traditional organization, employees are responsible for their individual performance, an orientation that can be a powerful inhibitor to teamwork. Teams work best when individual employees are held responsible for the performance of their team.
■ *Compensation and recognition.* The two most common stumbling blocks to teamwork are compensation and recognition. Traditional organizations recognize individual achievement and compensate on the basis of either time or individual merit. Teams work best when both team and individual achievement are recognized and when both individual and team performance are compensated.
■ *Planning and control.* In a traditional organization, supervisors plan and control the work. Teams work best in a setting in which supervisors and teams work together to plan and control work.

Organizations that are serious about teamwork and need the improved productivity that can result from it should remove structural inhibitors. In addition to the inhibitors described earlier, managers should be diligent in rooting out others that exist in their organizations. An effective way to identify structural inhibitors is to ask employees the following question: *"What existing procedures, organizational principles, or cultural factors will keep us from working effectively as a team?* Employees are closer to the most likely inhibitors on a daily basis and can, therefore, provide invaluable insight in identifying them.

=== APPLICATION AND DISCUSSION ===

The Redmon Company has been in business for fifty years. During this time, work has been done on an individual basis. Recognition, rewards, and incentives are all based on individual performance. One of management's favorite strategies is to pit individual employees against each other in performance competitions. Performance had been level or declining for two years when, six months ago, Redmon's managers decided to implement teamwork. This was done by calling all employees together to hear the CEO announce, "From now on we will work together in teams. Supervisors are now coaches, and employees are players. Now let's get to work and start winning."

■ Do you think teamwork is going to be effective at Redmon Company? Why or why not?

■ What can supervisors at Redmon Company do to help make the implementation of teamwork successful?

REWARDING TEAM AND INDIVIDUAL PERFORMANCE

Attempts to institutionalize teamwork will fail unless they include implementation of an appropriate compensation system; said another way, if you want teamwork to work, make it pay. This does not mean that employees are no longer compensated as individuals. Rather, the most successful compensation systems combine both individual and team pay.

This is important because few employees work exclusively in teams. A typical employee, even in the most team-oriented organization, spends a percentage of his or her time involved in team participation and a percentage involved in individual activities. Even those who work full-time in teams have individual responsibilities that are carried out on behalf of the team.

Consequently, the most successful compensation systems have the following components: (1) individual compensation, (2) individual incentives, and (3) team incentives. With such a system, employees receive their traditional individual base pay. Then there are incentives that allow employees to increase their income by surpassing goals set for their individual performance. Finally, other incentives are based on team performance. In some cases, the amount of team compensation awarded to individual team members is based on their individual performance within the team or, in other words, on the contribution they made to the team's performance.

An example of this approach can be found in the world of professional sports. All baseball players in both the National and American Leagues receive a base amount of individual compensation. Most also have a number of incentive clauses in their contract to promote better individual performance. Team-based incentives are offered if the team wins the World Series or the league championship. When this happens, the players on the team divide the incentive dollars into shares. Every member of the team receives a certain number of shares based on his perceived contribution to the team's success that year.

A four-step model can be used to establish a compensation system that reinforces both team and individual performance (Figure 15–3). The first step in this model involves deciding what performance outcomes will be measured (individual and team

Figure 15-3
It is important to reward team and individual performance.

```
        Four-Step Model for Establishing a
        Team and Individual Compensation System

  1. Decide what performance outcomes will be measured
     (team and individual).

  2. Decide how the performance outcomes will be measured.

  3. Decide what types of rewards will be offered (monetary,
     non-monetary, or a combination).

  4. Integrate the compensation system with performance-
     related processes.
```

outcomes). Step two involves determining how the outcomes will be measured. What types of data will tell the story? How can these data be collected? How frequently will the performance measurements be made? Step three involves deciding what types of rewards will be offered (monetary, nonmonetary, or a combination of the two). In this step, rewards are organized into levels that correspond to levels of performance so that the reward is in proportion to the performance.

The issue of **proportionality** is important when designing incentives. If just barely exceeding a performance goal results in the same reward given for substantially exceeding it, just barely is what the organization will get. If exceeding a goal by 10 percent results in a 10 percent bonus, then exceeding it by 20 percent should result in a 20 percent bonus, and so on. Proportionality and fairness are characteristics that employees scrutinize with care when examining an incentive formula. Any formula that is seen to be unfair or disproportionate will be ineffective.

The final step in the model involves integrating the compensation system with other performance-related processes. These systems include performance appraisals, the promotion process, and staffing. If teamwork is important, one or more criteria relating to teamwork should be included in the organization's performance appraisal process.

Correspondingly, the employee's ratings on the teamwork criteria in a performance appraisal should be considered when making promotion decisions. An ineffective team player should not be promoted in an organization that values teamwork. Other employees will know, and teamwork will be undermined. Finally, during the selection process, applicants should be questioned concerning their views on teamwork. It makes no sense for an organization that values teamwork to hire new employees who, during their interview, show no interest in or aptitude for teamwork.

Nonmonetary Rewards

A common mistake made when organizations first attempt to develop incentives is thinking that employees will respond only to dollars in a paycheck. In reality, nonmonetary rewards can be just as effective as actual dollars. Widely used **nonmonetary rewards** that have proven to be effective include: movie tickets, gift certificates, time off, event tickets, free attendance at seminars, getaway weekends for two, airline tickets, and prizes such as electronic or household products.

Different people respond to different incentives. Consequently, what will work can be difficult to predict. A good rule of thumb to apply when selecting nonmonetary incentives is "Don't assume—ask." Employees know what appeals to them. Before investing in nonmonetary incentives, organizations should survey their employees. List as many different potential nonmonetary rewards as possible and let employees rate them. In addition, set up the incentive system so that employees, to the extent possible, are able to select the reward that appeals to them. For example, employees who exceed performance goals (team or individual) by 10 percent should be allowed to select from among several equally valuable rewards on the "10 percent Menu." Where one employee might enjoy dinner tickets for two, another might be more motivated by tickets to a sporting event. The better an incentive program is able to respond to individual preferences, the better it will work.

─────── APPLICATION AND DISCUSSION ───────

Most of the work at Saladita Corporation is done by teams of employees. Both individual and team incentives are available, but there is no variety and there are no levels. Every individual and every team that exceeds its performance goals receives the same reward. Saladita's "one-size-fits-all" approach to incentives has failed to generate the performance improvements management had hoped for. A meeting of all supervisors has been called to discuss their problem.

- If you were a supervisor at Saladita, what advice would you offer during the meeting?
- List at least ten nonmonetary rewards (e.g. movie tickets, dinner for two, a day off, etc.). Ask at least five people to prioritize the items on your list. Make sure to ask a diverse group (i.e., old, young, male, female, etc.). How do the priorities of your respondents compare?

RECOGNIZING TEAMWORK AND TEAM PLAYERS

One of the strongest human motivators is *recognition*. People don't just want to be recognized for their contributions; they *need* to be recognized. The military applies this fact very effectively. The entire system of military commendations and decorations (medals) is based on the positive human response to recognition. No amount of pay could compel a young soldier to perform the acts of bravery that are commonplace in the history of the United States military. But the recognition of a grateful nation and grateful comrades-in-arms continues to spur men and women on to incredible acts of valor every time our country is involved in an armed conflict. There is a lesson here for nonmilitary organizations.

The list of methods for recognizing employees is extensive. For example, the following strategies can be effective:[4]

- Write a letter to the employee's family telling about the excellent job the employee is doing.
- Arrange for a senior-level manager to have lunch with the employee.
- Have the CEO of the organization call the employee personally (or stop by in person) to say, "Thanks for a job well done."
- Find out what the employee's hobby is and publicly award him or her a gift relating to that hobby.
- Designate the best parking space in the lot for the "Employee of the Month."
- Create a "Wall of Fame" to honor outstanding performance.

These examples are provided to trigger ideas, but are only a portion of the many ways that employees can be recognized. Every individual organization should develop its own locally tailored recognition options. When doing so, the following rules of thumb will be helpful:

- Involve employees in identifying the types of recognition activities to be used. Employees are the best judges of what will motivate them.
- Change the list of recognition activities periodically. The same activities used over and over for too long will go stale.
- Have a variety of recognition options for each level of performance. This allows employees to select the type of reward that appeals to them the most.

APPLICATION AND DISCUSSION

James Richmond was pleasantly surprised at the reaction of his direct reports to his military decorations from the "old days." As a birthday gift, his wife had his various service ribbons and medals mounted and framed and hung in the family's den. Richmond had supervised his team for just three months when he invited team members and their spouses to his home for a social get together. Richmond's team members expressed sincere interest in the military decorations. He found himself wondering if his company could implement a recognition system that would interest employees this much.

- What kind of recognition would motivate you as one of Richmond's team members?
- What would you recommend Richmond do to establish an effective recognition system?

ON-THE-JOB SCENARIOS

1. Mandy Walton has never been a supervisor, but as of tomorrow, she will be. Walton just learned she has been selected to replace the team's former supervisor who resigned last week. When she was selected, the managers of her division had given Walton the following advice: "Mandy, your new team isn't working well. I need you to find out what is wrong and fix it. I'd begin by getting to the bottom of what is causing the problems. Let's not waste time treating symptoms. Let's remove the root causes."

   - Put yourself in Walton's position. How would you determine what is causing problems in the team?
   - How should Walton proceed to build her team? What should she do first? Next? Next?

2. Tom Yader has two types of people on his team—those who disagree with each other most of the time and those who disagree all of the time. Yader does not mind his team members disagreeing. In fact, sometimes their disagreements actually reveal problems, issues, and possibilities he had not considered. But lately, disagreements have become personal and bitter. Team members have begun to divide themselves into warring cliques based on race, gender, and age. They complain about not knowing what the team is supposed to achieve or how it will be evaluated. They bicker with each other over even the smallest issues. Yader has a "tiger by the tail" and is not sure how to proceed.

   - Analyze this situation. What broad categories of problems will Yader have to deal with?
   - Put yourself in Yader's shoes. How would you proceed? What would you do first? Next? Next?

KEY TERMS AND PHRASES

Action plan	Needs assessment
Alignment	Nonmonetary rewards
Assessment	Proportionality
Celebration	Stretching tasks
Coaching	Structural inhibitors
Common language	Team
Conflict	Team building
Diversity	Teamwork
Institutionalized bias	Trust building
Interdependence	Trust and respect
Mentoring	

REVIEW QUESTIONS

1. What is a team and why are teams important?
2. When does a group of people become a team?

3. Explain the strategies for being an effective team leader.

4. List and explain the Ten Team Commandments.

5. What are the characteristics of a good team mission statement?

6. Describe how to promote diversity in teams.

7. Explain the concept of institutionalized bias.

8. Explain why some employees are not comfortable being team players.

9. List and describe four common structural inhibitors of teamwork in organizations.

10. Explain the concept of nonmonetary rewards.

ENDNOTES

1. Dennis King, "Team Excellence," in *Management for the 90's: A Special Report from SUPERVISORY MANAGEMENT* (Sarance Lake, NY: American Management Association, 1991), 16–17.

2. James R. Lucas, *Fatal Illusions* (New York: Perigree Books, Putnam, 1991), 24.

3. Michael Donovan, "Maximizing the Bottom Line Impact of Self-Directed Work Teams," *Quality Digest* 16(6) (June 1996): 38.

4. Bob Nelson, "Secrets of Successful Employee Recognition," *Quality Digest* 16(8) (August 1996): 29.

Web Site Linkages for Supervisors

For Legal Issues

www.aele.org

For Safety and Health Issues

www.osha.gov

For Management Issues

www.amanet.org

For Quality Issues

www.asq.org

For Staffing, Discipline, Termination, and Other Legal Issues

www.shrm.org

Success Tips For Supervisors

Becoming a supervisor can be like entering a new world where the rules and the expectations are different. New supervisors suddenly find themselves attending more meetings, dealing more frequently with executives, and needing to manage their time better. The following tips are provided to help new supervisors who find themselves in these situations.

TIME MANAGEMENT

1. Maintain a calendar of appointments and keep it with you at all times.
2. Write things down so you don't forget. Maintain a "To Do" list and prioritize the entries.
3. Set realistic deadlines for yourself. Then, promise small and deliver big. If you think your team can get a project done by noon, promise it for 2:00 P.M. but deliver it at noon.
4. When you are on a deadline, use your voicemail. Filter out all but essential telephone calls.
5. Use e-mail instead of the telephone whenever possible. This will avoid the tendency people have to talk longer than is necessary to convey their information.
6. With paperwork, practice the principle of "Do It Now."
7. Always plan to arrive at scheduled appointments ten minutes early. It almost always takes longer to get there than you think.
8. Practice gently helping people get to the point when they are talking to you. Save superfluous chatting for after work.
9. Hold impromptu and unscheduled "drop-in" meetings standing up. This will convey a sense of brevity to the person who wants some of your time.
10. When you call a meeting, specify both a starting and an ending time. This will keep participants on track and on schedule.
11. Get rid of unnecessary paper clutter. More than 80 percent of the paperwork filed is never used again. Ask yourself if you really need it before deciding to keep paperwork.

MEETINGS

1. Give yourself at least ten minutes of "wiggle room" when going to meetings. However, never show up in someone's outer office more than five minutes early. You want to arrive on time, but you don't want to convey the impression that you have too much time on your hands or that you waste time.
2. If you are going to be late for a meeting, call ahead and let someone know. Then get there as soon as possible. When you arrive, enter prepared but be quiet and unobtrusive.

3. If you miss a meeting, apologize but don't make excuses. You are responsible and accountable. Simply ask if there is anything you can still do to make a contribution.

4. When attacked in a meeting, never respond in kind. Remain calm and objective. Never lose your temper and fight fire with fire.

5. Stick to the agenda, save jokes and small talk for after work, and don't go off on tangents. In other words, set an example of respecting the time of the other participants.

DEALING WITH EXECUTIVES

1. Your promotion to supervisor was based on merit, not charity. You would not be in a supervisory position if your were not qualified and if your employer did not need you. Treat executives with the appropriate respect but don't be intimidated.

2. When in doubt, ask questions: What are your priorities with regard to these projects? How would you recommend I proceed with this project?

3. Use the method of communication preferred by the executive in question (e.g., telephone, e-mail, etc.). If you don't know what it is, find out.

4. Avoid wishy-washy words when talking to an executive. Be positive, direct, and forthright.

5. Schedule time with executives rather than just dropping in on them. When meeting with executives, be respectful of their time. Get to the point. Nuture a reputation as a supervisor who never wastes an executives time and asks for time only when it is truly necessary.

Checklists for Supervisors

This appendix contains brief checklists to assist supervisors in dealing positively with situations that might make them uncomfortable, especially the first time these situations are confronted.

COMMUNICATING WITH PEOPLE FOR WHOM ENGLISH IS A SECOND LANGUAGE

Many employees in today's workplace are immigrants. As such, English is not their native tongue. When trying to communicate with employees who still have trouble speaking the English language, try the following strategies:

1. Use visual aids (pictures, diagrams, signs, etc.) as much as possible.
2. Do not just tell, show (demonstrate).
3. Speak slowly and deliberately.
4. Use simple terms and avoid the use of slang.
5. Assume that there will be misunderstandings. Repeat yourself and ask the employee to paraphase and repeat back to you.
6. Try to put yourself in the employee's shoes. What would you like the supervisor to do?
7. Remain courteous, friendly, and patient. Never let exasperation show. It will make attempts at communication even more difficult.
8. Smile, but never laugh at the employee.
9. Never make the mistake of thinking an employee lacks intelligence because of a language barrier. Remember, you don't speak their language either.
10. If all else fails, find an interpreter.
11. Encourage higher management to provide on-site "English as a Second Language" classes in partnership with a community college or university.
12. Reward the acquisition of English-speaking skills.

INTERACTING WITH EMPLOYEES WITH DISABILITIES

Some people are uncomfortable interacting with others who have physical disabilities. If you are uncomfortable in these situations, try the following strategies:

1. Don't be afraid to ask the employee if you can help (open a door, press an elevator button, carry something, etc.). If the employee accepts your help, and you are unsure exactly what you should do to be helpful, ask.

2. Talk directly to the employee. Don't avert your eyes or stare at your feet.

3. Speak to the employee in an age appropriate manner. Never make the mistake of speaking to employees with disabilities as if they were children.

4. If you don't understand something about an employee's disability, don't act as if you do. Just say you don't understand and ask for clarification.

5. When planning meetings, get-togethers, or other events, keep the disabilities of the employee in mind and plan for them ahead of time.

DISCUSSING THE ISSUE OF SEXUAL HARASSMENT WITH EMPLOYEES

Supervisors are responsible for taking appropriate actions to prevent sexual harassment among their direct reports. One of the most important "appropriate actions" is talking frankly and openly about it with employees. If you are uncomfortable discussing this subject, try breaking the ice by using a checklist of actions that contains examples of behavior that might be considered "unwelcome" or that could be viewed as having sexual connotations. The attention of employees will be drawn to the checklist and away from you. The following types of items should be on such a checklist:

Physical Behaviors

1. Uninvited touching
2. Hugging
3. Kissing
4. Pinching
5. Patting
6. Leering
7. Grabbing
8. Gesturing
9. Pointing at intimiate body parts
10. Standing too close (assume this to mean closer than 18 inches)
11. Posturing
12. Assault

Verbal Behaviors

1. Suggestive or sexual jokes, comments, questions, or insinuations
2. Actual requests for sexual activities
3. Pressure for dates or inappropriate time together
4. Sexually explicit language
5. Comments about an individual's body
6. Assuming a suggestive or seductive tone of voice

Visual Behaviors

1. Displaying cartoons that have sexual connotations
2. Using sexual language in written documents
3. Displaying or distributing written material that is sexually explicit

4. Displaying sexually explicit calendars, posters, photographs, etc.
5. Displaying or sending sexually explicit computer images
6. Playing sexually explicit computer games
7. Displaying sexually explicit objects
8. Leaving sexually explicit magazines and other forms of literature in locations where they are visible to other employees or the public

LOOKING FOR PREDICTORS OF WORKPLACE VIOLENCE

It can be difficult to view employees as potential perpetrators of violence on the job. Some supervisors feel as if they are mentally intruding. This is understandable. However, it is better to be mentally alert to potential problems than to ignore the warning signs and let a disaster happen. The following warning signs can be effective indicators of a potential problem. If you have an employee who consistently displays any of these warning signs, alert higher management or the Human Resources Department.

1. More than ordinary interest in weapons
2. Inflexible attitude
3. Feelings of hopelessness
4. Co-workers fear the individual in question (are very uncomfortable dealing with this individual)
5. Signs of paranoia
6. A hypercritical attitude
7. A tendency to blame others for everything
8. A tendency to get overly wrapped up in causes and crusades
9. A record of problems with the police
10. A tendency to have grievances about everything

Index